THE EDUCATION DEBATE

WHAT EVERYONE NEEDS TO KNOW®

THE EDUCATION DEBATE

WHAT EVERYONE NEEDS TO KNOW®

DAVID KIRP AND
KEVIN MACPHERSON

OXFORD
UNIVERSITY PRESS

OXFORD
UNIVERSITY PRESS

Oxford University Press is a department of the University of Oxford. It furthers the University's objective of excellence in research, scholarship, and education by publishing worldwide. Oxford is a registered trade mark of Oxford University Press in the UK and certain other countries.

"What Everyone Needs to Know" is a registered trademark of Oxford University Press.

Published in the United States of America by Oxford University Press 198 Madison Avenue, New York, NY 10016, United States of America.

Library of Congress Cataloging-in-Publication Data
Names: Kirp, David L., author.
Title: The education debate : what everyone needs to know /
David Kirp & Kevin Macpherson.
Description: First Edition. | New York : Oxford University Press, [2023] |
Series: What everyone needs to know | Includes bibliographical
references and index.
Identifiers: LCCN 2022029909 (print) | LCCN 2022029910 (ebook) |
ISBN 9780197531334 (Hardback) | ISBN 9780197531327 (Paperback) |
ISBN 9780197531358 (epub)
Subjects: LCSH: Education—Research.
Classification: LCC LB1028 .K5165 2023 (print) | LCC LB1028 (ebook) |
DDC 370.72—dc23/eng/20220727
LC record available at https://lccn.loc.gov/2022029909
LC ebook record available at https://lccn.loc.gov/2022029910

DOI: 10.1093/wentk/9780197531334.001.0001

1 3 5 7 9 8 6 4 2

Paperback printed by Lakeside Book Company, United States of America
Hardback printed by Bridgeport National Bindery, Inc., United States of America

CONTENTS

PREFACE   IX

**Introduction: Education Policy in the
Twenty-First Century**   1

What is the K–12 education system?   1
What is education policy?   4
What is equal educational opportunity?   6
What is the role of the courts?   10
How do major social changes affect the schools?   11

1 Big Ideas to Equalize Educational Opportunity   15

What is racial integration?   15
What is socioeconomic integration?   20
How are schools financed?   22
How does additional funding affect student outcomes?   27
What is school choice?   28

2 Strategies Designed to Improve the Quality of Education   31

What is a magnet school?   31

What is a charter school?   32

What is a school voucher?   37

What is early childhood education?   39

What is a community school?   44

What is homeschooling?   47

What is high-stakes accountability?   48

What is the "no excuses" strategy for closing the achievement gap?   51

What is standards-based education?   52

What is the No Child Left Behind Act (NCLB)?   54

What is the Every Student Succeeds Act (ESSA)?   56

What is the systemic reform strategy?   58

What is the continuous improvement strategy?   59

3 The Key Players   61

What is an effective teacher?   61

How are teachers recruited and retained?   63

What is teacher preparation?   65

What is teacher professional development?   67

What is teacher evaluation?   69

What are teachers' unions?   71

Why do teachers strike?   73

What is the leadership role of the school principal?   75

What is the leadership role of the school district superintendent?   76

What is the role of the school board?   79

What is the influence of outside money on school board elections?   81

What roles do parent-teacher associations and school-based foundations play?   82

What is the influence of philanthropy on education policy?   83

4 Life Inside the Public School   87

How can schools reduce the achievement gap?   87

What are tracking and ability grouping?   89

Does class size affect student achievement?   91

What is school climate?   92

What is student discipline?   95

What is bullying?   98

What are school shootings?   102

How do extracurricular activities affect academic
performance?   104

How is technology used in schools?   105

What is deeper learning?   109

What is STEM education?   110

What are noncognitive skills and social-emotional learning?   111

How are nudges used to improve educational outcomes?   113

What are social-psychological strategies that improve
student outcomes?   114

What is high school completion?   116

What is career education?   117

5 The Composition of the Classroom   121

What is special education?   121

What is the immigrant students' experience?   125

What is the most effective way to teach English
Language Learners?   129

What is the Native American students' experience?   130

What are individual students' legal rights?   132

What is LGBTQ students' experience?   135

6 The Impact of the Pandemic   139

How have schools responded to Covid-19?   139
What will Covid's long-term impact on schools be?   144

NOTES   147
INDEX   205

PREFACE

At the turn of the twentieth century, philosopher Lester Ward offered a course at Brown University called A Survey of All Knowledge. While this venture is considerably less audacious, any book that looks across the prekindergarten through high school landscape is necessarily broad in its scope. The topics range from racism in education to bullying, multilingual instruction to school finance, and standards-based education to school discipline. Though the full impact of the pandemic remains uncertain, Covid-19 has highlighted long-standing inequalities rooted in race and social class, leading educators to reassess policies and practices, like the ubiquity of classroom (rather than online) instruction, that have long been taken for granted; those questions are addressed as well.

To keep a book about a topic as sweeping as pre-K–12 educational debates and policy within a manageable length, choices had to be made about what to include and what to omit. There is no discussion of curricular specifics or the design of achievement tests, and nuts-and-bolts matters like how school cafeterias operate are omitted. Books have been written about many of these topics, but we have aimed for brevity in order to make the book widely useful, and the reader who wants to go deeper can turn to the notes. There is overlap among some of the topics—for instance, between the No Child Left Behind Act and the "no excuses" strategy. The importance of race, ethnicity, and poverty in equal educational opportunity figures throughout the book.

We approach each topic in the same way, describing the issue and appraising the evidence. Where ideology or politics comes into play, as is often the case in education policy, we summarize the positions of the parties. Although we came to this enterprise with our own experience as students, our perspectives on controversial topics, our blind spots, and our biases, throughout the course of research and writing we have critically examined each issue and nudged one another into fully justifying a conclusion. We have striven to be neutral, leaving it to the readers to draw their own conclusions.

The book examines education policy through three overlapping perspectives, starting with the broadest and then narrowing the lens, from broad questions regarding equal educational opportunity and strategies to achieve it to a narrower focus on school districts, schools, and classrooms. From politicians and policymakers to teachers and parents, there's a lot of useful information to digest.

The introduction paints a picture of the K–12 education system and simultaneously highlights key ethical debates when examining the K–12 system.

From the first years of public education, with the emergence of the American invention the "common school" in the mid-nineteenth century, policy rhetoric, though not always reality, has emphasized the importance of securing equality of educational opportunity.[1] This is the framework of chapter 1.

The chapter's title—and a recurring theme in the book—references the landmark study "Equality of Educational Opportunity" (1966), usually referred to as the Coleman Report after its principal author, James Coleman. The aspiration to equalize educational opportunity for all children emerged more than fifty years ago. It remains an elusive goal. The strategies to secure it vary greatly. Whether the focus is on racial integration, school finance, or market-based reforms, the debates are perennial and are often rooted in ideology, not data. While the substance of policy conversations varies from one era to the next, there is a *Groundhog Day* quality to these debates.

In the wake of the landmark Supreme Court decision in *Brown v. Board of Education* (1954), racial integration became the all-consuming equity concern for a generation. During the 1970s, integration shared the spotlight with inequities in the financing of education; it largely receded from view during the 1980s when, after an influential government report, the focus shifted to workforce preparation. A generation later, however, integration was once again on the agenda, but the focus had shifted from race-based to social class–based integration.

The school finance story is somewhat similar. The reformers initially sought to equalize school funding: "one dollar, one scholar." Later, the emphasis was on securing funding adequate to provide all children with an adequate education.

Chapter 2 narrows the lens, examining school models and specific education policies. Debates over some of these matters, such as "no excuses" schools versus community schools, have been vociferous and perennial.

The high-stakes reform and "no-excuses" strategies concentrate on improving reading and math achievement test scores. The community school strategy is based on entirely different premises: academic performance is necessarily linked to other aspects of students' lives, and the role of the schools reaches beyond developing math and language proficiency.[2] In tandem with this debate, educators have developed strategies to strengthen the system of schooling, including standards-based reform and systemic change.

Chapter 3 focuses on the practitioners within the school system and relevant education policy actors. What is the role of the principal? How are teachers recruited, trained, and retained? Why do schools rely on mentoring and coaching to improve teaching? How are teachers evaluated? What is the role of teachers' unions? What issues prompt teacher strikes and walkouts?

Chapter 4 examines life inside the public school as it shapes the learning process. How is "school climate" defined? What is restorative justice, as a mode of student discipline? What is the school-to-prison pipeline, and how can it be broken? How are noncognitive outcomes measured? What is the school-to-college or -career transition?

Chapter 5 highlights distinct categories of students, including those with disabilities in special education, multilingual and English Language Learners, Native American students, and LGBT youth. We have highlighted the discrimination faced by Black and Latino students throughout the book.

Chapter 6 examines issues that are surfacing in the aftermath of the Covid-19 pandemic. What has the pandemic revealed about racial and social disparities in the provision of education? What is "Covid loss"—understood in academic and social-emotional terms—and how have schools attempted to overcome it? How can the Covid experience encourage educators to incorporate modes of teaching honed while schools were closed, as well as new ways of connecting with parents and communities?

INTRODUCTION

EDUCATION POLICY IN THE TWENTY-FIRST CENTURY

What is the K–12 education system?

Public education is an immense enterprise. Public schools in the United States enroll 65.2 million students in prekindergarten through grade 12. They are taught by 3.2 million teachers in 16,800 school districts. Private schools enroll 10.83 million students, and 3.7 million students are homeschooled.[1] The national education budget exceeds $700 billion, and while that is a tidy sum, the impact of public education reaches far beyond dollars-and-cents calculations, for the ways in which children are educated and the quality of the education they receive will profoundly affect the nation's economic and political health over the next generation.

As a starting point, we might think of this system as a layer cake: the school is the bottom layer; the other layers, from bottom to top, are the school district (and county school system, in states where that exists), the state government, and the federal government. To be sure, reality is somewhat more complicated. The scope of a school district's policy-making authority differs from state to state. At the state and federal levels, the three branches of government—the executive, legislative, and judicial—have different responsibilities. Other players from the community, such as parent-teacher organizations

(PTAs), teachers unions, and philanthropists, influence the K–12 system as well.

The school is, for the most part, tasked with implementing, not making, policy. It may emphasize a particular field of study, like arts education or STEM (science, technology, engineering, and mathematics). It may be designated as a magnet school, which draws students from across the district. Charter schools have greater flexibility than regular public schools in defining their mission and program. Often, but not always, schools are organized by districts and have centralized offices that provide financial, operational, and programmatic support.

The school board charts a course for the district. Its responsibilities include calculating the local tax rate; deciding how to spend funds; approving the budget; hiring and firing personnel; and ensuring that district practice, such as how it educates children with special needs, is consistent with state and federal law. The superintendent, together with their colleagues in the central office, is tasked with implementing these decisions. That office also plays a role in selecting curriculum materials and distributing equipment such as computers.

Every state constitution includes a provision guaranteeing a first- through twelfth-grade education for its children. Thirty-nine states also require districts to offer either full or half-day kindergarten.[2]

The language that defines the state's constitutional obligations varies. The most frequently used descriptions of the state's role include providing a "thorough and efficient education" or a "free education." Some constitutions require the state to "secure to the people the advantages and opportunities of education"; some reference the importance of a "general diffusion of knowledge." While these constitutional provisions are vague, they have been the basis of lawsuits that challenge how the state funds school districts.

State education agencies, whose role is defined by state and federal legislation, typically regulate public preschool, primary, and secondary education; license private preschool, primary, and secondary schools; establish curricular guidelines; and set standards for homeschooling. The state sets the formula for allocating tax dollars among districts, establishes the metric by which students' and districts' performance is evaluated, and defines the criteria for high school graduation. In some instances, the state determines the specifics of the curriculum (as in the recent case of critical race theory) and generates a list of approved textbooks. In the main, the state's role has shifted from a compliance orientation to a focus on supporting districts.

Historically, the federal government had a modest role in education. The first major federal legislation, the 1917 Smith-Hughes Act, underwrote vocational education. It was intended to address the dropout problem by enabling schools to provide instruction that would engage disaffected students. In the wake of the launch of Sputnik and the accompanying fear that the country was lagging behind the USSR in science, Congress passed the National Defense Education Act in 1958.

The passage of the Civil Rights Act, in 1964, and the Elementary and Secondary Education Act, in 1965, thrust Washington onto center stage. Washington underwrites programs targeted for students from low-income families, minority students, students with disabilities, and English Language Learners. The US Department of Education drafts and implements regulations that add specificity to broad congressional mandates. It shapes public discourse; for example, the secretary of education during the Bush and Obama administrations focused on high-stakes testing and charter schools, while during the Trump administration, the secretary emphasized school vouchers. The Office of Civil Rights enforces federal laws that prohibit discrimination on the basis of race, color, national origin, sex, disability, and age in schools that receive federal aid.[3] The department also conducts and funds research.

Until the landmark decision in *Brown v. Board of Education* (1954), outlawing segregation, federal and state courts were reluctant to decide cases that had policy ramifications. Since *Brown*, the courts have played a pivotal role in interpreting the US and state constitutions, statutes, and regulations.

What is education policy?

Education policies are enshrined in legislation and regulations, crafted by politicians and policymakers, that specify the goals of the pre-K–12 system and the strategies for achieving those goals. Policy disputes about how best to educate this generation of students have often been waged as high-stakes battles, characterized by partisans as nothing less than a struggle for the soul of the nation. Politics may influence these determinations, as exemplified by the 2021 headline-making debates over "critical race theory" or the requirement, set by states and districts, that students and teachers must wear masks.[4]

"When it comes to education, everyone thinks she or he is an expert because everyone has had one"—that old saw reflects the widespread belief that expertise is irrelevant in setting policy. But hard thinking about policy choices is essential, for decisions about how the structure and content of schooling must be made, and disagreements are often bitterly contentious.

Here are some examples of policy choices:

- Should the public school system be strengthened or replaced, either by public charters or vouchers for private schools?
- Should race and/or socioeconomic status be taken into account in assigning students to schools?
- Should students be tracked by some metric of ability, or should classes be heterogeneous?
- Should discipline be premised on "zero tolerance" for infractions of school rules, or should reconciliation be emphasized?

The decisions that districts make about such issues will have a profound effect on students' futures, not only while they are in school but also after they graduate (or drop out). These topics are discussed in later chapters.

All too often, politicians and school officials operate in a data-free zone, basing their judgments on a hunch (this ought to work) or ideology (discussions of homosexuality lead students to become gay). That's invariably a mistake.

To be sure, ethics or constitutional principles, rather than data, are sometimes the right drivers. For example, because racial equality is a foundational belief, enshrined in the Fourteenth Amendment, it is ethically and constitutionally unacceptable to separate students on the basis of race. The fact that evidence shows that racial integration increases tolerance among both White and Black students and boosts the performance of Black students is relevant, because it should allay the concerns of White parents, but it is not determinative.

Here's another example: it's a basic ethical principle that the amount of money spent on students' education should not depend on the wealth of their family or community. Even though the US Supreme Court, in *San Antonio Independent School District v. Rodriguez* (1972), ruled that a system of financing that disadvantages poor school districts does not violate the Constitution, that ruling is not ethically decisive, because legal and ethical reasoning do not always lead to the same result. (The deciding vote, in this case, was cast by Justice Potter Stewart, who castigated the Texas funding scheme as "chaotic and unjust," because it preserved inequalities between rich and poor districts, even as he upheld it, because he thought it was constitutionally inappropriate for the courts to intervene.) Research shows that additional funds have a positive effect on students' performance, and while this is pertinent in deciding how best to allocate funds, it isn't the basis for an ethically rooted decision.

In most instances, policy decisions should rely heavily on research, because evidence-based choices are most likely to benefit students. To return to the example of school discipline, the fact that suspension increases the likelihood that a student will drop out of school and enter the school-to-prison pipeline offers a good reason to be chary of a "zero-tolerance" approach.

The research may yield conflicting results. In this text we lay out the relevant evidence and identify these conflicts.

What is equal educational opportunity?

Education has long been regarded as the way to realize the American dream. As nineteenth-century public school crusader Horace Mann declared, public schools should serve as the "balance wheel of the social machinery" of society. For some children this promise has been realized, as education has altered the course of their lives. Still, inequities persist; instead of being engines of social mobility, public schools can have the perverse effect of reinforcing barriers to success that exist even before children enter school.

The gap between the aspiration to provide equality of educational opportunity (EEO) and the reality emerges in many of the topics that this book addresses, including how schools are funded, which schools students attend, whether and how they are grouped, how they are evaluated, and how they are disciplined.

Racial justice figures prominently in securing equality of opportunity. Beginning in 1954, with the Supreme Court's epochal decision in *Brown v. Board of Education*, which held that racially segregated schools were inherently unequal, desegregation was at the forefront of the campaign for EEO. But that effort stalled in the 1980s, in large part because of a shift in constitutional doctrine that has made racial integration difficult to accomplish, even when school districts have voluntarily integrated their schools.

What's more, the impact of zoning laws and covenants in property deeds that prohibited racial and ethnic minorities from buying a home in certain neighborhoods still lingers, even though these restrictions have long since been declared unconstitutional. In most states, students can only attend public schools in the district in which they live, and there are substantial racial and socioeconomic disparities among districts. Within a school system, attendance zones are often geographically based, and students are assigned to the school in their neighborhood. That practice also limits the possibility of desegregation, because zip codes (a proxy for neighborhood boundaries) typically coincide with the wealth of the residents. With racial integration essentially foreclosed because of the Supreme Court's reading of the Constitution, some school systems have focused on securing socio-economic integration instead. In short, nearly seven decades after *Brown*, schools remain heavily segregated by race and ethnicity. Overcoming racism in the schools is critical to securing EEO for minority students.

Even in elementary school, children are aware of racial animus.[5] Two-thirds of educators have witnessed a hate or bias incident in their schools, but administrators seldom intervene.[6]

A US Justice Department investigation in 2021 found a heinous example in the Farmington, Utah, school district. There, Black and Asian American students were seriously and frequently harassed, while school officials ignored the students' behavior or engaged in harassment themselves. "Black students were called the n-word, referred to as monkeys and told their skin looked like feces," the Justice Department's report stated. "The investigation also uncovered slurs aimed at Asian American students, who were called 'yellow' and 'squinty' and told to 'go back to China.' . . . Peers taunted Black students by making monkey noises at them, touching and pulling their hair without permission, repeatedly referencing slavery and lynching, and telling Black students 'go pick cotton' and 'you are my slave.' . . . [S]taff members ridiculed students in front of their peers, endorsing pejorative stereotypes of people of color in class and retaliating against students of color for reporting harassment."[7]

Incidents like these are not isolated cases that occur in a handful of "bad apple" school districts. They are symptomatic of embedded beliefs, policies, and practices that have generated and normalized racial inequities.[8]

Equal educational opportunity has also been defined in terms of school funding, and here too aspirations have not been matched by reality. In forty-five states, funding formulas have been challenged in court as violating the state constitution. Nonetheless, in many states that formula still favors districts that are whiter and wealthier. The combination of two factors—how district boundaries are drawn and where accessible housing is located—often has the effect of concentrating lower-income families into some districts and separating more affluent families into others. This results in a gap that averages $6,355 in district funding per pupil and affects 12.8 million students across the country.[9]

High-quality pre-K enables children to enter kindergarten ready to learn. Research shows that it has a positive, long-lasting impact, especially for low-income children and minority children. The quality of early education is decisive, and while Black children are more likely to attend preschool than White children, the caliber of those preschools is often lower. Latino children are far less likely to go to preschool than White youngsters.[10]

The federal government partly levels the playing field by underwriting educational initiatives targeted at children from low-income families, children with disabilities, American Indian and Alaska Native children, migrant children, bilingual children, English Language Learners, foster children, and homeless children. However, these funds account for less than 10 percent of the $739 billion expenditure for public elementary and secondary school education. In short, inequities in educational inputs persist. There are also substantial gaps in educational outcomes.

The landmark Coleman Report (1964) concluded that a family's income is the major predictor of student success. The impact is greater when it intersects with race and ethnicity. While disparities among racial and ethnic groups have shrunk in recent years, sizeable differences in high school graduation rates remain. In 2018–19, Asian students had the highest graduation rate (93 percent), followed by White (89 percent), Hispanic (82 percent), Black (80 percent), and American Indian/Alaska Native (74 percent) students.[11] Children in foster care and students experiencing homelessness graduate at substantially lower rates.[12]

Whether a student earns a high school diploma and goes to college will likely have a substantial impact on their life chances. Over the course of their lifetimes, college graduates earn, on average, $1 million more than students who leave education after high school, and high school dropouts earn less than half what students with a bachelor's degree do.[13] Although the racial and ethnic gaps in college enrollment have decreased in recent years, White high school graduates are likelier to enroll in college (66.9 percent) than Latino (63.4 percent), and Black (50.7 percent) students. Low-income students, as well as students of color, are more likely to attend community college, where graduation rates are far lower than in four-year institutions.[14]

While they are in school, students' experiences may vary, depending on their race or ethnicity. High-achieving students of color are frequently overlooked by teachers and administrators. The odds of Black and Latino children being referred to gifted programs are 66 percent and 47 percent lower than White students, respectively.[15] Beginning as early as preschool, Black students are disproportionately, and more harshly, disciplined than White students. They are overrepresented, by 22 percent, among students who are suspended or expelled from public schools, a punishment that marks the start of the school-to-prison pipeline.[16]

Summarizing the findings of a host of studies, *New York Times* columnist Thomas Edsall concludes that "education, training in cognitive and noncognitive skills, nutrition, health care and parenting are all among the building blocks of human capital, and evidence suggests that continuing investments that combat economic hardship among Whites and minorities—and which help defuse debilitating conflicts over values, culture and race—stand the best chance of reversing the disarray and inequality that plague our political system and our social order."[17]

What is the role of the courts?

On issues ranging from student rights to school desegregation, courts have had a significant influence on education policy. The role of the judiciary is discussed in detail throughout the book in the context of specific topics. Following is a brief overview.

Historically, courts took a hands-off approach, as state lawmakers were deemed responsible for designing systems of public education. *Brown v. Board of Education* (1954) marked a sea change in the courts' role. It generated litigation about issues, such as what constitutes an "adequate" education, which previously would have been off limits to the judiciary.

Court rulings can have a symbolic as well as substantive impact, drawing attention to a problem, such as the exclusion of children with special needs or the mistreatment of Native American youngsters, that previously received little public scrutiny. What's more, the mere threat of litigation can alter educators' and politicians' actions. The possibility of school finance litigation, for instance, prompted several states to reform their school funding laws.

Heated education debates about policy, coupled with the growing reliance of the federal government's executive and legislative branches on the courts to enforce civil rights legislation, contributed to greater judicial involvement during the 1960s and 1970s. State courts entered the policy arena as well, striking down their states' funding systems.

This judicial activism was controversial. Supporters argued that court decisions safeguarded students' rights and promoted equal opportunity. Critics insisted that the courts had fashioned themselves into a "super-school-board," an "imperial judiciary" that ruled on matters properly left to legislators.[18]

The heyday of federal judicial activism ended in the early 1980s, as the Supreme Court became increasingly conservative, not only with respect to education but also with regard to social issues generally. Since then, litigants have mainly turned to the state courts, which have proven more receptive to rights-based arguments.

Whatever position one takes in this debate, the courts' biggest challenge is implementing their decisions. Judges are not education experts. While they issue decrees, they need the active participation of educators in order to turn those rulings into on-the-ground reality.

How do major social changes affect the schools?

Society evolves in a host of ways, and those changes necessarily affect public schools.

For one thing, the demography of the nation is changing. The Mather School, founded in 1639 in Boston, was the first free public school in North America (in the postcolonization era). At that time, all the students were White. Nearly four centuries later, the Mather School is still operating. Its student body is now 38 percent Black, 31 percent Asian, 21 percent Latino, and 5 percent White; 5 percent are identified as mixed/other.[19]

In many ways the story of the Mather School exemplifies changes in the composition of the nation's public schools. The country has become increasingly multicultural and multiracial, and so have the schools. Since 2014, White students have composed less than half of the nation's student population. Now 15 percent are Black, 29 percent are Latino, and 5 percent are Asian. The number of non-White students will increase substantially in the coming decades.[20]

Almost one out of four students came from an immigrant household in 2015; as recently as 1990, that figure was 11 percent.[21] Many of these youths are English Language Learners.

In the past twenty years, the percentage of students who have been eligible for free and reduced lunch has increased from 38 to 52 percent. Children from low-income households require an array of supports that in the past were not delivered by the schools.

In the 2019–20 school year, 7.3 million students—14 percent of the public school population—received special education services, and the number of these students continues to grow as more children are identified as having special needs. These children's needs, coupled with the fact that many of them are "mainstreamed" in regular classes rather than being assigned to separate classes, oblige the schools to deliver an effective education to them and their classmates.

What's more, the economy is evolving in ways that affect students' education. The ever-growing demand for technologically sophisticated "knowledge workers" in the digital age is prompting schools to expand their STEM offerings. The Covid-19 pandemic has led schools to make smarter use of technology.

It is estimated that by 2030, 85 percent of the jobs in artificial intelligence, machine learning, augmented reality, and quantum computing fields will have been created since 2020.[22] Despite fears that robots will replace humans, present trends indicate that artificial intelligence and robotics will generate more jobs than they destroy.[23] To respond effectively to this transformation, the education system needs to cultivate lifelong learners who can adapt quickly and effectively.

Schools are also tasked with fostering civic knowledge and political engagement. That's a demanding assignment in an ever more fractured and politically polarized nation.

Civic participation is essential in maintaining representative and responsive political institutions. Students need to understand how the government works and have the tools to participate in an increasingly partisan political system. Delivering the basics of civics presents its own set of challenges in a nation where a majority of adults cannot name the three branches of the federal government.

1

BIG IDEAS TO EQUALIZE EDUCATIONAL OPPORTUNITY

What is racial integration?

Racial integration represents an effort to end systematic separation. That segregation may be legally mandated, as it was during the Jim Crow era (often defined as the years between the Supreme Court cases *Plessy v. Ferguson*, 1896 and *Brown v. Board of Education*, 1954 in the South, when there were "White" schools and "Colored" schools. Since the 1960s, segregation has resulted in practices, such as setting attendance boundaries, that while seemingly neutral have the same racially isolating effect.

Although *integration* and *desegregation* are sometimes used as synonyms, integration generally refers to social and educational strategies that complement efforts to overcome racial isolation. Desegregation becomes a starting point, a springboard for promoting equal opportunity.

Until 1954, public schools in southern states were segregated by law. In *Plessy v. Ferguson* (1896), the US Supreme Court upheld the constitutionality of segregation in railway cars; that decision was relied on in later cases that upheld segregation in schools and public facilities.[1]

The *Plessy* "separate but equal" doctrine remained the law of the land for more than a half century. The segregationists claimed that the schools were equal, but this was rarely, if ever, the case. Black children often attended rundown schools, with few if any qualified teachers and fewer facilities than in White schools. Their school year was truncated, as schools were closed when Black children were expected to work in the fields during harvest season. During the first half of the twentieth century, scores of court decisions ordered that these inequities be rectified, but they did not confront the constitutionality of segregation itself.

Beginning early in the twentieth century, the National Association for the Advancement of Colored People (NAACP) devised a legal strategy to chip away at the "separate but equal" doctrine. The first cases challenged segregation in higher education. Later, relying on the Supreme Court's rationale in those cases, the NAACP challenged the constitutionality of "separate but equal" public schools.

In *Brown v. Board of Education* (1954), the Supreme Court unanimously held that school segregation was unconstitutional. "In the field of public education the doctrine of 'separate but equal' has no place," the justices declared, because segregated schools are "inherently unequal."

Southern resistance to the ruling was "massive," and the pace of desegregation was slow. Over the course of a generation, the Court elaborated on the *Brown* ruling. "There can be neither colored schools [n]or White schools, just schools," the justices decreed in *Green v. New Kent County* (1968).

After the passage of the 1964 Civil Rights Act, the federal government became a key partner in desegregating school districts, filing scores of lawsuits to enforce the law. In *Swann v. Charlotte-Mecklenburg County* (1971), the Supreme Court upheld a desegregation remedy that required a substantial amount of busing. The justices ruled that remedial plans were to be judged by their effectiveness, and mathematical ratios were a "legitimate starting point."

Segregation wasn't confined to the South. Beginning in the late 1960s, numerous lawsuits were filed against northern districts, challenging de facto segregation: racial separation that, while not required by law, resulted from a school board decision that had the effect of segregating students. In *Keyes v. Denver Unified School District* (1974), the Supreme Court decreed that the district had to be desegregated because "the [School] Board, through its actions over a period of years, intentionally created and maintained the segregated character of the core city schools."

Across the country, desegregation became a hot-button issue. In Boston, a 1974 ruling that because the school district had deliberately segregated its students, busing was necessary to promote racial balance, prompted riots in White neighborhoods.

Keyes was the high-water mark for desegregation in the North. One year later, in *Bradley v. Milliken*, a 5–4 decision, the Supreme Court overturned a metropolitan desegregation decree in Detroit, despite evidence that the boundaries between the city and suburbs were drawn with the intention to promote residential segregation.

During the 1980s, the Supreme Court grew more skeptical about the constitutionality of integration. It ruled that busing could be used as a remedy only where there had been "deliberate" or "intentional," not simply de facto, segregation. By the late 1980s, an increasingly conservative Supreme Court ruled that desegregation decrees issued by lower courts had to be lifted when everything "practicable" had been done to eliminate the vestiges of past discrimination.

In 2007, a sharply divided Supreme Court overturned voluntary desegregation plans that Seattle, Washington, and Louisville, Kentucky, had adopted in order to maintain school-by-school racial diversity. The majority concluded that districts could not be integrated by using a formula that took explicit account of a student's race. Such programs were "directed only to racial balance, pure and simple," a goal that the majority opinion said was forbidden by the Constitution's guarantee of equal protection. To dissenting justice John Paul Stevens, the majority's invocation of *Brown v. Board of Education* was "a cruel irony," because the opinion actually "rewrites the history of one of this court's most important decisions."

Justice Anthony Kennedy, who cast the deciding vote, specified the strategies that could legitimately be used to foster school diversity, such as drawing attendance zones that take into consideration the demographics of students' neighborhoods and "allocating resources for special programs" like magnet schools. "The nation has a moral and ethical obligation to fulfill its historic commitment to creating an integrated society that ensures equal opportunity for all of its children."

At that time, scores of districts had similar plans in place. The ruling led many of them to rely on socioeconomic factors, instead of race, in drawing attendance zones. In the political and legal landscape of the 2020s, some integration advocates argue that this is the most feasible approach, while others point out that the benefits of socioeconomic and racial integration are not equivalent.

Racial integration advocates have their work cut out for them. Black and Latino students are increasingly likely to attend racially and economically segregated schools. Nationwide, 40 percent of students of color are enrolled in schools where more than 90 percent of their classmates are non-White, while 20 percent of White students attend a school where more than 90 percent of their classmates are White. The number of high-poverty schools that serve primarily students of color doubled between 2000 and 2014.

Between 2000 and 2017, the last year for which data are available, seventy-one neighborhoods attempted to secede from their school districts. These were mostly White communities that sought to extricate themselves from lower-income Black and Latino districts; forty-seven of those secessionist efforts were successful.

Although suburbia is typically regarded as a mostly White, middle-class enclave, the racial and ethnic composition of many districts has been transformed during the past generation. Between 2000 and 2015, the number of low-income families living in the suburbs of America's largest metropolitan areas grew by 57 percent; in the 2020s, more than half of the racial minority population in major metropolitan areas lives in suburbia. Schools in those communities have become increasingly segregated, and within-school segregation is common in racially diverse schools.[2]

Despite judicial decisions that limit how school systems can integrate their schools, some districts have adopted a variety of tools that promote integration. These include

- altering school attendance zones to promote racial and/ or socioeconomic integration;
- giving preference to school transfer requests that increase the racial and/or socioeconomic diversity of the affected schools;
- assigning students based on "controlled choice," in which students are assigned to schools, based mainly on family preferences, that also increase racial and/or socioeconomic diversity; and
- authorizing charter schools to promote racial and/or socioeconomic diversity in admissions.

Opposition to racial integration has sometimes been grounded in the claim that it is detrimental to White students. The research says otherwise.

The 1966 Coleman Report, the launching pad for research on education policy, concluded that the most important predictor of school success, apart from students' family background, was their classmates. Black students benefited from an integrated educational experience, while White students did neither better nor worse.[3] Those findings have been confirmed in subsequent studies.[4]

African American students enrolled in integrated schools record higher test scores, are less likely to drop out, and are more likely to go to college. Attending an integrated school also reduces racial bias and counters racial stereotypes among both White and Black students. Integration also generates economic benefits; economists calculate that implementing programs to reduce socioeconomic segregation by 50 percent results in a three-to-one return on investment.[5]

Recent research demonstrates that integration also has life-long benefits for African American students, including higher earnings and improved health outcomes. What's more, these benefits extend to the second generation, moving those who attended integrated schools, as well as their children, into the middle class.[6]

Moving to Opportunity, a randomized social experiment that began in 1993, offered housing vouchers to families living in high-poverty neighborhoods that they could use to move to lower-poverty neighborhoods. An evaluation of the experiment showed that there was little impact on children whose families moved after the children were thirteen. However, college attendance rates rose, and earnings significantly improved, for children who were younger than thirteen when their families moved. Those gains have persisted: as adults, they live in higher-income neighborhoods and are less likely to become single parents than those youngsters, otherwise identical, who didn't move. These benefits will likely extend to the next generation.[7]

What is socioeconomic integration?

During the past quarter century, the Supreme Court has made it harder for school districts to use race as a factor when assigning students to schools.[8] Confronted with these judicial rulings, an increasing number of districts have switched their focus to securing social-economic status (SES) integration, since that policy doesn't pose obvious constitutional concerns. The goal is to "bring about the benefits of economic and racial diversity without running afoul of legal requirements that limit the use of race in student assignment."[9] The fact that socioeconomic integration is less politically controversial adds greatly to its appeal.

Since the "common school" movement of the nineteenth century, socioeconomic integration has been on reformers' policy agendas. Today, the chief argument for eliminating social class barriers is that diversifying the student body benefits all children, well-off and low-income alike, both academically and socially.

The SES integration movement has rapidly gathered steam. In 1996, only two school districts, with a combined enrollment of 30,000 students, had adopted socioeconomic integration plans. A generation later, one hundred school districts and charter school chains in thirty-two states, educating 4.4 million students (about 8 percent of public school students), have followed suit. These districts have adopted a variety of approaches in order to promote SES integration, including changing school attendance boundaries to allow students to transfer between schools only if doing so leads to greater SES integration.

In most school systems, attendance boundaries are drawn to reflect neighborhood boundaries, which conform to segregated residential patterns. This puts both low-income and middle-class students at a disadvantage.

Students in middle-class schools perform better, partly because they have access to their families' economic and social capital, which is associated with academic achievement. One study found that the test scores of fourth-grade students from low-income families who attended middle-class schools were two grades higher than those of their peers who attended high-poverty schools.

Regardless of their racial or socioeconomic background, students benefit from attending SES-integrated schools. They are less likely to develop racial stereotypes and the accompanying prejudices, their families are more likely to be engaged, their teachers have higher expectations for their success, and they have access to more advanced placement classes.

Economists have shown that SES integration is a cost-effective strategy. Schools in which socioeconomic segregation is half the national average have graduation rates 10 percent higher than more segregated schools, and the saving attributable to having to spend less on health care, crime, and welfare is more than $20,000 per student.[10]

SES integration plans may not generate a great deal of racial integration. In implementing such plans, school districts need to take political realities into account, weighing meaningful diversity against political feasibility. What's more, there are questions about the needs of English learners and Black, Latino, and Native American students that need to be addressed in tandem with SES integration.

How are schools financed?

Public education is financed by local, state, and federal taxes. Nationwide, 48 percent of a typical school district's budget comes from state revenue raised through income and/or sales tax and fees.[11] Most state funding formulas are designed to put rich and poor school systems on a more equal financial footing. Some states provide additional support based on the number of low-income students in a district as well as those with special needs.[12]

On average, 44 percent of a school system's budget is raised locally. In most states, property taxes are districts' primary revenue source. How much money a school system raises depends on its per-student assessed property wealth and its tax rate. Some states set a uniform or minimum tax rate, while in other states each district makes its own determination.

The federal government contributes 8 percent of a typical district's budget. The emphasis of federal programs is on promoting equity by providing additional resources to educate specified categories of underserved students, including those from low-income families and those with special needs.

Starting in the early twentieth century, schools depended mainly on property tax revenues. With local funding came local control; as one commentator observed, tongue in cheek,

"[L]ocal control is 'The Battle Hymn of the Republic.'" In some states, the wealthiest districts spent as much as fifteen times more than the poorest districts.

In that era, the state's share of a district's budget rarely exceeded 20 percent. Some states gave every district an equal amount for each student, a formula that preserved the budgetary disparity. While other states' funding formulas guaranteed a minimum level of expenditure, that approach was insufficient to close the gap.

Until *Brown v. Board of Education* (1954) declared segregation unconstitutional, southern states provided as much as ten times more funding to White than to "Colored" schools. The closing of these schools after *Brown* reduced this disparity, although predominantly Black schools are still less well funded.

Nationwide, state funding increased during the 1970s. Taxpayer revolts, such as Proposition 13 in California, forced communities to reduce property tax rates, making school systems more financially dependent on the state. State funding formulas were challenged on constitutional grounds, and where this litigation was successful, disparities in funding were reduced.

While these developments shrank the funding gap, inequities persist. Expenditures per student vary among the states: per pupil spending in Utah was $7,179 in 2020, less than a third of the amount spent in New York, a disparity that cannot be entirely accounted for by the cost of living. Nationwide, an average of 15 percent less per pupil is spent in the poorest school districts than in the most affluent.[13] The gap ranges from 5 percent in Florida to 36 percent in Alaska. While many states have reduced this gap, it is actually increasing in some states. What's more, fewer states allocated funds to equalize expenditures among districts in 2018 than was the case a decade earlier.[14] Federal funding has only a modest equalizing effect.[15] These persisting differences in expenditure led former education secretary Arne Duncan to conclude that "we have, in many places, school systems that are separate and unequal. Money by itself is never the only answer, but giving kids who start out already behind in life, giving them less resources is unconscionable, and it's far too common."[16]

The amount of money received by individual schools in a district also varies. Teachers' salaries are the major factor—experienced teachers, who typically cluster in wealthier neighborhoods, earn more. Additionally, in many wealthy communities, PTAs raise substantial sums to support their children's schools.

Federal policy has also shaped school districts' educational priorities. The Smith-Hughes Act (1917) marked the first time that the federal government funded a K–12 program. It underwrote vocational education for high school students in order to keep disaffected students from dropping out, enabling districts to offer classes that these students would regard as relevant. During the 1950s, the Cold War stimulated investment in science, mathematics, and foreign language and technical training programs, as the United States sought to catch up with the Soviet Union.[17]

In the 1960s, the federal government launched what President Lyndon B. Johnson promoted as the War on Poverty. Head Start and Early Head Start, which provided preschool for children, toddlers to age five, from low-income families, were critical to this strategy. Hopes ran high; President Johnson pledged that Head Start would end the "cycle of poverty." That year, Congress also passed the Elementary and Secondary Education Act (ESEA). Title 1 of that legislation provided funding for schools that enrolled mostly low-income students. Each time Congress has renewed ESEA, it has renamed the legislation; it became the No Child Left Behind Act in 2001 and is currently the Every Student Succeeds Act (2015).

Courts have also played a key role in school finance. The opinion in *Brown v. Board of Education* (1954) asserted that "education is perhaps the most important function of state and local governments. . . . In these days, it is doubtful that any child may reasonably be expected to succeed in life if he is denied the opportunity of an education."

Civil rights lawyers read this language as a blueprint for challenges to other inequities, especially in school funding. In *Serrano v. Priest* (1971), the California Supreme Court ruled that the state's school finance formula violated the equal protection clause in both the state and US constitutions. The court held that education is a constitutionally "fundamental" interest and that the "wealth" of a school district was a "suspect classification" that demanded "strict scrutiny" from the court. In order to prevail, the state had to show a "compelling" state interest, and the justices found no compelling reason to tie education expenditures to a district's tax base.

In *Rodriguez v. San Antonio Independent School District* (1974), a closely divided US Supreme Court reached the opposite conclusion: wealth, unlike race, is not a "suspect classification," and education is not a "fundamental right." For that reason, Texas had only to show that the state had "reasonable grounds" for its policy, a constitutional standard that invariably leads courts to uphold state legislation. Justice Potter Stewart, who cast the deciding fifth vote, described the state's school finance formula as "chaotic and unjust"—but constitutional.

Shut out of the federal courts by the *Rodriguez* decision, advocates turned to the state courts, challenging school finance formulas on the grounds of state equal protection clauses and right to education provisions. By 1980, more than twenty states had modified their education finance laws, because of either political pressure or judicial rulings.

By 2020, twenty-three state courts had ruled that their states' school finance formula violated the state constitution. The result was greater equity in per-pupil spending in states where the school financing system was overturned.[18] Courts in seventeen states rejected the plaintiffs' contention, concluding that the state's formula passed constitutional muster or that the state constitution did not give the court the authority to make that determination. In 2020, there were pending legal challenges in at least nine states.

Lawyers have relied on a variety of theories in attacking state legislation. School finance cases in the 1970s and 1980s, like *Serrano v. Priest*, focused on the unequal allocation of resources. But beginning in the 1980s, advocates started questioning whether even successful litigation was achieving enough for poor districts. While many of these decisions led to the provision of additional resources, in some states the political climate and fiscal capacity proved at least as important as court rulings.

The advocates began to formulate a different strategy. Rather than comparing the education that children in poor, mainly low-income districts receive with what was provided to children in wealthier districts, the new line of reasoning focused on the inadequate education that many children receive, as judged by an absolute standard of "adequacy." Under this theory, children were entitled to a "high-minimum quality education for all."[19]

In 1989, the Kentucky Supreme Court adopted this approach, holding that every student had a constitutional right to an "adequate education that promised to teach them to reasonably high standards."[20] Since then, more than twenty state courts have struck down school funding formulas because they failed this "adequacy" test.

Adequacy has many possible meanings. One way to define it is to seek a consensus of educational professionals regarding what's needed for an adequate education and then price those inputs. Another approach entails an assessment of how much additional money schools need to address high-cost problems like special-needs pupils or high wages. Courts have used a variety of approaches, but it's unclear whether any of them have resulted in improved student achievement.[21]

In 2020, a federal appeals court recognized education and literacy as a constitutional right for "children relegated to a school system [Detroit] that does not provide even a plausible chance to attain literacy." In a joint statement with the governor, plaintiffs asserted that the settlement "will help secure the right of access to literacy for students in Detroit who faced obstacles they never should have faced."[22]

Judicial rulings rarely inquire into the quality of education that students receive. Whatever legal theory guides the courts' decisions, state lawmakers, not judges, are tasked with deciding how to design and implement practices to achieve equal opportunity.

How does additional funding affect student outcomes?

There has long been a contentious debate about whether providing additional resources improves student achievement. *Equality of Educational Opportunity*, colloquially known as the Coleman Report (1966), was the intellectual launching pad for those committed to evidence-based education policy. Rather than focusing on educational inputs, like the school building, it examined the forces affecting the outcome of education. It concluded that "schools bring little influence to bear on a child's achievement that is independent of his background and general social context. . . . [T]he inequalities imposed on children by their home, neighborhood, and peer environment are carried along to become the inequalities with which they confront adult life at the end of school."[23]

Since then, opinions about the report's policy implications have differed sharply.[24] Critics of increased educational spending read this finding as meaning that "money doesn't matter" and use it as a rationale for opposing programs like ESEA, which are meant to close the achievement gap.[25] Econometricians critiqued the Coleman Report's methodology, arguing that the analysis was premised on an outmoded approach that relied on comparisons between school districts at a single moment, rather than following the progress of students who, over a period of years, attended better-funded schools.

Recent research, which has taken the latter approach, concludes that increasing funding for schools does in fact improve both educational outcomes and life chances, especially for children living in poverty.[26] One study found that a 10 percent increase in K–12 per-pupil spending led to 7.25 percent higher wages and a 3.67 percent reduction in adult poverty.[27] The impact on children from low-income families was even greater. Another study concluded that states that spent more on districts with high concentrations of students from low-income families shrank the achievement gap by 20 percent.[28]

In California, increases in district revenue attributable to a change in the state's school finance formula have had a "strongly significant" impact on high school graduation rates. Black students and students from low-income families benefit most. The impact is greatest when the additional money is spent on evidence-based strategies like smaller class sizes, early childhood programs, and increased teacher compensation.[29]

What is school choice?

Equity-driven strategies, previously described in this chapter, rely heavily on the racial and socioeconomic integration of public schools and school finance reform to equalize outcomes across race, wealth, and ethnicity.

While school choice strategies have the same objective, they are driven by market-based assumptions. They rely on generating competition among schools, rather than on improving traditional public schools, to eliminate racial, income, and wealth gaps in school performance.

In a choice-based scheme, rather than funding only public schools—the traditional approach—public dollars follow students to whatever learning environment their parents favor, whether that's a public school, private school, charter school, or homeschooling.[30] Choice plans are premised on the argument that competition will improve school quality and boost student outcomes.[31] If parents and students can select from a number of schools, the argument runs, those schools that attract students will thrive, while unpopular schools will either adapt and improve or close. What's more, advocates contend that choice levels the playing field by offering options to families in poverty akin to those available to wealthier families.

The mechanisms for increasing choice include charter schools, magnet schools, and school vouchers. Each is discussed in chapter 2.[32]

2

STRATEGIES DESIGNED TO IMPROVE THE QUALITY OF EDUCATION

What is a magnet school?

Magnet schools are public schools, open to all students living in the school district, that focus their curriculum on a theme such as performing arts, STEM, or international languages. Nationwide, there are an estimated forty-three hundred magnet schools, which enroll more than 3.5 million students.[1]

The magnet school concept was introduced during the 1960s as a way to encourage voluntary racial integration. A decade later, the rationale changed. Magnet schools were promoted as a way to attract students with specific interests and to keep students who otherwise would enroll in private schools in the public school system.[2]

Proponents note that magnet schools provide students with choice within the public school system, enabling students to select a school that matches their interests. The fact that magnets are publicly run is seen as an assurance of quality. Furthermore, these schools offer districts the opportunity to try out new curricula and pedagogy. If those innovations prove effective, they can readily be implemented across the school system.

Critics contend that because magnet schools are closely scrutinized by the district and governed by the same rules that apply to all public schools, opportunities to innovate are constrained. Unlike a charter school, the magnet school cannot create an extended-day program or select its teachers.

Another concern is that magnets siphon off the ablest students, in much the same way as ability grouping in elementary school and tracking in high school. When a magnet school is oversubscribed, a third of such schools rely on a student's academic record in determining whom to admit. Consequently, low-performing students, who benefit from having high-performing classmates, are worse off.

What is a charter school?

Charter schools are privately run, publicly funded schools. Depending on state law, teachers, parents, nonprofits, universities, and government agencies may create charters. The contract between the charter school and the local school board or the state education agency outlines its mission, how it will accomplish that mission, and the measure of its accountability.[3]

Charters exercise greater autonomy than traditional public schools. A charter may, for example, offer an extended school day, a distinctive pedagogy, or a specialized curriculum, and it can recruit its own staff. Charters are accountable for both academic outcomes and fiscal management.

In 1988 American Federation of Teachers president Albert Shanker proposed that teachers be offered the opportunity to innovate in schools that were more autonomous than traditional public schools.[4] That proposal attracted considerable attention, and three years later, Minnesota passed the first charter school law.[5] As of 2020, forty-five states and the District of Columbia had passed charter legislation.[6] Some states, such as Massachusetts, have detailed standards for application and renewal, while others, such as Arizona, are far less prescriptive. Amid reports of ineffective charters, many states have set more rigorous accountability standards.[7]

Charters were initially envisioned as stand-alone schools that would function as laboratories for educational innovation. Today, however, these independent charters enroll approximately 57 percent of the charter school students; 24 percent attend schools managed by nonprofit organizations such as the Knowledge Is Power Program (KIPP), Imagine Schools, IDEA Public Schools, Uncommon Schools, and Aspire Public Schools. The rest attend schools managed by for-profit entities.[8]

Nationwide, seven thousand charter schools enroll more than 3.3 million K–12 students. Most charter schools are located in urban areas, and about 60 percent of the three-fifths of charter students are Black or Latino. Enrollment increased by 7 percent in 2020, largely because of the impact of Covid on parents' decisions.[9]

Virtual charter schools, the fastest-growing type of charter, enrolled two hundred thousand students in 2019.[10] Students who attend these schools generally fare poorly: a 2015 report found that, during a single school year, students who enrolled in online charters lost 72 days of learning in reading and 180 days of learning in math, compared to their public school counterparts.[11]

The charter school model initially garnered bipartisan support, but popular opinion has become polarized, in large part because of the Trump administration's strident criticisms of traditional public schools and its ardent support of charters. A nationwide survey in 2020 found that 61 percent of Republicans, but only 40 percent of Democrats, support charters.[12]

Advocates argue that charters level the playing field. Wealthy families already make choices—they can move to communities with high-performing schools or send their children to private schools—that aren't available to low-income families, who must send their children to neighborhood schools. Charters enable all parents to decide what's best for their children.

What's more, the evidence indicates that many urban charters do a good job of boosting academic achievement.

One study found that students enrolled in charters in big-city districts gained approximately one month in math and reading over the course of a school year, compared to their peers in conventional public schools. English Language Learners made even bigger gains: seventy-two days of learning in math and seventy-nine days in reading.[13] A random-assignment experiment found that charters outperformed public schools in urban districts that served mostly disadvantaged students, while middle-class and higher-achieving students fared better in public schools.[14] Research also shows that the longer a student remains in a charter school, the greater the benefit.[15]

Several charter networks have compiled exemplary track records. For instance, the KIPP model emphasizes high expectations; focuses on character development; assiduously recruits talented teachers and leaders; and creates a structured, nurturing environment.[16] A 2019 study concluded that a middle school student who, following a lottery, was able to attend one of the 255 KIPP schools was 12.9 percent more likely to enroll in college than a peer who didn't have the same opportunity.[17]

What's more, the fact that charters are typically smaller than traditional public schools is said to enable them to offer a more personalized education and respond more nimbly to students' individual needs.

Charter school critics advance a number of counterarguments. Some base their objections on the theory that a private entity should not be able to use public funds to operate a school.[18]

Most anti-charter arguments are rooted in evidence. Freedom from many of the regulations governing traditional public schools was supposed to make charter schools hubs of innovation that could be adopted by public schools. But there is little evidence that this has happened; instead of working in tandem with mainstream public schools, they compete for dollars and students.[19]

Accountability is another source of concern. Some states, such as Massachusetts, closely monitor the performance of charters and close those that fail to meet the state's standards. But many states afford charters excessive latitude, which enables underperforming schools to survive.[20] Lax accountability has also failed to detect fiscal mismanagement and embezzlement.[21]

While market theory assumes that parents will withdraw their children from underperforming charters, this rarely happens; most parents trust the schools to which they send their children to do a good job.[22]

Many charter schools fail; between 1999 and 2017, more than half of all charters closed during their first five years of operation.[23] Those schools often close during the school year, disrupting students' education and requiring public schools to act quickly in order to adjust to these fluctuations in enrollment.

School funding is a zero-sum game, with dollars following enrollment, and when students move from their neighborhood school to a charter school, those funds are allocated to the charter. While defenders argue that this practice shows that the market is working, opponents have called for a moratorium on charters in large districts. There, declining enrollment, attributable to families' moving away or enrolling their children in charters, has led to a financial crisis.[24] What's more, many charter schools receive substantial philanthropic support to augment their budgets, which is seen as giving them an·unfair advantage.[25]

Critics note that while public schools must accept all students living in the district, parents who want their children to attend a charter must navigate the complex admission process. This requires information to which minority and low-income families may not have ready access. Although urban charters enroll many students of color, the profile of their students may differ from those who attend public schools.

Charters also enroll fewer students with disabilities. Although all schools that receive federal funds must admit these students, a 2018 survey found that one student in eight received special education services in public schools, compared

to one charter student in ten.[26] One explanation for this difference is that families are less likely to enroll their children in a
charter school if, as is often the case, the school doesn't have
an established special education program suitable to their
children's needs. This is especially the case for children with
severe disabilities.

The fact that few charter schools (one in ten, by one estimate) are unionized draws the critics' ire.[27] They see the model,
initially advanced by a progressive union leader, as having become a way to privatize public education. The fact that these
schools aren't unionized means they can require teachers to
work unreasonably long hours. Consequently, rapid teacher
turnover is the norm.[28]

Many charter organizations take a "no-excuses" approach
to academics, treating reading and math achievement as the
sole metric of success and disciplining students who fail to
follow rigid rules. That approach doesn't take into account
the impact of students' background on their performance and
behavior. Those students struggle in the less structured college environment, and many drop out. For this reason, some
charter networks have shifted from the "no-excuses" approach
to pedagogy informed by social-emotional learning, which is
designed to foster greater autonomy. Similarly, some charters
have replaced the "tough love" approach to discipline with
a "restorative justice" strategy—students who break school
rules meet with their teacher (and classmates, if they have
been affected) to discuss what occurred and agree on a suitable response.[29]

The fact that public funds can be diverted to charter school
founders, rather than being used to educate students, is trou-
bling. Although Arizona is the only state that permits for-
profit charters, nominally nonprofit charters can operate in
the same way by outsourcing all expenses, from instruction to
cleaning, to a for-profit management firm.[30] Students enrolled
in for-profit charters generally do considerably worse than
their peers in public schools.[31]

What is a school voucher?

School vouchers (sometimes referred to as education vouchers) give parents the opportunity to choose a private school for their children. In *Capitalism and Freedom* (1962), Nobel Prize–winning economist Milton Friedman popularized vouchers, arguing that vouchers would end the "monopoly" of public schools.

In the 1960s, southern states instituted voucher plans in order to perpetuate racial segregation. More than two hundred private "segregation academies" had opened by the end of the decade. In 1976 the Supreme Court struck down state laws that kept these schools financially afloat through government subsidies and tax exemptions.[32] As a result, segregation academies either changed their admission policies or closed.

By 2019 twenty-nine states and the District of Columbia were operating voucher programs. In 2020 a divided US Supreme Court held that a voucher plan must include religious schools.[33]

Some 188,000 students used vouchers in 2019, substantially fewer than those enrolled in charter schools or magnet schools.

A widely cited evaluation of the Milwaukee, Wisconsin, voucher program showed modest improvement in high school graduation and college enrollment rates. Students attending voucher schools did better in math and reading in the program's fourth year, compared to similar public school students.[34] One possible explanation, the study's authors note, is that weaker students dropped out or were counseled out of private schools. The researchers also cautioned that most of these gains could be attributed to the accountability measure imposed by the state legislature the year the plan was initiated, requiring private school students to take the state achievement tests, and the private schools' adoption of a teach-to-the-test curriculum.

Research findings are mixed. In Indiana, Louisiana, and Ohio, students who attended a voucher school had moderate to large declines in achievement compared to their peers in public school.[35] In Louisiana, a student who started at the fifty-third percentile in math dropped to the thirty-seventh percentile after two years in a voucher school. In Indiana and Ohio, this adverse effect persisted for four years. The Washington, D.C., results were more positive—while students' test scores fell during the first two years of the program, in the third year there was no clear affect on achievement.

Voucher proponents, including former president Donald Trump, contend that parents should receive public dollars for whatever school they choose, and taxpayers should be able to determine how their tax dollars are spent. They emphasize the fact that vouchers promote market competition among private as well as public schools, forcing schools to keep improving in order to attract students. There is some evidence to support this claim. Students in public schools that compete with voucher schools made greater test-score gains than those in public schools that didn't face such competition. What's more, students in both public and voucher schools did better on achievement tests in districts where vouchers were available.[36]

Critics advance a host of arguments. They note that the common school—free, secular, publicly supported schools, open to all children—is a bedrock institution. Vouchers reduce public school funding and reallocate the money to private schools; they deliver a windfall to well-off families that send their children to private schools.

Opponents also question the claim that private schools are more efficient, contending that the research shows that a voucher plan simply weakens public schools. They point out that public schools are held accountable for improving student achievement. Private schools are not accountable to any government agency if their students are underperforming; what's more, their finances are not audited, so there is no way to determine whether funds are being misused. While the "segregation academies" have long since vanished from the scene, vouchers typically increase racial and economic segregation.[37]

The curriculum of religious schools that participate in voucher programs is another cause for concern. It's estimated that more than three hundred schools teach creationism, instead of the theory of evolution, and some religious schools teach religious theology along with or instead of science. In June 2022, the Supreme Court ruled in *Carson v. Makin* that when states offer school voucher programs, they must include religious institutions.

Title VI of the Civil Rights Act bars all private schools from discriminating on the basis of race, color, or national origin in admissions and hiring, but Title IX, which prohibits sex-based discrimination, does not apply to private schools unless they receive federal funds, and they can be single-gender institutions. Private schools that accept vouchers cannot exclude a student based on disability if, "with minor adjustments," such a student could participate in the private school's education program. However, if the school does not offer programs designed to meet a student's special needs, its inability to serve that child is not considered discrimination. Sectarian schools may consider religion in admissions and hiring decisions.[38]

What is early childhood education?

The term *early childhood education* (ECE) refers to teaching, both formal and informal, from birth through age five, when children typically enter kindergarten.

ECE varies with children's developmental stage as well as the mode of teaching—that is, whether instruction relies on purposeful play, academic preparation for kindergarten, or a combination of the two pedagogical approaches. ECE programs incorporate a focus on children's socio-emotional development and physical development.

The teacher-child relationship distinguishes ECE from parenting programs, such as the Nurse-Parent Partnership, which are designed to strengthen parents' understanding of the rudiments of child development and give them the tools they may need to enrich their children's lives.[39] ECE also differs from traditional child care, which is carried out in daycare centers or else through informal arrangements such as babysitting, in which children's safety, not learning, is of paramount concern.

In recent years the distinction between early education and child care has become blurred. The National Association for the Education of Young Children (NAEYC) describes quality child care as emphasizing play-based learning that's designed to develop motor, social, language, and cognitive skills.[40] The Harvard Center for the Developing Child specifies that child care should be provided in a well-maintained environment specifically designed for children, with an adequate number of trained staff; time for both active and quiet play; and opportunities to develop motor, social, and cognitive skills.[41] Policies and services should support responsive relationships for children and adults; strengthen core skills for planning, adapting, and achieving goals; and reduce sources of stress in the lives of children and families. Similar criteria apply to high-quality ECE.

Providing quality early education to minority children and children from low-income families contributes substantially to equalizing educational opportunity. By the time they enter kindergarten, children of color are, on average, nearly nine months behind in math and almost seven months behind in reading, compared to their White classmates. A similar gap exists between children from low-income and middle-class families.[42] Children's literacy and numeracy skills at the time they start kindergarten are powerful predictors of later school success, and those who enter kindergarten without those skills find themselves at a substantial disadvantage.

The potential of preschool can only be realized if programs are of high quality. A high-quality program, according to early childhood education experts, features small classes and low student-teacher ratios, with well-trained teachers; an evidence-based curriculum that emphasizes hands-on learning, not eat-your-spinach instruction in the ABCs or coloring inside the lines; and lots of time for play. The focus is on kids' physical, social, and emotional growth as well as their cognitive development. In that setting youngsters, preferably from different social backgrounds, are solving problems together, while their teachers talk with, not at, them. Well-designed ECE has been shown to enable all children to enter kindergarten with the basic academic and social-emotional tools (sometimes called soft skills) they need for success.[43]

The Learning Policy Institute identifies the "building blocks" of quality as including comprehensive early learning standards and curricula, sufficient time, well-trained professionals, appropriate assessments, ongoing support for teachers, support for students with disabilities, and appropriate class size and student-teacher ratios. The National Institute for Early Education Research's quality benchmarks are similar.[44] NIEER issues an annual "report card" that shows how many of these benchmarks each state is meeting.[45]

Studies of high-quality ECE programs show long-term positive outcomes. The iconic Perry Preschool experiment compared three- and four-year-old children who went to preschool in the early 1960s with a control group of youngsters, identical in every other way, that didn't have this experience. The Perry children have been followed into middle age, a rarity in social science research, and the research has shown decades-long impacts. During their school years, these children were significantly less likely to repeat a grade or to be assigned to special education; they were significantly more likely to graduate from high school than the control group.[46] Later, significantly more of them went to college, had jobs, and were more likely to own their own homes; significantly fewer have been on welfare or been imprisoned.[47] A 2021 study found that these benefits are intergenerational, reaching the children of the Perry youngsters.

The Perry Preschool Project, as well as other early studies, evaluated the impact of small-scale initiatives.[48] Contemporary evaluations of large-scale pre-K programs confirm the finding that quality pre-K has substantial and sustained benefits.

Critics of prekindergarten argue that its effects fade in a year or two.[49] Initial evaluations of Head Start, the federal government's ECE program, seemed to confirm this contention. However, subsequent analyses have shown that the program increases the likelihood that participants will graduate from high school; attend college; and receive a postsecondary degree, license, or certification. Head Start also enhances social, emotional, and behavioral development, particularly among Black participants; the positive effects become evident years later, in adulthood measures of self-control, self-esteem, and positive parenting practices.[50]

An evaluation of the Tennessee prekindergarten (TN-VPK) program, undertaken during the first year of the program, found that by the under of kindergarten the participants no better than their peers who did not participate in the program. Furthermore, by the end of second grade, students who participated did *worse* in math and on a broad achievement test. This finding seemed to bolster the "fadeout" contention, inspiring critics to question the value of early education, but a closer examination of the program revealed that the teachers had neither experience nor training in the field and had little time to prepare their classes. Those factors indicate the most likely explanation for these results is that the program was of low quality.[51]

A randomized study in Boston found that over the course of a school year, prekindergarteners from low-income families gained between four and seven months in reading and math; those gains persisted through third grade.[52]

In the late 1990s and early 2000s, Boston couldn't meet the demand for pre-K, so a lottery was used to determine which children to accept. Economists Guthrie Gray-Lobe (University of Chicago), Parag Pathak (MIT), and Christopher Walters (UC Berkeley) tracked more than four thousand students from preschool through high school, comparing the outcomes of those who won a pre-K seat to those whose lottery number wasn't high enough.

"If you were to judge Boston pre-k by students' achievement test scores in sixth grade [the focus of the Tennessee study], it would look unimpressive," wrote Professor Pathak. Yet life-changing experiences, not test scores, are what matter, and the impact of attending Boston pre-K confirms the value of good early education. Those who attended preschool were less likely to be suspended or become entangled with the juvenile justice system. They were 6 percent more likely to graduate from high school and 8 percent more likely to enroll in college. The "soft skills" that children develop in preschool—wait your turn, share, use your words—are what drive academic and life success.[53]

Research in neuroscience and genetics confirms the importance of early experiences. Neuroscience has shown that the brain evolves more rapidly during the first years than at any other time in life. Using magnetic resonance imaging, researchers have learned that a child's brain has a hundred billion neurons at birth. What happens in the lives of infants and toddlers affects the architecture of a child's brain, as neural synapses are created and discarded at astonishing speeds. Although deficits in early experiences can be overcome, it is an arduous process. And while learning occurs throughout the life cycle, especially during adolescence, the brain's early development is crucial.[54]

Until the 1990s, geneticists conceptualized children's mental development in terms of heredity versus environment, or nature versus nurture. Only in extreme circumstances, as in the infamous case of the Romanian orphanages, did a child's early environment make much of a difference.[55] Arthur Jensen, a leading proponent of this position, contended that Head Start, the federal government's preschool program, was destined to fail because early education couldn't overcome inherited intelligence.[56] However, a spate of more recent research has shown that the correct frame of reference isn't nature *versus* nurture but nature *through* nurture and nurture *through* nature; much of what is described as hereditary becomes meaningful in the context of experience.

Across a wide array of disciplines in the natural and social sciences—developmental and behavioral neuroscience, program evaluation, genetics, medicine, and cognitive and behavioral psychology—researchers are converging on an understanding of human development that emphasizes the interplay of nature and nurture. These findings bolster the conclusion of the researchers who have evaluated the long-term impact of programs such as Perry.[57]

What is a community school?

In the late nineteenth century a social worker named Jane Addams opened a center called Hull House in a low-income, largely immigrant Chicago neighborhood. Hull House offered an array of services for children and families that supplemented the schools' offerings. It was the forerunner of the community school.[58]

Traditional public schools typically operate from 8:00 a.m. to 3:00 p.m., Monday through Friday, 180 days a year. They are stand-alone institutions, often unconnected to other public and private agencies. Their main focus is academics, and their success is often measured by achievement test scores.

The National Coalition of Community Schools reports that there are about five thousand community schools, and many districts have expanded the strategy throughout all their schools.[59]

The community school significantly expands the scope and role of a traditional public school. It addresses myriad aspects of children's development, including their social, emotional, physical, and psychological, as well as academic, development. It rejects the contention, often heard during the "No Child Left Behind" era (2002–2015), that schools should focus exclusively on academic performance and that personal, family, or community concerns do not "excuse" failure.[60]

The community school is most usefully thought of as a strategy, not a model. Its components vary, depending on what the community needs. Its essential components are student supports, such as counseling; activities such as art and sports; expanded learning time and opportunities; and family and community engagement. These activities are not add-ons but are integrated into the life of the school.

Structurally, most community schools open before the start of the regular school day and remain open until the evening; many of these schools are also open on Saturdays and during the summer. Using the school as a hub, the community school connects partners that range from health, dental, and optometry clinics to local businesses and cultural institutions.

The community school serves not only children but parents and the surrounding community as well. It may direct parents to job-training opportunities; deliver clothing, food, furniture, and bikes; and enable teenage mothers to stay in school by providing day care for their infants. Parents are enlisted in their children's education. In some programs, they have the opportunity to take classes that, depending on their interest, may range from cooking and computer literacy to citizenship test preparation. Parents also play an active role in charting the direction of the community school.[61]

Here's what one such school looks like: "A dentist comes by regularly. So does an optometrist, and students who need glasses get them free. Parents are ubiquitous at the school, learning computer skills, attending a 'caring for the caregiver' class or picking up groceries from the food pantry. The school gives coats to their children, and washing machines on the premises allow them to keep their kids' uniforms looking sharp. Pro bono lawyers are available to counsel families on immigration, housing and health insurance."[62]

Research indicates that community schools improve the lives of students.[63] The Learning Policy Institute's review of copious studies concludes:

> Integrated student supports provided by these schools are associated with positive student outcomes. [They] often show significant improvements in attendance, behavior, social functioning, and academic achievement. . . . Longer school days and academically rich and engaging after-school, weekend, and summer programs are associated with positive academic and non-academic outcomes. . . . The meaningful family and community engagement found in community schools is associated with positive student outcomes, such as reduced absenteeism, improved academic outcomes, and student reports of more positive school climates. Additionally, this can increase trust among students, parents, and staff, which in turn has positive effects on student outcomes.[64]

A rigorous evaluation of Boston's City Connects (CCNX), a community school initiative for third, fourth, and fifth graders, found that students in that program had higher reading and math grades than a matched sample of peers. The magnitude of these positive effects was sufficient to overcome the negative effects of poverty, and the impact of the program lasted long after it ended. In middle school, these students performed better on statewide tests than the control group. They were less likely to be left back or drop out and more likely to graduate from high school, enroll in college, and earn a degree.[65]

As with all educational initiatives, how well the program is implemented determines its success. A nationwide evaluation of Communities in Schools (CIS), which operates twenty-five hundred community schools in twenty-five states and the District of Columbia, found that the impact of the program on student performance depended on how frequently students participated in CIS programs.[66]

What is homeschooling?

Children who are homeschooled are educated by their parents, rather than by a public or private school.

There were 3.7 million homeschooled students in 2020–21, about 6 percent of school-aged children. Those numbers had been increasing annually, between 2 and 8 percent, in recent years. The number of homeschooled students grew substantially from 2019–20 to 2020–21, in large part because most public and private schools were closed due to Covid.

Many parents choose to homeschool their children in order to provide them with religious instruction, and a large part of the growth has come from Christian fundamentalist sects. Concerns regarding the climate of public schools—for instance, the prevalence of drugs or fears about safety—and unhappiness with the quality of academic offerings are the other frequently cited explanations. The growth in the number of homeschooled children has led to a proliferation of instructional resources and networks that support homeschooling.[67]

Conservative and religious White families are not the only group opting to homeschool their students: "Black homeschooling families found they were often pushed out of traditional school systems when their children encountered racist treatment in the classroom. In interviews, Latino families expressed similar concerns. And Asian families sought to influence their children's cultural education."[68]

Disputes have arisen over whether homeschooling families are entitled to state resources. Every state has compulsory education laws, and the legally legitimate reach of government control over curriculum and standardized testing is another controversial issue. The extent to which homeschooling is regulated varies among the states.

Critics argue that children who have been educated by their parents have fewer social skills and are being brainwashed.[69] In *Homeschooling on the Right*, political scientist Heath Brown argues that by opting out of public education and organizing politically, homeschoolers have advanced conservative goals of reducing the size and influence of government generally.[70]

Some of these concerns may be misplaced. A literature review concludes that "the majority of peer-reviewed studies reveal a positive effect for the homeschooled students compared to institutional schooled students, while a few studies show mixed or negative results. Regarding social and emotional development, a large majority of studies show clearly positive outcomes for the homeschooled compared to those in conventional schools. A majority of the studies on the relative success of the home-educated who later became adults show positive outcomes for the homeschooled compared to those who had been in conventional schools."[71]

The academic performance of homeschooled children depends on the quality of education that their parents provide. A Canadian study found that children whose parents adopted a "school-at-home" approach, with a well-structured curriculum, outperformed their public school counterparts on standardized achievement tests; children whose parents took the "unschooling" view that education emerges from a child's day-to-day activities did substantially worse.[72]

Homeschooling parents are increasingly collaborating with public and private schools. Their children divide their time between being homeschooled and attending traditional schools. Parents turn to the schools to teach difficult subjects, such as foreign languages and science, and their children may participate in extracurricular and athletic activities.

What is high-stakes accountability?

High-stakes accountability is a strategy designed to improve student achievement and narrow the achievement gap by rewarding or penalizing teachers and schools, based on students' performance on state achievement tests. The No Child Left Behind Act (NCLB, 2001) was premised on the efficacy of this approach: beginning in the third grade, students were tested annually in reading through the eighth grade, then once during high school.

The strategy is highly controversial. Supporters assert that schools and teachers should be held accountable for their performance. Because businesses and their employees are evaluated this way, the argument runs, they function efficiently. Similarly, a performance-based accountability system in schools compels educators to focus on improving student achievement.

What's more, proponents assert that teachers are motivated to improve their students' achievement only if they are threatened by punishment or promised a reward. Otherwise, the argument runs, low-income and minority students in schools with weak test scores are victimized because their teachers and administrators believe those results are inevitable. President George W. Bush memorably described this as the "soft bigotry of low expectations."[73]

Critics point out that high-stakes testing leads teachers to teach to the test. Skills such as critical thinking and working with others are better measured by performance-based assessments.[74] The comparison with business is inapt, they assert, because focusing on rewards and punishments undermines the caring relationship between teachers and students essential for authentic student learning. What's more, educators, unlike business employees, have a moral responsibility to promote students' overall growth that may be at odds with prioritizing higher test scores. It is difficult, the critics contend, for good teaching to flourish in a high-stakes testing and accountability regime that punishes students and teachers.[75] The best way to improve student achievement isn't through high-stakes tests but by distributing resources more equitably.

The pressure on students may be overwhelming and counterproductive to their development. Reliance on high-stakes tests is associated with higher dropout rates because those who fail experience an increased "sense of discouragement."[76]

The strongest evidence of the positive effects of high-stakes accountability comes from a study that showed substantial increases in reading and math test scores in Texas public schools following the introduction of this strategy. The results were so impressive that the strategy was dubbed the Texas miracle.[77] In other states, high-stakes testing has also been linked to improved test scores.[78]

A subsequent study of the Texas program concluded that pressure to teach to the tests led teachers to focus on aggregations of facts and meaningless exercises in order to prepare students to answer the test questions. As a result, students who passed the reading test were unable to use those skills to understand what they were reading.[79]

What critics call the "drill and kill" approach was widely used during the NCLB era. In a national survey, 79 percent of teachers reported that they devoted class time to teaching test-taking skills such as filling in bubbles on multiple-choice questions. Only when assessments "encourage more ambitious teaching—for example, by asking for written arguments or applications of knowledge"—did teachers "attempt changes beyond practicing test-like multiple-choice items."[80]

In a high-stakes accountability environment, teachers felt pressured to show that their students' test scores were consistently improving. Some of them resorted to cheating in order to meet the expectations of district administrators. In 2015, an Atlanta jury convicted eleven teachers in a test-cheating scandal. Superintendent Beverly Hall was alleged to have run a "corrupt" organization that used test scores to financially reward and punish teachers, depending on their students' achievement test scores, which led some teachers to change their students' answers in order to obtain better results.

Similar allegations of cheating were reported in nearly forty states and the District of Columbia.[81] This epidemic of cheating was driven by the requirements of NCLB, which mandated that if "annual yearly progress" benchmarks were not met, schools, teachers, and principals would face sanctions, ultimately including school closure. Similarly, Race to the Top, a competition among states for federal funding, tied teacher evaluations and pay to students' test scores.

What is the "no excuses" strategy for closing the achievement gap?

The "no excuses" strategy is premised on the belief that children's experiences outside the schoolhouse are irrelevant to their academic performance. Schools should concentrate exclusively on achievement, as measured by test scores. "Poverty is not destiny" was the motto of advocates of this approach, including Arne Duncan, President Obama's education secretary. It is the premise on which the high-stakes accountability regime, Obama's Race to the Top initiative, and NCLB were based.[82]

Michelle Rhee, chancellor of the Washington, D.C., school district (2007–10), was the poster child for the "no excuses" approach. Rhee was featured on the cover of *Time*, and the Gates Foundation spent $2 million to promote the film *Waiting for Superman*, which portrayed her as a savior of public education.

Rhee demanded results, measured by constantly improving students' achievement test results. Poverty, substance abuse, crime, or lack of access to health care in the neighborhood where a student grew up didn't affect her calculations. "You can never, ever, ever let [poverty] be an excuse for the kids not achieving at the highest levels."[83] Rhee presided over substantial test score irregularities during her term as D.C. schools chancellor. Nearly two-thirds of D.C.'s public schools had unaccountably high erasure rates on standardized tests, as wrong answers were erased and changed to right ones.

A cursory review by a consulting firm absolved every school of wrongdoing.[84]

Prominent charter school networks, including KIPP, Uncommon Schools, Success Academy, YES Prep, and Achievement First, adopted the "no excuses" model. They developed elaborate behavioral regimes, starting in kindergarten, that demanded submission and obedience.[85] Some charter networks continue to champion this approach, pointing out that test scores are robust and parent demand remains high. Critics have described these schools as militaristic, rigid institutions that concentrate on rote learning.[86]

Although the Every Student Succeeds Act (2017) broadened the NCLB criteria for evaluating school performance, advocates of the "no excuses" model continue to battle with those who believe that students' out-of-school life affects achievement.

What is standards-based education?

Standards-based education specifies the content that students are expected to have mastered at a particular grade level. Tests are aligned with these standards, and test results are the metric of accountability.

The standards are intended to influence curriculum, assessment, and professional development. The teacher determines how students acquire the skills; for example, a ninth-grade standard in reading may require students to cite specific evidence to support an argument, and a teacher can choose to generate that skill by using a novel or a magazine article.

Standards-based education was initially proposed during President George H. W. Bush's 1989 education summit, where experts set national education goals for 2000. In 2001, after many schools fell short of meeting these goals, Congress passed the NCLB Act. Rather than setting national standards, the legislation required each state to adopt its own reading and math standards, administer tests to assess student outcomes, and review each school's results to ensure "adequate yearly progress."

Common Core State Standards (CCSS) are the most recent iteration of standards-based education reform. Those standards, championed by the Council of Chief State School Officers and the National Governors Association, were drafted in 2009 by K–12 educators and subject matter experts.[87] Advocates argued that well-designed standards would encourage the creation of more rigorous assessments and prepare students for college and twenty-first-century careers. Arne Duncan enthused that the standards "may prove to be the single greatest thing to happen to public education in America since *Brown v. Board of Education*."[88] They were adopted by forty-one states and prompted collaboration in designing suitable curricula.[89]

Despite bipartisan initial support for the CCSS, their rollout provoked criticism. Right-wing political groups like the Tea Party warned of federal overreach. Influential commentators like Diane Ravitch argued that the development and implementation of the standards had been rushed, and that the standards reduced teachers' flexibility in designing courses.[90] In some states, parents organized boycotts of standards-based state exams.

Rigorous evaluations have found little if any improvement in reading and math achievement in states that adopted the CCSS.[91] Researchers acknowledge that it is difficult to estimate the true impact of these standards, as states adopted them at different times and implemented them with varying degrees of fidelity. Some analysts have argued that the problem is not with the standards themselves but the inadequate amount of time allotted to preparing suitable course materials and strengthening teacher training.[92]

While some states have officially opted out of CCSS, most of them simply changed the name without changing the substance of the standards.[93]

What is the No Child Left Behind Act (NCLB)?

The No Child Left Behind Act of 2001 (the federal education legislation in the years 2002–2015) reauthorized the 1965 Elementary and Secondary Education Act. NCLB expanded the federal government's role in holding schools accountable for student outcomes. The goal was to boost the performance of low-performing students, including English Language Learners, students in special education, minority youth, and those from low-income families. The strategy to achieve this goal was to identify schools that needed help and incentivize them to improve. If that didn't have the desired effect, the state was required to step in or risk the loss of federal funds.

States were required to administer annual reading and math tests in grades 3–8, and once in high school; science assessments were added later. The states designed and administered the tests and determined what constituted proficiency, while the federal government specified what results were expected and the consequences of failing to meet those expectations.

Schools were expected to show that students made adequate yearly progress, as measured by improved test scores. The goal was 100 percent "proficiency" in reading and math by 2014; each state was tasked with determining what that meant. A school that didn't meet this standard for two consecutive years had to give its students the option of transferring to a high-performing public school and was required to offer private tutoring. A school that did not meet the adequate yearly progress standard for five consecutive years had to replace its teachers and administrators, be reconstituted as a charter school, or be taken over by the state. A state that did not comply with these requirements risked losing federal funds.

It is difficult to isolate the impact of NCLB because that would require disentangling the multiple factors that affect student achievement, including funding, teacher quality, poverty, and students' motivation to do well on exams. Still, student performance on the National Assessment of Educational

Progress (NAEP), often described as the nation's report card, indicated that NCLB didn't generate the hoped-for gains in student achievement for all children, as well as for students living in poverty and minority students. Those students had recorded substantial gains between 1986 and 1999, well before the passage of NCLB, but their performance did not improve in subsequent years.

What's more, NCLB focuses only on reading and mathematics, ignoring art, social studies, physical education, music, and other academic subjects as well as character development. The results indicate only how well students were prepared to take certain kinds of tests, which may not translate into usable skills. Crucially, there was no evidence of any long-term effects.[94]

NCLB initially had strong bipartisan support. Civil rights groups saw it as a way to close the race and social class achievement gap; the business community regarded it as a way to promote American competitiveness in the global market by increasing the number of well-trained workers. In Congress, Senator Ted Kennedy led the charge.

Soon after the legislation took effect, bitter arguments erupted among the partisans. Proponents argued that NCLB focused on children with the greatest needs, incentivizing schools to identify students with poor test scores and give them extra help. Because a school's aggregate test scores were public information, parents had a better understanding of the education their children were receiving. If their children were attending "failing" schools, the transfer and tutoring options gave parents a chance to secure a higher-quality education for them.

Opponents criticized NCLB for treating students' performance on reading and math tests as the sole measure of a school's success. Consequently, less time was devoted to subjects that weren't tested. Because NCLB used student proficiency to rate schools, it was almost inevitable that those ratings would be closely linked to poverty, which, in the eyes of the critics, unfairly penalized schools because of the students they served. And while NCLB created an elaborate system of sanctions for "failing" schools, it didn't specify what interventions would help a struggling school.

Critics also noted that the law led schools to rid themselves of students who were not doing well, harming the very students it was designed to help. Researchers found that districts held back, suspended, expelled, or counseled out students who had not met the proficiency benchmark, in order to boost districts' test scores.[95]

Previously, it had been common practice to assign instructors to teach subjects with which they were unfamiliar. Because NCLB required schools to hire "highly qualified teachers," the overall quality of teachers was supposed to improve, but the requirement led to teacher shortages in math, science, and special education.

Testing wasn't the way to remedy the achievement gap, opponents argued—more money was essential, in order to counter the impact of generations of neglect and strengthen schools with concentrations of low-income and minority students. Although the proponents of NCLB anticipated that major increases in the federal education budget would offset the cost of reaching the student achievement goals, those funds were not forthcoming; NCLB funds were less than 10 percent of most districts' budgets.

In 2015 the Department of Education concluded that NCLB-driven testing regimes were "draining creative approaches from our classrooms," "consuming too much instructional time," and "creating undue stress for educators and students." The Every Student Succeeds Act is an effort to address some of these objections.

What is the Every Student Succeeds Act (ESSA)?

The Every Student Succeeds Act (ESSA), passed by Congress in 2015 with bipartisan backing, replaced the NCLB Act.

ESSA reduces the federal role in decision-making, enabling the states to eliminate practices such as teach-to-the-test pedagogy. It softens the "high-stakes" approach by giving states greater say over their goals and standards.

Instead of relying entirely on math, reading, and science tests, some states have developed academic standards for other subjects, including social studies, music, and art. The legislation requires that those standards be "challenging," so that students are prepared for college.

ESSA requires that in rating schools, states must include at least one schoolwide measure, such as kindergarten readiness, absenteeism, school climate, and student engagement.[96]

NCLB relied mainly on sticks, rather than carrots, to assure that schools were making "adequate yearly progress." ESSA leaves it to the states to determine how best to support low-performing schools, defined by the legislation as those in the bottom 10 percent of high school graduation rates in the state or with test scores that the state deems not "proficient." When a school is rated as "struggling," states and school districts, in collaboration with parents, must design a strategy to help it improve.

States must also create school "report cards," which include test scores, graduation rates, and school funding, as a way of communicating to parents how their children's schools are performing.

Key elements of the NCLB approach remain intact. ESSA mandates annual testing for third through eighth grades, and once during high school. Because "much greater weight" must be placed on these achievement tests than on schoolwide measures such as school climate, teach-to-the-test instruction persists. What's more, because high-poverty schools are likeliest to record low achievement scores, the spotlight—and the accompanying obligation to make changes—still focuses on those schools. Some states emphasize academic growth, rather than absolute achievement, in rating schools, and that measure is less closely linked to poverty.

ESSA, like NCLB, does a much better job of defining, measuring, and proscribing than of showing schools how they can
improve. The law has not led states to propose new ways of
assisting low-performing schools. Instead, they have created
vague plans that do not specify what support they will deliver.[97]

What is the systemic reform strategy?

Systemic reform, an approach developed in the 1990s, is
designed to improve student outcomes, align policy approaches
and institutional strategies to promote these outcomes, and re-
structure the public education governance system to support
improved achievement.

Systemic problems require systemic solutions: a continuous improvement approach focused on the quality of education for underserved students as well as the quality of the
educational system that targets interventions focusing on key
transitions (for example, from middle school to high school)
and stronger ties between schools and other organizations that
affect students' development and well-being.[98] One way to
achieve this last objective is through community schools.

Advocates argue that piecemeal interventions such as
ending tracking ignore the underlying systemic factors that
generate deep and pervasive inequities. They argue for an
approach that incorporates a system-wide focus on quality
improvement within a standards-based framework, targeted
interventions to address pervasive disparities, and coordi-
nation between schools and other child- and family-focused
agencies and organizations.[99]

An evaluation of systemic reform efforts in three states
identified "a tension between enacting the reform vision
and maintaining current practice." The evaluation identified
four major challenges: aligning curriculum between grades,
aligning the curriculum being taught with the assessments
used to measure students' knowledge of that curriculum,
linking teacher preparation and professional development

with other elements of systemic reform, and creating a stable political environment that's essential in maintaining state reform efforts.[100]

What is the continuous improvement strategy?

School systems are notoriously difficult to manage. The well-known "garbage can" model of organizational behavior aptly describes how some of them operate. There is no organizational process for solving problems, and decision makers, "disconnected from problems and solutions," change frequently. Amid the resulting chaos, many possible solutions—"organizational garbage"—emerge. "Choice opportunities are treated like garbage cans. Various problems and solutions are thrown into these opportunities—just like garbage."[101]

The continuous improvement strategy takes a diametrically opposite approach. Developed by management guru C. Edwards Deming in the context of industry (Deming is widely credited with the 1980s "Japanese miracle" in manufacturing), it has been adopted by a wide range of complex organizations, including school systems.[102]

In the continuously improving school system, teachers and administrators are perpetually scanning the educational landscape for promising new ideas. The district learns from experience, testing and refining these ideas, discarding those that don't work, and bringing to scale those that evidence-based evaluation shows are effective.[103]

One of the primary tools of continuous improvement is the Plan-Do-Study-Act (PDSA) inquiry cycle. Ideas are rapidly tested, resulting in efficient feedback. A key aspect of the PDSA approach is small-scale testing of new ideas, which enables quick learning and nimble adjustments with minimal cost. Over time, and with repeated cycles of small-scale testing, an organization can identify ways to improve and bring those strategies to scale. Improvement science—developed by Anthony Bryk, the former director of the Carnegie Foundation for the Advancement of Teaching—is a closely related approach.[104]

The continuous improvement strategy is baked into many statewide school accountability systems. Some states require low-performing schools to conduct a root cause analysis of the school's problems, interviewing stakeholders such as teachers and parents. Based on this feedback, the school creates a plan to boost outcomes like reading scores or attendance. Proponents of this approach argue that schools and districts should base their strategy, in part, on the perspectives of those who work directly with students.

The way in which the Union, Oklahoma, school district introduced the community school approach shows how continuous improvement works. Beginning in the 1980s, the makeup of the student body began to change: middle-class White families were leaving the school system, and a growing number of low-income and immigrant families moved into the district. Assessing the situation, school officials realized that because of the difficulties these families encountered in adjusting to their new homeland, focusing entirely on academics wasn't enough. Turning traditional schools into community schools looked like a plausible, promising approach because that strategy encompasses an array of nonacademic supports that the neighborhoods needed. Instead of making rapid change districtwide, Union tested the model in two schools. When an evaluation of the pilot community schools showed that attendance and test scores soared while suspensions plummeted, Union converted all its elementary schools into community schools.[105]

3

THE KEY PLAYERS

What is an effective teacher?

Highly effective teachers—those who expand students' academic knowledge and foster noncognitive skills—are invaluable to student success. Decades of research have confirmed that students with high-quality teachers have better learning outcomes.[1] High-performing teachers generate five to six more months of student learning each year than their low-performing colleagues.[2]

A teacher's impact on their students is not limited to the time that students spend in their classroom. Students with high-quality kindergarten through third-grade classroom teachers are more likely to attend college and receive higher pay in adulthood. Similarly, ninth-grade teachers, tasked with supporting students during the stress-filled transition to high school, affect students' subsequent attendance, suspension, and graduation. Students with highly effective teachers are also less likely to become pregnant as teenagers.[3]

Research specifies the attributes of high-quality teachers, including the following:

- *High expectations of all their students*: these shape how teachers relate to their students. Teachers with high expectations acknowledge differences in students' background and socio-economic status. They address students' needs while setting a high bar for all learners.[4]

- *Strong teaching pedagogy*: high-quality teachers know how to plan lessons with clear outcomes, organize ideas and content, and create engaging and accessible learning experiences for all students.
- *Content knowledge*: high-quality teachers must have a background in the material that's being taught and know how to connect pedagogy to content.
- *Skill at building relationships with students*: this is essential. Effective teachers empathize with students. They "see their perspective, communicate it back to them so that they have valuable feedback to self-assess, feel safe, and learn to understand others and the content with the same interest and concern."[5]
- *Responsiveness to student needs*: even when using a prescribed curriculum, strong teachers adapt and tailor instruction.
- *Continuous improvement and professional collaboration*: high-quality teachers strive to improve their practice through ongoing reflection and collaboration with other professionals.

Teachers with very different personalities exhibit the requisite skills. Having an advanced degree does not predict teacher quality or student outcomes.[6]

It is easier to specify the attributes of high-quality teachers than to identify them by using evaluation rubrics. Value-added modeling methodology is intended to capture the increase in student test scores in a given school year, and researchers use those data to determine a teacher's effectiveness. Whether this is a useful approach has been a topic of debate among researchers. Those who embrace it argue that the data show that teachers with higher value-added scores have a significant impact on students' test scores, noncognitive skills, and long-term outcomes.[7] Critics counter that the methodology is flawed and does not accurately measure a teacher's impact.[8]

How are teachers recruited and retained?

Most new teachers are recruited from university-based teacher training programs, while experienced teachers are hired from other school districts. Although recruiting excellent teachers is essential for student success, it matters even more that they be retained, for teachers continue to improve with experience.[9]

Every year, one teacher in twelve leaves the profession. That's nearly twice the rate in countries like Singapore and Finland, whose students excel in the international Programme for International Student Assessment (PISA) exams.[10]

High rates of teacher turnover are linked to lower student performance.[11] A comprehensive system of recruitment and retention—a recruitment strategy that generates a diverse pool of highly qualified teacher candidates; ongoing professional development; and strategies to support veteran teachers, including continued coaching and professional advancement to supervisory positions—can encourage teachers to remain in the classroom.

School districts' conventional hiring practices shrink the pool of talented candidates.[12] New teachers are usually recruited through job postings on school district websites and in job fairs. This approach typically results in a hyperlocal and homogeneous group of candidates.[13] Some districts have learned to project the number of teacher openings early in the hiring season, increase the applicant pool through social media outreach, and gather feedback from candidates about their hiring experience.[14]

Not surprisingly, teacher compensation contributes to teacher retention. The prospect of higher earnings may keep some teachers on the job. Although increased pay is associated with a modest reduction in turnover, there is no consensus regarding what salary scale is most effective in inducing high-quality teachers to remain in the classroom.[15]

When the Covid-19 pandemic magnified the national teacher shortage, more school systems offered signing bonuses to attract new teachers. This appears to be a Band-Aid solution; bonuses may help the district hire more teachers in the short term but have little if any effect on retaining teachers.[16] In communities where housing is expensive, districts are experimenting with housing subsidies to recruit and retain teachers. In Oakland, California, the school system has gone one step further: it plans to repurpose unused vacant school district buildings and transform them into housing for teachers.[17]

The climate of the school also has an impact on whether a teacher remains in the classroom. New teachers need advice and support from fellow teachers, through mentoring, as well as from principals who see themselves not simply as administrators but as education leaders. Teachers are more likely to remain in the classroom when they receive ongoing training, which is best delivered not in conferences, but by coaches who work with them in their classrooms.[18]

The demographics of the 3.2 million public schoolteachers do not reflect the racial and ethnic diversity of students. A 2016 survey from the US Department of Education found that 80 percent are White and 77 percent are female.[19] Despite the growing racial and ethnic diversity of students, only 9 percent are Latino, 7 percent are Black, and 2 percent are Asian. This disparity suggests that there may well be talented prospective teachers, particularly from underrepresented demographic groups, who are not being recruited into the profession.[20] The failure to hire and retain a diverse pool of teachers contributes to the nationwide shortage.

Maintaining a teaching staff that reflects the student body's racial composition has a significant impact on student performance.[21] One study found that low-income Black male students were nearly 40 percent less likely to drop out of high school if they had a "role model" Black teacher in third, fourth, or fifth grade.[22]

What is teacher preparation?

Each state issues a teaching credential (also called a license or certificate), which is based on tests, coursework, and/or teaching experience. Depending on the grade level they plan to teach, teachers must demonstrate content knowledge in the field in which they are teaching as well as a grasp of effective pedagogy.

Designing a program that prepares teachers for today's classroom is a demanding task. As Covid vividly illustrated, teachers must become more technologically literate. Students with special needs and English Language Learners are often assigned to general education classrooms, and teachers must understand how to tailor their approach in order to include them. And because their students are likely to come from a wide array of backgrounds, teachers need to be trained in culturally responsive modes of teaching.

College and university education departments do the lion's share of teacher training, which includes both academic coursework and supervised teaching (also called clinical practice), with faculty and staff mentoring the aspiring teachers.[23] The time spent as a practice teacher is the most crucial component of teacher preparation. One study found that first-year teachers can be as effective as third-year teachers if they have ten weeks of practice teaching and are observed by an effective mentor who gives them written feedback.[24] Other professions, such as medicine, have a similar model—students shadow experienced doctors with hands-on training, repetition, and ample feedback.

Enrollment in these traditional teacher preparation programs has declined by one-third during the past decade.[25] The cost of these programs discourages candidates from entering the profession. Would-be teachers are also disheartened by the relatively low salaries and challenging working conditions such as large class sizes.[26]

Alternative pathway programs like Teach for America (TFA) and Mississippi Teacher Corps shrink the time devoted to academic coursework to as little as four weeks, after which trainees are placed in the classroom.[27] Because of the short duration, this crash course boot camp, which incorporates lesson planning as well as a modicum of developmental psychology and awareness of the relevance of sociocultural factors, has attracted more prospective teachers.[28] After completing the abbreviated training, teachers apply for a temporary credential, which enables them to start teaching immediately while pursuing the training and coursework required for a permanent credential.

Critics assert that teachers who enter the profession through these alternative routes start their careers underprepared and do their students a disservice. Research shows that traditional and alternative pathways teachers are equally effective in boosting student achievement. However, the turnover rate among teachers who enter the profession in this accelerated manner is higher than for those who have been trained in the customary way.[29]

Other training models, such as the Ozarks Teaching Corps in Missouri and Tartans Rural Teacher Corps, focus on a particular region. These programs partner with local universities, placing the newly minted teachers in high-need communities. They typically require a multiyear commitment from the students, who receive scholarships to cover all or part of the cost of securing a teaching license or degree.

Teacher residency programs represent another accelerated pathway to the classroom. As in the university-based model, residents take academic courses while teaching under the supervision of a mentor teacher. While these programs are shorter and less expensive than the traditional model, students may have to work or study as much as seventy hours a week in order to meet the credentialing requirements.

Residency program graduates are less likely to leave the field, come from more diverse backgrounds, and are more sought after by school administrators than traditionally trained teachers.[30]

What is teacher professional development?

Teachers have customarily worked alone, behind the closed classroom door, where their word is law. But numerous studies have shown that teachers, like other professionals, benefit from ongoing collaboration and training. That is why the typical district spends an estimated $18,000 to provide professional development (PD) for each teacher, and 10 percent of a teacher's time is devoted to PD.[31]

If training is going to improve teachers' skills, quality is the make-or-break factor. Unfortunately, the most widely used training model is ineffective. PD typically consists of brief workshops, irreverently referred to as "spray and pray." In theory, the teachers who attend such a workshop bring what they have learned back to their schools, sharing it with their fellow teachers. But research indicates that this form of PD doesn't develop the teacher expertise that's required to improve student learning.[32]

Researchers have identified the components of high-quality professional development:

1. *Content-focused*: teachers' skills and understandings are directly related to the extent that PD focuses on subject matter content.[33]
2. *Ongoing and extended*: PD should be continuous, not episodic, and include follow-up and support for further learning. Extended professional development experiences, rather than one-time sessions, allow for more substantive engagement with subject matter and more opportunities for active learning; they connect more coherently to teachers' daily work.

3. *Collaborative*: "Teacher learning is beneficial when they collaborate with professional peers, both within and outside of their schools, and when they gain further technical expertise through access to external researchers."

4. *Embedded in daily work*: PD should be largely school based and incorporated into the day-to-day work of teachers.

5. *Coherent and integrated*: PD should incorporate experiences consistent with teachers' goals; be aligned with standards, assessments, and other reform initiatives; and be informed by the best available research evidence.

6. *Inquiry-based*: PD should promote continuous inquiry and reflection through active learning.

7. *Teacher-driven*: PD should respond to teachers' self-identified needs and interests.[34]

Professional development is most effectively provided through mentoring and coaching. While coaching and mentoring are distinct activities, they are often used as complementary strategies.

Mentoring, sometimes referred to as peer coaching, involves an interaction between teachers that is intended to strengthen the mentees' skills. The relationship entails modeling: the mentee observes the mentor's teaching, then the mentor observes the mentee's teaching and offers feedback.

Mentoring commands widespread support among teachers and educators.[35] It is especially valuable for novice teachers because it can alleviate the pressure and insecurity that often come with being new to the classroom. That's likely the reason new teachers who receive intensive mentoring are far more likely than the typical teacher to remain in the profession.[36] Additionally, having become better teachers, they often serve as mentors to the next generation of novices.

Mentors usually teach in the same school as their mentees. By contrast, the coaching model brings an outside expert into the classroom, where, using evidence-based strategies, they work one-on-one with a teacher. Depending on the context, the coach offers the teacher a framework for managing the classroom, designing the curriculum, improving the quality of teaching, and/or assessing students' progress. The interaction between the coach and the teacher is tailored to the individual teacher's needs and sustained over an extended period of time.

When coaching is well implemented, it has a substantial impact on the quality of instruction, enabling teachers to become more skillful practitioners. The effect on students' achievement, while smaller, is nonetheless significant.[37] Those outcomes compare favorably with the standard PD model.

Coaching is effective only in a school where teachers are respected, are free to take risks, and have the backing of the principal—in short, a school with a learning-friendly culture. If effective one-to-one coaching becomes a schoolwide practice, the relationships forged during coaching may contribute to a better school climate, which in turn encourages teachers to continue working in the profession.[38]

What is teacher evaluation?

Evaluation is intended to determine a teacher's pedagogical effectiveness and their students' academic progress. Feedback from evaluation is supposed to generate a prescription for improvement. Evaluation is also a tool for identifying teachers who are struggling in the classroom.

School principals traditionally appraised their teachers by observing their classes.[39] Now most evaluations also include an assessment of a teacher's lesson planning and the classroom environment, as well as students' academic performance. During the "high-stakes" accountability era, teachers were held accountable for students' test scores, with their livelihood on the line.

Unfortunately there is no evaluation instrument that reliably predicts either teacher quality or student outcomes.[40] The New Teacher Project (TNTP) reviewed thousands of evaluations from twelve districts. Its influential 2009 report concluded that schools could not identify exceptional teachers—99 percent were rated "good" or "great." Teachers reported that evaluation did not lead to feedback or opportunities for professional development. Novice teachers believed that because they had been insufficiently trained, the commonly used evaluations were an unfair measure of their skills.

The TNTP also found that teachers who received poor performance ratings were generally not held accountable. A popular documentary, *Waiting for Superman*, assailed teachers' unions for protecting poorly performing teachers.[41] The TNTP report, coupled with broader critiques of public school bureaucracy, sparked debates among union officials, reform advocates, private-sector philanthropists, government officials, and practitioners about how best to evaluate teachers. Union leaders, as well as many teachers, asserted that the tools commonly used to evaluate teachers did not fully capture strong teaching. Moreover, they pointed out that the weight given to test scores in the evaluation led teachers to adopt a rigid "teach to the test" pedagogy.[42]

The Obama administration's Race to the Top initiative fueled the demand for more robust evaluations. The Gates Foundation, which was closely aligned with the administration, invested $700 million in designing and implementing new measures.[43] The instrument developed by the Gates Foundation included several dozen performance indicators and two classroom observations. Using the instrument, each participating district categorized teachers, describing them as entering, effective, highly effective, or master teachers. An evaluation found that the Gates model, coupled with funding for professional development, did not result in meaningful increases in student achievement in school districts that participated in the experiment.[44] The districts concluded that the model was unusable because it imposed an excessive burden on teachers and administrators and was too costly.[45]

Another approach, pay-for-performance evaluation, is grounded in the belief that incentives are the only way to motivate teachers to improve. Advocates argue that incentives should lead to better teaching, entice the strongest teachers to remain in the field, and improve student learning. However, several studies have found that pay-for-performance had little, if any, effect on student outcomes.[46]

Entangled with the teacher evaluation debate is the related process of granting tenure to teachers. About half of the forty-five states with teacher tenure legislation include a teacher performance or evaluation component in the process.[47] Tenure is an up-or-out process. Often, after three years in the classroom, teachers earn tenure and (except for instances of moral dereliction, such as being in a relationship with a student) are rarely fired.

American Federation of Teachers (AFT) president Randi Weingarten contends that "tenure is not a job for life. It's ensuring fairness and due process before someone can be fired, plain and simple." Critics counter that tenure makes it nearly impossible to fire ineffective teachers. Nationwide, about one in five hundred tenured teachers is fired for poor performance.[48]

Evaluations have become more useful in recent years. An increasing number of districts have adopted a system that reflects the daily work of a teacher and is tied to professional development, coaching, mentoring, and timely feedback. A recent report found that districts with effective teacher evaluation systems focused on growth and thoughtfully weighted at least three measures, such as student learning, student surveys, and instructional observations. The report's methodology also defined "successful evaluations" as tools to encourage less effective teachers to leave the classroom.[49]

What are teachers' unions?

Teachers' unions advocate for improved working conditions, including higher wages, smaller class sizes, and more school support staff (e.g., teachers' aides, nurses, or counselors).

They also promote education reforms that coincide with their priorities.

The two largest unions are the National Education Association (NEA) (2.3 million members) and the American Federation of Teachers (AFT) (1.7 million members). The National Education Agency, the first teachers' union (renamed the National Educational Association), was founded in 1857. It sought to raise teachers' salaries, promoted the education of emancipated slaves, and called attention to the forced assimilation of Native Americans.

During the 1960s, the NEA and the AFT were key actors in the civil rights campaign. For the past sixty years they have engaged in collective bargaining with school districts, sometimes relying on strikes as a pressure tactic.[50] In states that prohibit public employee unions, professional organizations have a similar agenda, although they cannot engage in collective bargaining.

Teachers' unions have become a force in national politics. Between 1989 and 2014, the NEA spent more than $90 million on campaign contributions, contributing mainly to Democratic candidates. Unions have generally opposed charter schools, backing candidates who are sympathetic to their position.

Union advocates argue that without the protection of a union, teachers have no way to defend themselves against unfair treatment by school administrators. Critics contend that unions often come to the aid of incompetent teachers and have resisted needed reforms. A widely circulated 2009 *New Yorker* article, "The Rubber Room," criticized the New York City teachers union as hyper-protective guardians of the status quo who resisted needed reforms.[51]

Like all unions, teachers' unions focus on increasing their members' pay. Harvard professor Martin West notes that "teachers' salaries have been stagnant for nearly a quarter of a century, and even declined by 2 percent after adjusting for inflation since 1992. Teachers' take-home pay has fallen well behind other college graduates. . . . It makes sense for teachers to put the issue of pay on the table."[52] However, evaluations differ on whether they have been able to do so.[53]

Studies of whether unionization leads to improved student achievement have yielded mixed results.[54] This research is problematic, because it is difficult to disentangle the role of the union from factors such as the level of school funding, student demographics, and state labor laws.

Between 2000 and 2016, the percentage of teachers who belonged to a union decreased from 79 to 70 percent.[55] In *Janus v. American Federation of State, County, and Municipal Employees Council 31* (2018), the Supreme Court ruled that mandatory union dues violated the First Amendment rights of public employees. Dues underwrite collective bargaining, which benefits nonunion and union members alike; the *Janus* decision has doubtless led to the decline in union membership.

Why do teachers strike?

Strikes are a last resort for teachers. Educating students is their vocation; for many of them, it is their passion. But strikes have become increasingly common in states and districts where politicians have repeatedly rebuffed attempts to raise salaries and improve working conditions in the schools.

The history of teacher walkouts dates to the Second World War, when teachers' salaries were eroded amid increasing inflation; the average real income of factory workers rose 80 percent, while teachers' real income fell 20 percent. As strikes broke out across the country, legislatures reacted by passing anti-strike laws. But these measures haven't had the intended effect. Since the 1960s there have been well over three thousand teacher strikes lasting more than a single day.

A nationwide wave of walkouts and strikes began in 2018 in West Virginia, which ranks forty-eighth in teacher compensation. There, rank-and-file teachers, not the union, led the charge for higher wages and lower health costs. When teachers went on strike, the state attorney general asserted that the action was illegal because state legislation forbade public employee strikes. Teachers ignored that warning. They rejected a 2 percent raise approved by the lawmakers, noting that it was lower than inflation. Soon afterward, the lawmakers met the teachers' demand for a 5 percent raise.

Teachers elsewhere wore red clothing in solidarity with their striking colleagues, and grassroots social media campaigns used the hashtag #RedForEd. The West Virginia strike inspired teachers in other states, including Oklahoma and Arizona, to follow suit. Arizona's teachers were awarded a 20 percent pay raise, but Oklahoma, which ranked forty-ninth in teacher compensation, repeatedly rejected plans to increase state expenditures on education, boost teacher pay, and reduce class size. The situation became so dire that a Tulsa teacher began panhandling to raise money for her classroom.[56]

While increasing salaries was the teachers' top priority, they also demanded a bigger school budget, smaller class sizes, and more support staff. In 2019, more than a year after their strike, the teachers prevailed, receiving a $6,000 pay raise. Walkouts in Los Angeles and Oakland, California; Denver; and Virginia also resulted in substantial salary boosts.[57]

The public has overwhelmingly backed teachers who strike. In a 2018 survey, two-thirds of those polled agreed that teachers are underpaid. Seventy-eight percent of parents and 73 percent of the public said they would support teachers in their own community if they went on strike for higher pay.[58]

Scant research has been done on the impact of strikes on student performance. One study found that even short strikes may adversely affect student achievement.[59] In an attempt to alleviate this problem, some districts where teachers are on strike have provided students with materials like books and worksheets.

What is the leadership role of the school principal?

The principal is the school's administrative leader. Historically, the principal was a manager, the middle man between the central administration and the school. In that role, the principal was responsible for financial operations, building maintenance, student scheduling, evaluating teachers, discipline policy, and coordinating the instructional program.

As the accountability movement gained momentum, beginning in the 1980s, the principal's role began to expand.[60] In addition to retaining managerial duties, which in large schools are handled by an assistant principal, the principal's primary responsibility is to be the school's educational leader.

As the person empowered to oversee the entire school, the principal, in collaboration with teachers and parents, is in a key position to improve the school.[61] Linda Darling-Hammond, president and CEO of the Learning Policy Institute and a nationally recognized scholar and education policy leader, notes that "if you ask teachers, 'What kept you in a school that you're in?' or 'What caused you to leave?' administrative leadership and support is one of the most critical elements because everything the teacher does is framed by the way the leadership operates."[62] While most research indicates teachers have the greatest impact on student outcomes, research shows that effective principals contribute to improved achievement.[63] A growing base of research estimates that the impacts of effective principals on student achievement are nearly as large as those of effective teachers. However, the principals' effects are broader in scope because they are averaged over all students in a school, rather than concentrated in one classroom.[64]

Studies conclude that an effective principal does the following:

- Creates and communicates a vision of success.[65]
- Emphasizes the quality of instruction (if necessary, overcoming some teachers' desire to be left alone) and encourages professional learning.

- Shapes a healthy school climate.
- Implements an organizational structure that encourages teachers to be supportive and responsive to the needs of their students and assures them that they are respected members of a professional community.[66]
- Uses data to inform and guide strategy. Teachers as well as administrators can rely on data to spot problems and indicate where a shift in teaching strategy is necessary.
- Involves parents in decision-making. While the evidence of the impact of parent engagement on student performance is inconclusive, establishing these bonds increases their understanding of, and support for, the school's mission and strategy. Parents should also be encouraged to be partners in their children's education, which boosts achievement.
- Cultivates and shares leadership with teachers. "The higher performance of [successful] schools might be explained as a consequence of the greater access [teachers] have to collective knowledge and wisdom embedded within their communities."[67]
- Engages in frequent, spontaneous, and informal interactions with teachers and provides on-the-spot feedback.
- Stays on the job. Frequent turnover is associated with worse student performance. It affects the overall climate of the school, discourages a sense of shared purpose, and generates cynicism among teachers. Research has shown that in order to accomplish any meaningful change in the school and have a positive impact on students' math and reading achievement, a principal needs to remain for at least five years. However, the average tenure of a principal is less than four years.[68]

What is the leadership role of the school district superintendent?

The superintendent is the CEO of the school district. In tandem with the school board, the superintendent defines the district's mission, specifies its goals, and charts a strategy for reaching those goals. The superintendent is generally regarded as the person who bears the greatest responsibility for a district's successes and failures.[69]

Managing an organization as complex as a school district is an extremely hard job. Superintendents juggle multiple responsibilities that include drafting a budget, being a responsible fiscal manager, hiring and supervising central office staff, growing a pool of school principals and teachers, making quick decisions in the event of an emergency, and lobbying for additional resources.

Ineffective superintendents often get bogged down in detail. To be an effective leader, the superintendent has to grasp the bigger picture; be skilled at managing personal relationships, developing a rapport with multiple constituencies, including teachers, students, parents, staff, community leaders, and taxpayers; and be a good communicator, capable of publicizing the district's vision, needs, and accomplishments to the public.[70] Improving student outcomes and preparing students for engaged citizenship are the superintendent's top priorities.[71]

"A great superintendent has to have a real passion for the job," observes Frank Till, former superintendent in Broward County, Florida, who has received national recognition for his accomplishments. "He's the one who sets the tone. Whatever the superintendent neglects, that sends a message that it's not a priority. The superintendent has to be the conscience of the district. He has to be willing to make tough decisions and work with the diverse political forces—parent groups, unions, the community, and make them all work to be part of the solution."[72]

Some superintendents, such as former Boston superintendent Tom Payzant, have been lauded for their accomplishments. Others, such as former Washington, D.C., superintendent Michelle Rhee, gained national reputations for their advocacy of controversial strategies.

The popular perception of superintendents, their portrayal in the media, and their high salaries lead one to believe that they are critical to student success. Until recently, the evidence was consistent with that perception. However, this research consisted of case studies and surveys that identified the characteristics of effective district leadership. Both modes of research assume what is open to question—that the superintendent makes a major difference—and a quantitative Brookings Institution analysis reaches the opposite conclusion. "Superintendents associated with substantive improvements in district performance are quite rare. . . . The typical superintendent accounts for just 0.3% of student achievement."[73] Superintendents are more effective in improving the financial health of the district, increasing parent and student satisfaction, and gathering community support.

One reason most superintendents have limited impact on student outcomes is their high turnover rate. Three to four years is a superintendent's average tenure, and a big-city superintendent typically stays for an even shorter period. This churn makes it hard to be an effective leader of an organization as complex as a school district. Aiming to improve students' performance, school boards often change superintendents, but the Brookings study shows that this strategy does not lead to higher student achievement.

The research does not specify the characteristics of a transformative school district superintendent: a leader who raises student achievement and displays academic leadership, managerial talent, and political acumen. It's difficult to pinpoint the effects of a single individual—and their qualities as a leader—among the wave of confounding elements such as an activist school board, shifting demographic patterns of student enrollment, teacher quality, and the district community's economic health.[74]

What is the role of the school board?

A school board determines the policy direction of the district's public schools.[75] In partnership with the superintendent, the board articulates a vision for the school system. It is responsible for hiring a superintendent, who is tasked with turning that vision into a blueprint for action as well as managing the district on a day-to-day basis. The board also approves or modifies the budget that the superintendent submits.[76]

Typically, voters in the school district elect the school board members. These elections have usually been nonpartisan. A study of the nation's thousand largest school districts found that, in about a third of elections, candidates ran unopposed; more than four-fifths of incumbents who sought reelection were successful.[77] Being a school board member has often served as a springboard for higher office.

In recent years, conservative organizations such as the American Legislative Exchange Council (ALEC) have invested in school board races, training candidates who favor privatizing education. "If conservatives are truly concerned about influencing society, they must get serious about getting educated and involved with institutions that shape the next generation."[78]

While school boards are still elected in most communities, several big-city systems, including New York and Chicago, have switched to a system of mayoral appointment.[79] There is more debate than research about which model is preferable. The most rigorous study concludes that, compared to the typical school district, mayoral-run urban districts improve student performance and shrink the achievement gap. However, outcomes differ among districts, as well as with students' grade level and subject matter. The study also notes that turning control of the district over to an "education mayor" does not ensure a positive outcome. To be effective, the mayor must leverage resources and mobilize stakeholders.[80]

School board meetings used to be sleepy affairs that focused on the routine business of the district. That's no longer
the case. Boards are sometimes swept up in culture wars
whose reverberations reach far beyond the school district.
The controversy over "critical race theory" offers a good example. Beginning in 2020, conservatives weaponized this
forty-year-old academic framework, which holds that racism
is embedded in the country's history and institutions.[81] They
contended, without any evidence, that the public schools are
teaching children to hate one another, and White children to
hate themselves.

Events in Loudoun County, Virginia, illustrate the potential
volatility of the issue. The *Washington Post* reported: "An email
to members of the school board began: 'Loudoun County
Virginia is ground zero and we have not yet begun to FIGHT!'
It was titled, 'All of America is Watching YOU!' and it promised
action against the 'liberal LOONS' on the board. . . . The controversy turned violent, leading to arrests of the combatants. It
was the mildest of more than 94 emails threatening the life [of
the school board chair]. After one email targeted her children,
she asked the county sheriff to start regularly patrolling her
neighborhood." News stories, aired on Fox News, thrust this
school board into the national spotlight.[82]

In October 2021, amid the mushrooming of harassment,
intimidation, and threats of violence against school board
members, as well as teachers and staff, Attorney General
Merrick B. Garland directed the FBI and US Attorneys' Offices
to meet with federal, state, tribal, territorial, and local law
enforcement leaders to discuss strategies for addressing this
trend. "Threats against public servants are not only illegal,
they run counter to our nation's core values," he wrote. "Those
who dedicate their time and energy to ensuring that our children receive a proper education in a safe environment deserve
to be able to do their work without fear for their safety."[83]

Controversies over race, as well as Covid closures and mask
and vaccination requirements, have prompted an increase in

campaigns to recall school board members. Between 2006 and 2020, on average there were 23 recall efforts against 52 school board members each year. During the first ten months of 2021, 81 recall efforts against 209 board members were initiated.

What is the influence of outside money on school board elections?

School board elections used to draw little attention. Campaigns were run on a shoestring—in 2010, fewer than 3 percent of candidates reported spending more than $25,000—and voter turnout was low.

Most board elections still fit this model, but during the past decade the battle lines have been drawn between charter advocates and public school supporters, as well as over Covid and race-related issues. In urban school districts with high concentrations of low-income students and students of color, millions of dollars have been spent to sway the outcome of these elections. Out-of-state donors and political action committees (PACs) are pitted against teachers' unions and regard one another as threats to public education.

A study of school board elections in five such districts found that big-money campaigns "nationalized local education politics . . . enabl[ing] a new pathway for elite influence in local school district governance, and crowd[ing] out or overshadow[ing] some local voices." In these elections, "attention does not always turn to the most well-funded candidates, and outside funding does not always lead overall campaign coverage to become overly negative. In some cases, though, [the candidates] tend to focus on the same set of nationalized issues, sometimes at the expense of what may be significant local issues. Further, attention in the election often becomes fixated on the money itself rather than on more substantive policy issues."[84]

Los Angeles, the nation's second largest school system, provides the clearest example. In the 2020 race, the California charter school organization and the teachers' union combined to spend nearly $20 million. Charter supporters feared that a "hostile" school board would limit the number of charter schools in the district, while the union regarded a "friendly" school board as a buffer against the influence of pro-charter groups.[85]

Those who favor this influx of outside money argue that it can improve the quality of campaigns, draw more public attention to school board elections, and increase voter turnout. Critics counter that by increasing the cost of campaigns, outside money drives out those who can't afford to participate. They also contend that such campaigns are more negative and focus on issues that resonate nationally, like charter schools, rather than on those of mainly local importance.

What roles do parent-teacher associations and school-based foundations play?

The PTA is a familiar presence in many public schools. More than twenty thousand elementary and middle schools have a PTA; some high schools have a parent teacher student association, or PTSA. The PTA model has been adopted worldwide.[86]

The PTA's main role is to encourage communication among parents, teachers, and administrators. Its activities may include recruiting and coordinating classroom volunteers, organizing parent education events, and initiating community-level programs on issues like bicycle safety and energy conservation awareness. It can provide a forum for resolving conflicts over controversial issues.

Many local PTAs belong to a national organization, the century-old National Parent Teacher Association. Historically, that organization promoted school lunch and inoculation programs. More recently it has supported sex education and tobacco and alcohol education in the schools, and opposed school vouchers.

While public education is chiefly funded by taxpayer dollars, some PTAs or school-based nonprofit foundations raise money in order to augment the school's budget. "There have always been parent-teacher associations that raise modest or even not-so-modest amounts of money," notes Stanford political scientist Rob Reich. "But increasingly local school foundations are being created expressly for the purpose of raising private funds."[87]

In some wealthy communities, these foundations raise outsized sums. In 2013–14 the nation's fifty richest foundations raised $43 million to supplement the budgets of schools in the nation's most affluent communities.[88] For example, the foundation in a Palo Alto, California, public school that enrolls fewer than five hundred children raises about $2 million annually, or $4,000 for each child, to pay for smaller classes, librarians, art and music teachers, and technology. Elsewhere in the Bay Area communities, parents are expected to contribute as much as $3,400. By contrast, foundations in low-income California communities raise less than $100 per student.[89]

Reich argues that "private giving to public schools widens the gap between rich and poor. It exacerbates inequalities in financing. It is philanthropy in the service of conferring advantage on the already well-off."[90]

What is the influence of philanthropy on education policy?

Philanthropy has had a substantial impact on education policy. In 2016 major foundations gave about $800 million to K–12 education. More than half of these expenditures were made by the Bill and Melinda Gates Foundation and the Walton Family Foundation.

The Gates Foundation's most successful venture, in terms of its impact on policy, was underwriting the development of the Common Core State Standards. It built political support across the country, enabling states to work together, developing shared expectations for student outcomes. In the span of just two years, forty-five states and the District of Columbia adopted these standards. Reviewing the impact of this strategy thus far, Brookings Institution scholar Tom Loveless concluded that the standards were "built on a shaky theory"; he found no correlation between quality standards and student achievement.[91]

The Gates Foundation's efforts to change the way public schools operate has proven less successful. A $650 million "small schools" initiative, premised on the theory that students in urban school districts would be less likely to drop out in an intimate education setting, had mixed results.[92] After the foundation's support ended, some urban districts continued using the costly model, straining already cash-strapped school systems.

Subsequently, the foundation invested $200 million in a system that was designed to improve teacher evaluation. That initiative was controversial because it linked those assessments—and consequently, pay increases and job security—to student test scores in a way that assessment experts said was a misuse of the data. A 2018 RAND Corporation evaluation concluded that the venture didn't "achieve its goals for student achievement or graduation," and the foundation abandoned the strategy.[93]

The Walton Foundation has focused almost exclusively on charter schools. In 2018 it committed $100 million to organizations that create successful charters, with the explicit expectation that the funds will be used to launch hundreds of charter schools.

One of the primary critiques of philanthropic giving is that the resources are earmarked for specific initiatives, often without the input of teachers. For example, the $800 million provided in 2016 could have instead paid credential tuition costs (assuming $7,000 per year) for more than 110,000 novice teachers. Alternatively, each of the nation's nearly four million teachers could receive $200 to offset the $750 they typically spend out of their own pockets purchasing school supplies for their classrooms.[94] Where and how to allocate financial resources, such as philanthropic gifts, is contentious and constantly debated.

There is some evidence of a change in the direction of philanthropic giving. In 2021, the Gates Foundation, the Walton Family Foundation, and the Chan Zuckerberg Initiative jointly launched the Advanced Education Research & Development Fund, with $200 million initial funding. The goal is to engage educators in the process of design change rather than dictating changes in practice. "Its focus will be on what it calls 'inclusive R&D,' or bringing together people with different expertise, including educators, to design and test practical ideas like improving assessments and making math classes more effective."[95]

4

LIFE INSIDE THE PUBLIC SCHOOL

How can schools reduce the achievement gap?

White and Asian students, on average, outperform their Black, Latino, and Native American schoolmates on an array of math and reading tests. They are also more likely to earn a high school diploma and enroll in college. To fulfill the promise of equal opportunity, it's vital that these achievement gaps—perhaps better described as opportunity gaps—be effaced.

The following are the among the most promising strategies that school districts are using.

Make equity the priority: School districts that are committed to closing the achievement gap put it at the top of their list of priorities, devoting substantial resources and energy to the effort. These districts gather data that enable them to spot—and then address—gaps between racial and ethnic groups on a host of outcomes, including math and reading achievement scores, discipline, and assignment to special education.

While many school systems claim that graduating every student is their goal, districts that make it preeminent view every racial and ethnic disparity through the "100 percent graduation" lens. Rather than adopting a "deficit model" that blames students who are falling behind—for example, failing to reach proficiency in third-grade reading, a key predictor of high school graduation—they treat these gaps as problems that the district must solve.[1]

Improve staff training: Brief online experiences, grounded in social-psychological research, appear to reduce racism. For example, studies of large, heterogeneous school districts found that a forty-five-minute online experience (psychologists refer to them as interventions) showing teachers the importance of empathizing with their students reduced high school suspensions by a remarkable 50 percent.[2] To be most effective, such brief experiences should be paired with broader, systemic changes designed to improve the school climate.[3]

Show students that they "belong": Students are acutely sensitive to how their racial or ethnic group is regarded by teachers and classmates. Minority students are prone to what social psychologists term "stereotype vulnerability": the tendency to expect, perceive, and be influenced by negative stereotypes. The perception that White teachers and classmates consider them to be less academically able threatens their social and emotional well-being.[4] To overcome such stereotypes, schools need to foster an understanding that every student, especially those who have been historically marginalized, is valued by the community; as the psychologists put it, that they "belong."

Revamp the curriculum: A growing number of schools augment traditional English and history course materials with resources, including children's picture books and history texts, that include culturally responsive themes. These stories often center on the experiences of racial and ethnic minorities.[5] This material represents a marked change from mainstream textbooks, which give these experiences short shrift.

When students realize that their cultural heritage is acknowledged, they are more likely to be engaged in school.[6] By bringing their students' cultures into the classroom—celebrating, rather than effacing, differences; and incorporating activities and materials that treat those differences as assets, not deficits—teachers offer their students a sense that they have a valuable contribution to make.

Limited research on the impact of ethnic studies classes suggests that such a course can improve student engagement, increase attendance, and boost academic achievement, especially for male and Latino students.[7]

What are tracking and ability grouping?

Tracking is a system for grouping students based on their perceived ability or performance. Historically, high school students were assigned to college preparatory or vocational tracks, in which they took all of their courses. That practice died out in the United States in the late 1960s and early 1970s, though it is still in place in other countries. Now tracking is typically used for particular subjects, such as mathematics. Students are assigned to different classrooms, receive instruction from different teachers, and study a different curriculum—for instance, Algebra I or Pre-Algebra.

Ability grouping and tracking are often confused. While both are designed to match students with a curriculum based on their ability or prior performance, ability grouping, which is often used in elementary schools, takes place within, not between, classes. For example, during a math lesson, the teacher might divide the students into groups that differentiate between those who need to remediate multiplication facts and those who are ready for a more challenging assignment.[8] Sometimes a teacher gives each of these groups a name, like the Blue Jays and the Robins.

Tracking has been used in American public schools for nearly a century. It was introduced in order to provide immigrant children, many of whom fared poorly on the newly developed IQ test, with an education that was deemed suitable for their limited understanding of the English language and their inadequate preparation. Depending on their IQ scores, these youths were regarded as "fit" or "unfit" for the academic coursework that led students to higher education or jobs that required different levels of skill.[9] The result was internal segregation within public schools.

The most popular alternatives to ability grouping are whole-class instruction, in which every student in the class receives the same instruction, and small groups of heterogeneous students.

Tracking is a much-debated practice. Supporters argue that when tracking is based on ability and potential, it enables students to receive instruction targeted to their ability level for each subject. A gifted student may attend more advanced math classes, allowing them to be challenged at their own ability level. Tracking has shown benefits for above-average achievers.[10]

Those who oppose tracking point to the research showing that it often leads to the segregation of low-income and minority students, who are disproportionately assigned to low-track classes, thus widening the achievement gap. During the 1980s, Jeannie Oakes, the former dean of the UCLA school of education and a leading scholar in the field, labeled the practice "industrial schooling," noting that upper-class students received more educational opportunities, while lower-income students were funneled into vocational programs and given limited opportunities.[11]

Tracking decisions often have a lasting impact because it is difficult to switch tracks. Teachers have lower academic expectations for students who have been assigned to the remedial track, which leads to poorer academic performance among remedial track students.[12] Even if students do well there, they fall further behind their classmates in higher-level tracks, who are challenged with advanced content, and are much less likely to be placed in accelerated middle and high school classes.

Dividing students into groups according to their academic performance may lead students in the lower track to label themselves as inferior to upper-track students. Scholars who study stereotype vulnerability have shown that lower self-esteem can affect academic performance, thus functioning as a self-fulfilling prophecy.[13] When the screening process takes into account teachers' implicit bias, more students, regardless of race or class, are assigned to the advanced track.[14]

Does class size affect student achievement?

Common sense suggests that children will do better in smaller classes than in larger classes. There, teachers can pay more attention and give more feedback to students, either individually or in small groups. Yet large-scale studies of whether smaller class sizes improve academic performance reach mixed results.[15]

The widely cited Students-Teacher Achievement Ratio (STAR) study, a random-control experiment, examined the impact of a Tennessee class size reduction program for children in kindergarten through grade 3. Classes of twenty-two through twenty-six students were reduced to thirteen through seventeen students. Participating in smaller classes resulted in improved student academic performance in elementary school, particularly for low-income and minority children. The STAR study concluded that small classes led to "substantial improvement in early learning and cognitive studies," with about twice the effect for minority students. A follow-up study found that children who had been enrolled in smaller classes continued to outperform their classmates when they returned to regular-sized classrooms. However, reanalysis of the data showed that 35 percent of the improvement resulted from the fact that the smaller classes had teacher aides.[16]

Studies of similar programs have found that while removing one or two students has no impact, students fare better in substantially smaller classes, and those benefits are long lasting.[17] Critics counter that although substantially smaller classes are beneficial, the cost exceeds the benefits. Investing in additional qualified teachers and providing more support to teachers, they assert, would be more effective.

Skeptics claim that hiring more teachers to reduce class sizes is a drain of taxpayer resources and doesn't guarantee students will have a highly effective teacher. They argue that a more efficient use of resources would be to reward highly effective teachers with higher pay and assign a greater number of students to their classrooms. When researchers simulated the move of six students to a highly effective educator, they estimated students would still reap the benefits without overwhelming the teacher with an oversized class. The students who remain in the weaker teacher's classroom would also, theoretically, benefit because the teacher would have a smaller student load.[18] The researchers admit it would be difficult for practitioners to implement the strategy consistently, and at scale.

Class size reduction is a politically popular strategy, but it is difficult to implement because it requires a pool of high-quality teachers to staff the additional classrooms. In 1996, California voters passed a class size reduction referendum calling for a reduction in the number of students enrolled in K–3 classes by a third. Some educators and policymakers anticipated that this initiative would lead to large gains in student achievement. However, thousands of new teachers were needed to execute the measure, and the shortage of teachers was felt most acutely in low-income communities that were already having a hard time staffing their classrooms. An evaluation of the California program found that reducing class size by ten students raised the percentage of third-grade students who exceeded national median test scores by roughly 4 points. However, many of the teachers were new to the field, and having an inexperienced teacher reduced by 3 to 4 percent the number of students who exceeded national median test scores in mathematics and reading.[19]

What is school climate?

School climate refers to the culture—the heart and soul—of a school. It is a vaguely defined term, although researchers agree that it includes the "patterns of students,' parents' and school personnel's experience of school life and reflects norms, goals, values, interpersonal relationships, teaching and learning practices, and organizational structures."[20] Some definitions incorporate the physical, social, and academic characteristics of a school: the condition of the building; the depth and quality of relationships among staff and students; efforts to promote equitable treatment across race and class lines; and the quality of instruction, including teachers' expectations for their students' academic achievement and their responses to students' progress and performance.[21]

In a school with a positive climate, students might say, "I feel like I belong here," and "my personal background is celebrated," as well as, "at my school, I am physically and emotionally safe." Teachers report an understanding of, and a shared commitment to, the school's overall vision. They celebrate, rather than resist, the distinctive contributions that students from different backgrounds bring to the school.[22]

The result is a virtuous cycle. In a school that has established a positive climate, academic performance improves and motivation to learn increases; there are fewer instances of bullying, student suspensions, and mental health challenges.[23] That environment serves as a counterweight to the effects of poverty and trauma.

A positive school climate also reduces teachers' stress and burnout and increases the likelihood that they will remain in the profession. Conversely, teachers who report that they are working in a school where the environment is negative are far more likely to leave the classroom.[24]

Many states have adopted school climate measures to promote student outcomes. ESSA requires that states include at least one indicator of school quality or student success in their school accountability system, and as of 2020 eight states had integrated school climate data as part of the ESSA accountability system. A majority of states are informally collecting school climate data to improve the schools.[25]

Researchers and government agencies have developed a host of school climate measures. Surveys of all the members of the school community ask about the relationships among students, staff, and families, in topics that range from bullying, student safety, and high academic expectations to drug use.[26]

A national survey of principals, district leaders, and school climate coordinators from thirty-six states found widespread agreement that school climate was important. However, they were unclear about measurement and improvement strategies.[27]

Research-based guidance on how to improve school climate is similar to recommendations regarding other, broader school improvement efforts. Administrators, faculty, students, and parents are jointly engaged in this effort:[28]

- Create a core planning team of diverse stakeholders.
- Build and communicate a collective vision.
- Analyze multiple sources of schoolwide data drawn from parent interviews, student surveys, and teacher reports.
- Intervene in ways that are likely to improve school climate, such as implementing a behavioral system, restorative justice program, or social-emotional learning (SEL) curriculum, recognizing that change doesn't occur overnight.

Another recommendation from education experts is to focus on systems of developmental supports designed to promote a positive school climate. Examples include regular student feedback surveys, educator professional development to focus on building student relationships, and the removal of zero-tolerance discipline policies. Schools that are designed to be flexible and meet an array of student need also appear to be a critical component in schools with a positive school climate.[29]

What is student discipline?

Student discipline includes both preventative measures, such as offering incentives for completing classwork, and punitive measures, like detention, suspension, and expulsion.[30]

Corporal punishment was widely utilized in US schools during the nineteenth and twentieth centuries as a way to motivate students to perform better academically and behave appropriately. The practice was generally considered a fair and rational way to discipline schoolchildren, and teachers in the late nineteenth century were encouraged to employ corporal punishment over other types of discipline.[31]

The Supreme Court upheld the practice in *Ingraham v. Wright* (1977), holding that states had the constitutional authority to determine whether it is permissible.[32] At that time, only four states had outlawed the practice. Since then, suspension and expulsion have largely replaced corporal punishment. While (as of 2018) it is still legal in nineteen states and practiced in fifteen, in the 2013–14 school year, only 0.2 percent of students were disciplined this way.[33]

Suspension removes a student from school for a brief period—usually no more than two weeks—while expulsion keeps a student out of school for up to one school year. Suspended and expelled students are sometimes supplied with instructional materials.

During the "tough on crime" 1990s, federal policy encouraged zero-tolerance discipline for behavior like possessing drugs or bringing a weapon to school. Schools were obliged, under the threat of losing federal funding, to expel students for one year if they brought a gun to school. The number of suspensions ballooned from 1.7 million in 1974 to 3.1 million in 2000.[34] Students from low-income families, African American and Latino students, and students with disabilities have been disproportionately suspended.[35] According to the US Department of Education Office of Civil Rights, Black students continue to be suspended and expelled at a rate three times great than

White students. Students with disabilities are twice as likely as their general education counterparts to be suspended (13 percent compared to 6 percent).[36]

Studies of suspension conclude that the policy can have perverse implications; higher rates of suspension undermine student perceptions of caring adults, creating a negative school climate. Suspension often results in learning loss and, consequently, lower grades. Students who are suspended are substantially more likely to drop out of school and run afoul of the law, entering what has been termed the school-to-prison pipeline.[37]

Police are most likely to be assigned to schools in low-income neighborhoods. Many students feel safer with police on the campus, but Black and Latino students, as well as those from low-income families and those with disabilities, are much less likely to share that attitude.[38] The presence of police typically results in an increase in the number of suspensions and, subsequently, arrests, particularly among students of color; it is also linked to lower overall academic performance.[39]

The role of police in the schools has become a hot-button political issue, caught up in larger debates over racial justice and "defunding" the police. In the aftermath of George Floyd's murder in 2020, a handful of urban school districts removed police from their schools. The national teachers' unions support limiting the role of the police, but local unions have sometimes protested school districts' plans to cut their ties to the police, and the National School Administrators Association favors the status quo. In 2018, nearly half of pre-K–12 schools had an armed police officer on campus.[40]

In 2014 the Obama administration urged schools to minimize the use of suspensions and expulsions. Yet while the memo warned that the disproportionate suspension of students of color represented a potential violation of civil rights law, few districts changed their policy in response.

Policymakers seeking alternatives to suspensions and expulsions have turned to a variety of approaches. Replacing police officers with lay safety officers, social workers, and/or counselors—a step that a number of districts, including Denver and Minneapolis, have taken—has led to fewer suspensions and a healthier school climate.[41]

Several states, including Michigan and Illinois, limit the use of zero-tolerance discipline policies. California has gone further, forbidding school administrators to suspend elementary and middle school students who are "willfully defiant," an ambiguous standard that has often been used in a culturally biased manner.[42]

A growing number of schools have adopted a model called "restorative justice." Instead of suspending students who violate school rules, this approach focuses on supporting victimized students. In a meeting between the victim and victimizer, misbehaving students acknowledge their responsibility and apologize for the harm their actions have caused. The consequences of misbehaving are tailored to the harm that has been done; for instance, a student who bullies a classmate might be required to write a letter of apology and read it in front of classmates. One potential problem with this approach is that in this setting, the victimized student may feel threatened by the presence of the misbehaving student.

It can take several years to fully train staff and students in restorative justice, familiarizing them with how the process is supposed to work. When well implemented, this model can help to build a more positive school culture and encourage closer relationships among students as well as between students and teachers.

Educators and social psychologists have also developed ways of keeping students motivated and engaged in school, making them less likely to violate school rules. Positive behavioral intervention support (PBIS) incorporates such incentives as public praise for well-behaved students, whether as a feature of schoolwide announcements or in the public display of a "good character" honor roll. Behavior charts can be used to show how much work a student has completed or how well they have performed academically. When PBIS has the endorsement of teachers, administrators, and students, it has been shown to improve school climate, reduce the number of suspensions, and end the disproportionate suspension of low-income, minority, and special education students.[43] One study found that a positive school climate, partly attributable to PBIS, reduced suspensions by 10 percent.[44] The likeliest explanation for this improvement is the introduction of pedagogical practices that show teachers how to respond to challenging behaviors without escalating the situation and explain how to establish clear expectations for their students' behavior.

Strategies derived from social psychology are useful as well. Psychologists have created brief modules that are designed to build teacher empathy, making them less likely to rely on suspension in reacting to students who act out in class. One study, conducted in districts with diverse student populations, found that the online version of the empathy exercise, administered to eighth-grade math teachers, reduced suspensions by 50 percent.[45]

Progress in the nationwide effort to reduce negative disciplinary actions—including suspension, expulsion, and grade retention—has been gradual and continues to be a challenge. Between 2000 and 2016, the percentage of students retained in a grade decreased from 3.1 to 1.9 percent.[46] In a report (2015–18) from the Office of Civil Rights, there was a 13 percent reduction in expulsions under zero-tolerance policies, but overall disciplinary actions have only been reduced by 2 percent over that time period.[47]

What is bullying?

Bullying flourishes when there is an imbalance of power between the bully and the bullied that leads to repeated aggression. Verbal bullying includes taunting, name-calling, and threats of violence. Physical bullying ranges from kicking and tripping to attacks with a knife or gun. Cyberbullying, whether through texts, tweets, or other social media, has emerged in recent years as an especially noxious form of bullying, because it can spread instantaneously to a broad audience, inflicting substantial and continuous humiliation.

A host of perceived characteristics—weight, physical appearance, race, social class, sexual orientation, and disability—may trigger bullying. Students who are regarded as uncool or unable to fit in are also likely targets.

Bullying in schools has a long and sorry history. "I want to leave behind me the name of a fellow who never bullied a little boy, or turned his back on a big one," says Flashman, the bully who features in *Tom Brown's Schooldays*, an immensely popular nineteenth-century novel. It is an international phenomenon, documented in a 2015 study of eighty-three Organisation of Economic Co-operation and Development (OECD) nations, which concluded that in many countries, verbal and psychological bullying occur frequently.[48]

Teachers and staff used to regard bullying as a normal and unavoidable part of growing up. Whether they were made fun of, socially isolated, or beaten up, bullied students were told to toughen up or that being bullied builds character. But that "kids will be kids" attitude has been replaced by a concern for the bullied.

The 1999 shooting at Columbine High School in Colorado focused public attention on the issue, because the action was widely depicted in the media as revenge by victims of bullying. That year, in *Davis v. Monroe County Board of Education*, the Supreme Court ruled that a school could be held liable for failing to stop student-to-student sexual harassment, if school officials were aware of the bullying and were "deliberately indifferent" to it.[49]

Bullying is widespread. Two large-scale federal surveys of twelve to eighteen-year-old students found that 20 percent reported that they had been bullied in the previous year, and 41 percent believed that they would be bullied again.[50] Half of tweens (between ages nine and twelve) said they had experienced bullying at school, and a sixth had experienced cyberbullying.[51] According to the American Psychological Association, 40 to 80 percent of school-aged children experience bullying at some point during their school careers.[52]

Bullying can set off a cascade of consequences for the bullied. It may make the victims afraid to go to school and interfere with their ability to concentrate in class or participate in school activities. Those who are bullied are more likely to skip or drop out of school, reducing their chances of going to college as well as their job prospects.

Antibullying curricula abound, especially tailored to elementary and middle school students. Although these curricula are touted as evidence-based, there is limited evidence that they are effective.[53] By contrast, evidence-based strategies to promote SEL have a host of beneficial effects, including reducing "disruptive behaviors like conflicts, aggression, bullying, and anger."[54] To have the greatest effect, antibullying activities should be baked into the day-to-day life of the school—in research projects, for instance, or art projects.

Successful bullying prevention enlists the entire school community in creating a culture of respect. Schools with a positive climate build community, while a negative school climate is linked to higher rates of student bullying. Everyone in the school community—students, families, administrators, teachers, and staff such as bus drivers, nurses, cafeteria personnel, and front office staff—should have a role in combating bullying. Students and parents need to have a say in identifying what will be an effective approach. Students should let teachers and administrators know what is happening in the school bathrooms, playground, locker room, cafeteria, crowded hallways and school buses, where supervision is infrequent, as well as on cell phones and computers. Parents, teachers, and school administrators need to act as role models for positive behavior, while older students can serve as mentors. The school needs to make sure that students understand what bullying is and why it isn't okay, why reporting bullying isn't "tattling," how they can stand up to it safely, and where to get help. Lines of communication must stay open, so that teachers and administrators can understand what's happening in students' lives.

Government, at both the state and federal level, plays a significant role in combating bullying. Every state has adopted legislation that requires school districts and/or individual schools to devise policies that address bullying. Some of the most common provisions include investigation and reporting of bullying, disciplinary actions for students involved in bullying, and staff training. Three-quarters of the states require or encourage school systems to discipline students who bully.

In 2011 the federal Departments of Education and Justice sent advisory letters to the states, notifying them that bullying raises civil rights issues. Schools must "eliminate any hostile environment and its effects," as well as take steps to "prevent the harassment from recurring," when bullying based on race, color, national origin, sex, or disability interferes with a student's school experience.

Some antibullying strategies, though well-intentioned, make things worse. Many school districts have "zero-tolerance" or "three strikes and you're out" bullying policies, suspending or expelling students who bully others. In extreme instances, this course of action may make sense. But bullying is too widespread for this approach to work—surveys of elementary and middle school students show that about one in five students admit to bullying their peers, and the actual figure is doubtless higher than that—and the prospect that a student will be expelled for bullying may discourage children and adults from reporting an incident.

Conflict resolution and peer mediation represent the opposite end of the disciplinary spectrum. While this talk-it-out approach can be effective when there is a conflict between students, bullying is not a conflict. It is victimization, akin to child abuse, and there is no evidence that this strategy reduces bullying. Bullying is not an example of "each of you is partly right and partly wrong," the usual takeaway from mediation. The right message to a student who is bullied is: "No one deserves to be bullied, and we will do everything we can to stop it." The message for bullies is: "Your behavior is wrong and you must stop it."

Group therapy for bullies is another strategy that can backfire. The aim is to teach anger management and develop empathy and self-esteem, but group members may become role models for each other, which makes bullying more likely.[55]

What are school shootings?

We generally date school shootings—attacks on school campuses that involve the use of firearms—to the Columbine High School massacre in 1999, in which thirteen students were killed, but such events actually predate the American Revolution. In 1764, four Lenape Native Americans entered a rural Pennsylvania schoolhouse—in response to the ongoing conflict with colonists—and fatally shot the schoolmaster and killed nine or ten children.[56] During the following two centuries, shootings, which averaged one or two a decade, typically involved a student or parent killing a teacher or principal, but increasingly since the 1960s, students have usually been the victims.[57]

Columbine shocked the nation. The later massacres at Sandy Hook Elementary School (2012) and Marjory Stoneman Douglas High School (2018) had a similar impact, and in their wake advocates pressed for national legislation limiting the availability of firearms. After the Sandy Hook killings, President Barack Obama gave a televised address, declaring that "we're going to have to come together and take meaningful action to prevent more tragedies like this, regardless of the politics." In the wake of the shooting at Marjory Stoneman Douglas, thousands of students marched out of their classrooms, demanding action on gun violence. These efforts have been uniformly unsuccessful.

The number of school shootings has increased exponentially since Columbine. There were thirteen shootings in 2010, and more than ten times as many a decade later. Despite the fact that many schools were closed because of Covid, there were seventy-nine school shootings in the first half of 2021. While no single profile fits all shooters, the most common motives are being bullied (75 percent) and taking revenge (61 percent).[58]

In the spring of 2022, nineteen students and two teachers were killed by a school shooter at Robb Elementary School in Uvalde, Texas. More than a dozen others were wounded. After a wave of political pressure, federal legislators in Washington passed the Bipartisan Safer Communities Act, designed to bolster mental health resources available for states as well as expanding the review process to purchase a gun if the buyer is under twenty-one years old.

In an effort to protect themselves, many school districts are now relying on bulletproof school supplies, including backpacks, desks, silent panic alarms, and bullet-resistant door panels and windows. Some districts have gone further, redesigning schools to incorporate concrete barriers in hallways, so that students can hide in shooting situations, and building schools with curved walls to prevent a shooter from having a clear line of sight.

A growing number of schools (43 percent in 2015) have hired armed security guards to protect them against such attacks. UCLA professor Ronald Astor contends that bringing weapons into the schools likens them to prisons, intimidates students, and affects their academic performance.[59]

Although school shootings are a worldwide phenomenon, the widespread availability of firearms explains why shootings are far and away most common in the United States.[60] The National Rifle Association has argued that teachers should carry weapons to protect their students and themselves. There is no evidence that this approach is effective. In fact, that strategy generates the "weapons effect"—simply being in the presence of a gun increases feelings of aggression.[61]

Research has shown that building a positive school climate—reducing bullying and providing more psychological support—may well be the most effective strategy to prevent gun violence.[62] Union, Oklahoma (which, as we point out elsewhere, has made good use of other school reform strategies, including community schools) has adopted this approach. There, everyone who works in the schools understands the value of developing relationships, rooted in trust, between students and staff. Security chief Ty Wardlow and his team wear plain clothes, not uniforms. "We didn't want our officers to be perceived as police because some of the interactions that our kids have with police are not positive. If you're a child and the police have come and taken your father, you don't have a positive opinion of them."[63]

Superintendent Kirt Hartzler, like school chiefs everywhere, is acutely aware of the possibility that Union could be the next Parkland or Sandy Hook. While the district conducts firearm safety drills, Hartzler places more faith in personal connections. The perpetrators of violence are often disaffected students, and so "the relationships that our officers build with these kids are our biggest defense against a major tragedy. If they have a true concern, kids will let us know—but they've got to be able to trust somebody."[64]

How do extracurricular activities affect academic performance?

While schools focus most of their attention on academics, scores of studies show that youth also need opportunities to develop physically and socially. Because schools have a captive audience, they are an ideal venue for these activities.

An estimated 70 percent of high school students participate in some extracurricular activity. A review of the research concluded that nonacademic activities—sports, student government, school publications, and performing arts—and academic activities—focused, for example, on science and math—have positive effects on an array of outcomes, including grades, course selection, homework, substance abuse, and college enrollment. Students from low-income families, who often fare worse in traditional classes, are especially likely to flourish outside the confines of the classroom.[65]

The amount of time that a student participates in these activities has a long-term impact. A longitudinal study found that, eight years after high school, students who took part in an extracurricular activity for two years had greater educational, civic, and occupational success than those who did so for only a single year.[66] Other studies find similarly positive effects on mental health and relations with classmates. These findings are consistent with the studies of community schools, which show the benefit of engaging in an array of nonacademic activities.

A 2010 Centers for Disease Control and Prevention (CDC) report synthesized the findings of fifty studies that examined the association between school-based physical activity, cognitive skills, students' attitude toward school, and academic achievement.[67] The studies included research on physical education classes, elementary school recess, competitive extracurricular sports, and brief in-class activities (like five minutes of jumping jacks). Overall, half of the associations were positive, 48 percent were not statistically significant, and just 1.5 percent were negative. The report concluded that "increased time in physical education appears to have a positive relationship or no relationship with academic achievement."

Contrary to the stereotype of the "dumb jock," studies find that high school students who participate in competitive sports earn better grades, spend more time doing homework, have more positive attitudes toward school, and have higher educational aspirations than their classmates.[68]

How is technology used in schools?

Technology, in one form or another, has been used for generations. Beginning with the radio, it became evermore prominent with the advent of television, computers, software, and internet-based platforms. When used well, technology can deliver learning experiences that complement in-person teaching, reading, and experiential learning. When used poorly, however, it can impede learning.

The use of technology for educational purposes has not been confined to the schoolhouse. Public television programs like *Sesame Street* created educational material that was designed to expand children's vocabulary through language-rich content, while keeping them entertained.[69] But while such programs were intended to close the learning gap, they actually increased it, since middle-class children took greater advantage of the opportunity.[70]

In the early 1980s, computers began appearing in schools. A 1996 study of the effects of educational technology on national math achievement tests found that students' performance didn't improve when they used computers for math drills on basic math facts.[71] However, when teachers adopted computer-based programming as a tool for rigorous instruction, math outcomes did improve. In the mid-1990s, eighth-grade students in Union City, New Jersey, a low-income Latino community, were given personal computers. Research showed that they learned more and also became more enthusiastic about school.[72]

Computers became nearly ubiquitous in schools by the early 2000s. In 1984, the typical school had one computer for every 92 students; today, the ratio is closer to 1:5, and a growing number of districts provide a computer for every student.

Some school districts allow students to take their school-issued laptops home, to be used for homework. This strategy helps to close the digital divide, the gap between affluent and low-income students' access to technology.[73]

Researchers specify four ways in which technology potentially benefits students: it promotes active student engagement, increases interaction and feedback, forges connections to real-world contexts, and enables group participation.[74]

But while incorporating technology in the schools has often been useful, it has not been problem free. Skeptics worry that online learning may be more difficult than learning in face-to-face environments; students who procrastinate or who are not skilled in self-directed learning may do badly unless there's a teacher on hand. Other students lack broadband or other technological resources, though this gap was substantially narrowed during the pandemic, and even those with adequate technology may lack the skills needed to take full advantage of course material.[75]

Technology can cause more problems than it solves if it is not thoughtfully integrated. In 2013 Los Angeles Unified School District (LAUSD) gave every student an Apple iPad that was stocked with material supplied by a single publisher. But the software was beset by bugs, frustrating teachers, and high school students hacked the iPads, using them for purposes that the district never contemplated. Some criticized the venture as a waste of money. As one student wrote: "My mom's [LAUSD] school isn't even able to afford a janitor to clean the bathrooms. The kids themselves avoid using them. But hey, they get iPads! Yay! This is such a great example of ignorance at the top."[76]

The ed-tech market is a huge business; in 2019, schools spent $43 billion on hardware and software. Google dominates the field because it combines inexpensive hardware and free software for teachers. Internet-connected Chromebooks can replace paper-based school supplies such as worksheets and notebooks. Between 2012 and 2019, Chromebooks soared from less than 1 to 60 percent of mobile devices shipped to K–12 schools.[77]

Other online programs deliver a personalized curriculum, potentially enabling students to become self-directed learners. For example, a math program might include a brief video lesson with written instructions, additional hints when a learner is stuck, and embedded quizzes that provide instantaneous feedback. Such an approach can be a notable improvement over one-size-fits-all instruction, for it gives teachers more time for discussion with the class and conversations with individual students.

Because the evidence base for these learning programs, as well as the quality of their implementation, varies significantly, it is difficult to generalize about their effectiveness. The best-designed study of such a program found small but positive effects in math but no effect for reading.[78] The impact on performance was the same for students who were lagging and those who were doing well.

The ed-tech field is still new, and as with every educational strategy, implementation is the make-or-break factor. Personalized learning programs are most effective when teachers are adequately trained and students have ample time to adjust to the new mode of instruction. Their performance improves after a school has implemented the program for several years.[79]

Virtual learning is a catch-all term for instruction that takes place on digital platforms, transmitting a classroom lesson to a student's home either synchronously or asynchronously. The pandemic put virtual learning front and center, but this method of teaching was already being used in some districts. Nearly three million K–12 students took courses online in 2019.[80]

A 2010 US Department of Education report concluded that high school students who received their instruction online did as well as students who attended school; this wasn't the case for elementary or middle school students.[81] However, because students were not randomly assigned, the results may be attributable to the fact that those who opted into virtual learning differed from their classmates who learned in person.

Teaching students how to make responsible use of technology, a crucial task, has proven challenging. While the internet gives students access to nearly unlimited information, potentially increasing the pace and scope of learning, websites can be misleading, false, not age appropriate, or like the dark web, unsafe. Educators need to model critical-thinking skills, showing students how to appraise the source and credibility of the information they find on the web. They also should make clear the harm that results from cyberbullying.

What is deeper learning?

Deeper learning is an umbrella term for learning experiences that are designed to richly understand academic content, while also practicing academic skills and mindsets such as collaborating, self-directed learning, problem-solving, and thinking critically.[82] This model of teaching pushes students, often working in groups, to do the heavy cognitive lifting and problem-solving rather than passively listening to a lecture. It requires a highly skilled teacher, a supportive school environment, a demanding curriculum, and the time to plan and execute.

For example, a middle school robotics teacher enlists her class to build a motorized prosthetic hand for a local disabled war veteran. Students are split into small groups to independently research, test, prototype several models, and present their findings. During the unit, students will apply math, engineering, and the scientific method aligned with academic state standards.

Deeper learning is what many practitioners, policymakers, and researchers argue *should* be the mode of instruction. It often incorporates active engagement in real-world and personally meaningful projects. But shallow learning predominates: students fill out worksheets, summarize historical events from textbooks, and memorize facts. Unsurprisingly, many students report feeling bored and disengaged when they describe their classes.[83]

Researchers have found that deeper learning was most likely to take place in elective courses and extracurricular activities; students preparing for a theater production or debate competition are deeply motivated, invested by choice, and consistently engaged.

Advocates argue that this mode of teaching is the best way to align students' experience with twenty-first-century demands.[84] Evaluations show that when it is implemented well, students record higher scores than their peers on international achievement tests as well as state-mandated English and math exams. Students report that they become more skilled at collaborating, more involved academically, and more motivated. Schools that participate in a deeper learning network have recorded higher graduation rates than comparison schools; their students are more likely to attend four-year institutions and selective colleges and universities.[85] It is difficult to disentangle the extent to which these results can be attributed to the pedagogy rather than the quality of the schools that have made use of it.

What is STEM education?

STEM is an acronym for science, technology, engineering, and mathematics. STEM fields include behavioral sciences, agricultural sciences, engineering, math, biology, psychology, and economics. Each of these disciplines promotes technological fluency and is also relevant to a host of societal problems. In some schools, the acronym STEAM is used because art has a symbiotic relationship to the STEM sciences.

When executed well, STEM classes make use of deeper learning, with hands-on experiences that require students to think critically about topics as socially significant as mitigating global warming.[86]

Although the STEM fields have become increasingly important in the economy, there is a shortage of STEM professionals in the United States.[87] American students lag behind students from other countries in the STEM subjects; in a 2015 report, the United States ranked thirty-eighth of seventy-one countries in math and twenty-fourth in science in the PISA exams.[88] ESSA, the current iteration of the ESEA, emphasizes the need for additional STEM courses, especially in schools in low-income communities.

What are noncognitive skills and social-emotional learning?

Schools focus mainly on academic or cognitive skills, paying little attention to the noncognitive, or soft, skills that partly determine how well a student performs in school and after graduation. *Noncognitive* is an umbrella term that describes attitudes, behaviors, and coping strategies, as distinguished from academic knowledge. Different disciplines refer to these skills in various ways: social-emotional competencies, soft skills, personal qualities, personality traits, character traits, twenty-first-century skills. A few examples of noncognitive skills are empathy, perseverance, grit, and growth mindset.[89]

Noncognitive skills may matter more than academic performance. This is widely understood—polls show that Americans place a higher value on schools' turning out good citizens, who possess these traits, than academic high-achievers. Research confirms the popular intuition; econometric studies find that these character traits do a better job of predicting future earnings than achievement test scores.[90] Employers report that a lack of noncognitive skills is more common and more problematic among their employees than deficiencies in academic achievement. In a company-wide survey, Google found that the best predictors of performance were soft skills like good communication and empathetic leadership, not technical excellence.[91]

A 2020 study conducted in Chicago's public high schools showed that students who attend schools that build soft skills, such as learning how to resolve conflicts, recorded higher grades than their peers who are enrolled in schools that focus almost entirely on improving test scores. They were absent less frequently, less likely to be suspended, and more likely to graduate and enroll in college.[92]

Despite the voluminous evidence that shows these skills' importance, policymakers pay far less attention to fostering noncognitive skills than to honing academic talent. One reason is that soft skills are far harder to measure than academic competency. A student's ability to solve for "x" on an algebra test doesn't depend on external factors. By contrast, noncognitive skills are often measured through student reports and teacher questionnaires. Racial, cultural, and socio-economic factors may affect how particular noncognitive skills are measured and how students express them.[93]

A student's background and the characteristics of the school affect the importance that they attach to particular noncognitive skills. For example, grit—defined as passion and perseverance toward long-term goals—became a buzzword among urban educators, who adopted curricula designed to foster that trait among their students. Although students' self-reported scores indicated that they were lacking in grit, the fact that they had to cope with poverty and discrimination should be seen as ample demonstration of their grit.[94] Students' self-appraisal did not predict their academic success.[95]

Brief SEL experiences, designed by psychologists, to promote characteristics such as a sense of belonging or a growth mindset, are intended to help students acquire positive identities, manage their emotions, achieve their goals, demonstrate empathy, build positive relationships, and make responsible decisions.[96]

If SEL is to realize its promise, it has to be embedded throughout the curriculum rather than be treated as a one-off exercise. Teachers need to learn how best to respond to student conflicts. The school needs to create a positive classroom climate, crafting organizational structures that support close relationships among the students and teachers. SEL can also provide a framework that helps students respond to out-of-school problems like substance abuse and bullying.[97] In this sense, the aspirations of SEL are akin to strategies for improving school climate.

Several large-scale studies have found that when SEL is well implemented, reading and math achievement tests, as well as grades, improve substantially, by 11 percentile points.[98]

How are nudges used to improve educational outcomes?

Nudges are positive reinforcements and brief, indirect suggestions that are meant to influence the behavior of individuals in situations that range from increasing voter turnout to energy conservation.[99]

Educators are increasingly using nudges. While nudges in education are meant to change behavior in a particular situation—for example, ensuring that students complete financial aid forms—related strategies are designed to bring about broader behavioral changes, such as promoting an individual's sense of belonging or developing a growth mindset.[100]

Nudges are inexpensive, usually costing less than $10/student, and make modest demands on students' and teachers' time. Seemingly small changes can bring about outsized changes in behavior, helping students make smarter choices and perform better in school.[101]

Nudges have been used to address school-based problems such as expanding parental involvement in their children's education and increasing enrollment in advanced placement classes. For example, chronic absenteeism—missing more than 10 percent of days in a given school year—is a sure ticket to academic failure. In California, one of eight students is chronically absent, and more than ten million school days are lost each year. The absenteeism problem starts very early; one kindergartener in six misses at least fifteen days. These children are much less likely than their classmates to be reading proficiently by third grade and four times more likely than adept readers to drop out of school.[102]

Nudges can reduce absenteeism by enlisting parents as allies to keep their youngsters in school. Many parents know very little about how their offspring are faring. The information gap helps to explain why parents underestimate how many days their youngsters have been out of school and how that figure compares with their classmates' attendance records. They aren't aware of the situation until their children are academically at risk.

In two studies, families in Chicago and Philadelphia whose youngsters had met the chronically absent standard the previous year received attendance information five times during the year.[103] That information was accompanied by a personalized letter signed by the superintendent: "Billy has missed more school than his classmates—16 days so far in this school year. . . . Students fall behind when they miss school. . . . Absences matter and you can help." This simple, inexpensive strategy reduced chronic absenteeism by 15 to 20 percent.[104]

What are social-psychological strategies that improve student outcomes?

Social-psychological strategies focus on the thoughts, feelings, and beliefs of students and staff. In contrast to nudges, which are intended to alter a specific negative behavior like absenteeism, these interventions specifically target psychological processes that prevent people from thriving or contribute to social problems.[105] Like nudges, they are brief, inexpensive, and scalable. Researchers have also found that the benefits stemming from these brief experiences may increase over time. Two of the most widely used strategies are growth mindset and belonging.

A growth mindset is the belief that intelligence is not static but can be developed through hard work, good learning strategies, and help from others. The model posits that individuals have either a fixed mindset (intelligence is a static trait), growth mindset (intelligence can be cultivated), or mixed mindset.[106] Students with a growth mindset, for example, will attribute a failing grade on a math test to a lack of effort, preparation, or understanding. If, after persisting, they don't understand the topic, they seek help. In contrast, students with a fixed mindset believe they lack the innate intelligence to master math concepts, and they stop studying.[107]

Growth mindset experiences (psychologists refer to them as interventions) have been shown to lead to improved student performance.[108] In a large-scale study of a nationally representative sample of students in secondary education, a forty-five-minute online growth mindset intervention led to higher grades among lower-achieving students and increased enrollment in advanced mathematics courses, a reliable predictor of graduation.[109] Some researchers argue that a growth mindset can affect the way individuals experience the hardships of economic disadvantage on a systemic level.[110]

The benefits attributable to growth mindset interventions have recently been questioned by researchers who have been unable to replicate the positive outcomes.[111] Critics also argue that commercially available curricula that claim to teach a growth mindset have little if any effect.[112] Despite the criticism, growth mindset researchers remain optimistic about the benefits of growth mindset, yet acknowledge the need to understand why certain students in particular schools respond well to these interventions, while others do not benefit similarly.[113]

Belonging experiences are intended to help students feel more connected to the school. Some students believe that they don't belong or are uncertain about whether they belong. Research shows that these feelings depress students' academic achievement and increase the likelihood of their dropping out.[114]

Fortifying a student's sense of belonging can have other positive effects. For instance, many high school students who are eligible for federal or state college financial aid don't apply. When California officials redrafted the letter that notified students of their eligibility, making it more reader-friendly by simply adding two sentences—"You have shown that you're the kind of person who *belongs* in college. We've been working hard to help you get there!"—more students applied for aid.[115]

Like every strategy meant to improve student outcomes, social-psychological interventions are not a panacea.[116] Researchers agree that the interventions should be timely, tailored, and integrated in the life of the school.[117]

What is high school completion?

The most common pathways to high school graduation are completing the requisite number of courses or passing a General Educational Development (GED) test.

In 2018–19, 86 percent of K–12 students graduated from high school in four years, 7 percent more than in 2010–11.[118] Graduation rates differ widely, ranging from 69 percent in the District of Columbia to 92 percent in Iowa and Alabama. A considerable number of students take more than four years to complete high school—93 percent of eighteen- to twenty-four-year-olds have completed high school.[119]

The GED is an alternative route to graduation for students who have dropped out of high school. Though the GED performance expectations are the high school graduation requirement, GED recipients have lower lifetime earnings. "High school graduates outperform GED recipients in terms of their earnings, employment, wages, labor market participation, alcohol use, self-reported health, crime, college completion, welfare receipt, and other meaningful outcomes."[120] University of Chicago economist James Heckman, who conducted the research, speculates that the gap may be due to noncognitive skills honed in high school, which are not reflected in the GED, that contribute to a student's successful transition to adulthood.

Poor attendance and an inability to master academic content leads to failing grades, which prompts some high school students to leave school before graduating.[121] Surveys of these students show that they do not find their coursework interesting and prefer to focus on having a job. Dropouts earn $9,200 less a year, are far more likely to live in poverty, and have higher rates of incarceration than high school graduates.[122]

Schools need to intervene early, rather than waiting until high school, to keep at-risk students on track to graduate. The warning signs emerge as early as third grade; students who aren't proficient in reading are four times more likely to drop out. Poor grades and absenteeism in fifth grade are another flashing red light.

Failing three or more courses in ninth grade is a better predictor of dropping out than either race or social class.[123] Chicago initiated a program to reduce the number of dropouts by focusing on students who, prior to starting ninth grade, failed several courses and were frequently absent. Between 2010, when the program was launched, and 2020, the percentage of students who graduated on time increased from 57 to 82 percent.[124]

What is career education?

It is politically popular to talk about "college for all." However, 30 percent of students do not attend college, and well over half of those who do enroll drop out before graduation.[125]

Career education, sometimes called vocational education, is intended to prepare non-college-bound students for the world of work. Coursework often includes hands-on training that leads directly to a non-dead-end job or a postsecondary vocational training program. Auto mechanics, cosmetology, and STEM fields such as computer programming are among the fields for which career education students are trained.

The origins of high school vocational education programs can be traced to the Smith-Hughes Act (1917), which underwrote school-based vocational programs as a way to keep disaffected students in school. Since the 1980s, enrollment in vocational courses has declined, as students are required to take more traditional academic subjects, like math and science, in order to graduate.

Critics argue that career education segregates students who are regarded as unable to do college-prep course work, funneling them into blue collar jobs. A disproportionate number of low-income students attend vocational high schools or enroll in vocational tracks in high school.[126]

When executed well, career education programs live up to their promise. Roanoke, Virginia's, school system's program is a good example.[127] "We want to see that our kids are ready to go to work or go to college, whichever they want to do," says Julie Drewery, the district's chief academic officer. This dual focus prompted the school system to bulk up its career offerings while simultaneously making college a realistic option for students who otherwise would not have given it a second thought.

Roanoke's career-focused classes are nothing like traditional vocational education, which deservedly earned a bad rap for teaching out-of-date skills that left students ill-equipped to join the workforce. These courses are as rigorous as those designed for college-bound students. They afford students the chance to explore careers in a host of fields, including architecture and construction, culinary arts, education, health and medical sciences, and engineering. A suite of courses can lead to a professional certification. Many of the courses receive credit at a local community college as well as the high school, giving students a jump-start on a college degree. Nearly every Roanoke student who has completed the career and education program has earned a diploma.

A randomized control trial conducted across a diverse group of high schools across the United States found no differences between the control group, who were placed in general education classes, and students assigned to Career Academies (the vocational pathway) in their graduation rate or enrollment in college.[128] However, students who attended Career Academics earned 11 percent more than their peers.

Students who take advanced vocational courses reap economic benefits. A recent study found that "students earn about 2 percent more each year for each advanced vocational class they take," but students who take only introductory classes don't experience a bump in their wages.[129]

5

THE COMPOSITION OF
THE CLASSROOM

What is special education?

Special education is an umbrella term that describes the array of support for students' disability-related needs, ranging from mild learning disabilities to profound developmental problems. The disability categories include learning disabilities, such as dyslexia; autism; emotional disturbance, such as anxiety and depression; speech or language impairment, such as stuttering; visual and hearing impairment; and intellectual disability, such as Down syndrome.[1]

Specialists, including school psychologists, speech and language pathologists, and occupational therapists, help school teams and families determine if a student is eligible for special education services. According to the National Center for Education Statistics, between 2009–10 and 2019–20, the number of students, ages three to twenty-one, who received these services increased from 6.5 to 7.3 million, or 13 to 14 percent of total public school enrollment. More recent estimates of the 2020-201 school year estimate 15 percent of all public students receive special education services.[2]

Until the early 1970s, school districts in most states had the legal right to exclude children with disabilities from school. In the aftermath of *Brown v, Board of Education*, which declared that all children were entitled to a public education, that long-standing practice was challenged in the courts. A landmark settlement agreement in *Pennsylvania Association for Retarded Citizens (PARC) v. the Commonwealth of Pennsylvania* (1972) required the state to provide a free public education for all students with intellectual disabilities.[3] In *Mills v. Board of Education of District of Columbia* (1972), a federal district court, relying on *Brown*, held that all students with disabilities had the constitutional right to an education.

Congressional action soon followed. The Individuals with Disabilities Education Act (IDEA), passed in 1975 and amended in 2004, specifies the policies and procedures that schools must follow:

- *Free and appropriate education*: Initially, schools were required to demonstrate that a child with a disability was making some or minimal academic progress. In *Endrew F. v. Douglas County School District* (2017), the Supreme Court raised the bar, ruling that a school must design an educational program that enables the student to make progress that is appropriate in light of the child's circumstances.
- *Appropriate evaluation*: Qualified evaluators are to conduct empirically validated and nondiscriminatory assessments intended to lead to a long-term educational strategy for the student.
- *Individualized Education Plan (IEP)*: The type of education that a special education student receives is defined by the IEP, a contract drafted by the school staff and the child's parents, that is responsive to the distinct needs of each student. The plan, which is updated at least annually, establishes goals for a student's education, documents the specific accommodations (such as allowing a student to take additional time in completing an exam or providing access to magnifying equipment) that are needed, and specifies the services (such as a teacher's aide) that are to be provided. The IEP team decides on the most

fitting placement for the student, such as a separate special education class, a general education class (with or without an aide), or a combination of the two.

- *Least restrictive environment*: Historically, students with disabilities were rarely assigned to the same classroom as their nondisabled peers. The legislation requires the IEP team to assign a student to the least restrictive educational environment. In other words, these students should be "mainstreamed"—assigned to general education classes—whenever possible.
- *Parent participation*: Parents play an important role in the IEP process. They must consent before their child is tested for special education, participate in meetings to develop the IEP, and sign the IEP before it is enacted.
- *Due process*: Parents who disagree with the school's decision may appeal to a third-party arbitrator seeking additional assistance, such as an independent evaluation, tutoring, or placement in another school.

Section 504 of the Rehabilitation Act (1973) and the Americans with Disabilities Act (1990) complement the requirements of IDEA, mandating that schools ensure students with disabilities access supports and services that make it possible for them to "obtain the same result, to gain the same benefit, or to reach the same level of achievement [as students without disabilities]." For example, a school must provide a ramp or elevator to a classroom on a school's second floor, offer extended time to students who have trouble focusing during tests, and ensure that students have access to a keyboard if their disability makes handwriting difficult. A student with a disability may have a 504 plan that identifies the impact of the disability and specifies the accommodations or modifications that the school has made in response to that need.

Implementation of IDEA has been problematic. Lack of adequate federal funding has been a major issue. In 1975, when IDEA became law, Congress estimated that it cost twice as much to educate a student with disabilities as it did to educate a general education student. While the legislation authorizes the federal government to contribute up to 40 percent of that additional cost, Congress has never appropriated more than 19 percent of the estimated cost. Consequently, states and school districts have had to devote a sizeable portion of their budgets to special education programs.[4] Resentment on the part of district officials and overworked school staff has been the predictable result.

The demands that IDEA imposes on teachers pose another problem. Because of the obligation to educate students in the "least restrictive environment," special education teachers must redesign the curriculum to take students' special needs into account, have a working knowledge of disabilities, satisfy legal requirements, collaborate with parents, and coordinate with agencies that provide supplementary services. General education teachers, who typically receive little training in teaching these students, are often ill-equipped to effectively meet the needs of all students with disabilities in their classroom. Many special education teachers, experiencing burnout, have left the field, and it has been difficult to recruit replacements. The teacher shortage has forced districts to use less-qualified teachers; in California, for example, only 40 percent of first-year special education teachers are fully credentialed.[5] Since this is a chronic shortage, all teachers need to be trained in the fundamentals of special education.

Special education has been criticized as a "rich man's game." Affluent families may hire a lawyer who can pressure the school district to provide additional services or pay the tuition at a private school that the parents regard as the appropriate alternative.[6] Districts may bend to parents' requests because they fear the threat and the cost of a lawsuit. In any event, parents must balance the need to maintain a positive relationship with their child's teacher with insisting that their child needs additional services.

The accuracy of diagnoses—especially dyslexia and autism, which increased 140 percent between 2008 and 2018—has been questioned by those who point out that public pressure, policies, and local practices shape these decisions. The debate is magnified when discussing the disproportionate percentage of Black and Latino students who qualify for special education.[7]

The line between ideology and evidence-based arguments about the merits of special education can become blurry. Special education professor Soyoung Park contends that special education pathologizes a child's disability, treating it like a disease; the interventions are designed to reduce "undesirable" behaviors and replace them with more "desirable" ones. Other scholars vehemently disagree. Special education professors Andrew Wiley, Dimitris Anastasiou, and Jim Kauffman vigorously counter that special education is not designed to punish or stigmatize, and it is important to acknowledge differences and diversities when designing each child's educational program. These researchers conclude that the field would benefit from theories that are testable, confirmable, and refutable based on reliable data. Special education is technically complex, and policymakers and the public would benefit from clarity rather than ideological debate.[8]

What is the immigrant students' experience?

Immigrant families come to the United States for a host of reasons. Some are fleeing violence in their home countries; others are desperate to escape from poverty. They share the common desire to provide a better future for their children.[9]

Public schools have a constitutional obligation to educate all students, including immigrant children whose parents are undocumented immigrants.[10] Schools cannot prevent students from enrolling because they do not have a birth certificate or because their parents do not have Social Security numbers.

The number of immigrant students has dramatically increased in recent years. In 1994, 12.5 million children, 18 percent of the total public school enrollment, were first- or second-generation immigrant students. By 2017 they numbered nearly twenty million and accounted for more than a quarter of all students.[11] This increase has come from the proportion of second-generation immigrants, which increased from 14 to 23 percent from 1994 to 2017.

These youth come to the United States from around the globe. While three-quarters live in Spanish-speaking households, more than four hundred native languages—including Arabic (2.7 percent), Chinese (2.1 percent), and Vietnamese (1.6 percent)—are represented. This diversity of background presents challenges, since districts cannot find teachers with correspondingly varied language proficiency.

This influx has profoundly affected the public education system. Immigrant students are also more likely to enroll in schools with less-experienced teachers or brittle school infrastructure to help students learn English and adapt to their new community. The needs include teacher training, development of specific programs, allocation of resources, and curricula.[12]

Immigrant children are more likely to live in poverty (households with incomes below the federal poverty level) than nonimmigrant children. Worst off are the first-generation children—in 2017, 25 percent of the first-generation and 22 percent of the second-generation immigrant students lived in poverty, compared with 17 percent of nonimmigrant youth.

Immigrant students confront three challenges: they must learn English, keep up academically, and navigate among American cultural norms and customs.[13] They also have to balance the competing demands of family and school. At home they are often "encouraged to learn English, but at the same time may be asked to keep the new language and cultural ways out of the home. If they do not do so, children may be accused of 'becoming American.'"[14] And while nearly 90 percent of immigrant students were born in the United States, and for that reason are US citizens, when one parent is undocumented, children live in fear that their undocumented parent will be deported.

What's more, these students have to contend with the reality that immigration is a hot-button political issue; in some regions of the country, there is widespread opposition to their presence. While earlier waves of European-origin immigrants encountered prejudice and discrimination, enduring racial tensions—specifically for immigrants of color—are arguably more challenging for immigrants today.[15]

This hostility surfaces in the schools. A recent study found that, compared to their US-born classmates, immigrant students had poorer health, fewer close friends, and weaker family relationships, and reported feeling lonely. Those who are undocumented or come from mixed status families are a particularly tempting target for bullies. The malevolent behavior that these students must deal with makes it more likely that they will drop out of school.[16]

The biases of teachers can also shape these students' experience in school. Many teachers grow impatient when students for whom English is not their first language cannot fully express themselves. Some teachers have lower academic expectations for children of immigrants. They assign rote tasks instead of giving them opportunities to be creative and solve problems.[17]

Not all immigrant groups have the same experience. Asian immigrants are more likely to take college preparatory courses and attend college when they graduate than their nonimmigrant classmates. Latino immigrants—the group rapidly becoming the nation's largest minority—are least likely to attend high school and college. This has tremendous consequences for the future labor force and the demand for public services.[18]

Those opposed to the growing number of immigrant students have asserted that their presence depresses the rest of the class. In fact the opposite is true: having an immigrant student as a classmate is associated with higher academic achievement for both nonimmigrant and immigrant students, an effect that is especially striking for nonimmigrant students from families living in poverty.[19]

Immigrant children who start school in the United States in preschool or elementary school usually catch up with their peers before they enter high school. But immigrant students who arrive when they are teenagers have a very limited time to learn English, master the curriculum, and pass state achievement tests before they can graduate. That's why these students are substantially more likely to leave before graduating from school than their classmates.

This need not be the case. The Internationals Network for Public Schools (not to be confused with International Schools, which prepare highly educated students for the international baccalaureate) has demonstrated that students who arrive as adolescents and have been in the United States for fewer than three years—the category least likely to graduate—can flourish in the right academic environment.

Many of the Internationals Network school students spent time in detention camps. About 70 percent have been separated from one or both parents at some point in their lives. They often live with distant relatives, in shelters, or on the street. They are poor—more than 90 percent are eligible for federally subsidized lunches. Despite those barriers, in New York City in 2015, 64 percent of the students graduated in four years, and 70 percent earned a degree in six years. Statewide, the rates for all English Language Learners were far lower: 34 percent graduate in four years; 50 percent in six years. More than 90 percent of these students reported that they had been admitted to college.

Instead of teaching English as a separate course, in an Internationals Network school every class, from science to gym, is a language class. The lessons are taught in English. Those with a grasp of the language translate for newcomers who speak the same home language, and students can discuss complex ideas in their native languages. In a matter of months, these students start speaking English.[20]

What is the most effective way to teach English Language Learners?

English Language Learners (ELLs) are students whose home language is not English.[21] Some researchers describe them as emergent bilingual or multilingual learners, because English is a second or third language for ELLs.

Researchers have differed on how best to teach English to nonnative speakers. Some are fearful that cultivating a language other than English in school will make mastery of English more difficult. They argue that these students are best taught in an English-only classroom. However, the research generally concludes that immersion in a student's native tongue before transitioning to English or providing instruction in both the home tongue and English is a more effective approach. Language immersion and bilingualism appear to yield long-term benefits.[22] Studies comparing English-only and immersion programs find that immigrant students in language immersion classes typically catch up academically with students in the English-only classes by the end of elementary school and outperform them by the end of middle school.[23] Being bilingual is valuable for another reason—it's linked to noncognitive skills such as working memory, flexible thinking, and self-control.

Since the 1980s, politics has played an outsized role in shaping policy on bilingual education. An organization called U.S. English, founded by California senator S. I. Hayakowa, argued that English should be the nation's official language; a counter-group, English Plus, promoted bilingualism. During the late 1990s, California, Massachusetts, and Arizona banned bilingual education. Those who favored this position argued that the California measure was overwhelmingly supported by Latino families, who were dissatisfied with poor-quality immersion programs. As the quality of language immersion instruction improved and long-term evaluations demonstrated its worth, voters' attitudes changed; in California and Massachusetts, the ban on immersion has been repealed.[24]

What is the Native American students' experience?

The 700,000 Native American, Alaska Native, and Native Hawaiian students who attend public schools fare worse academically than any other group. They are more than twice as likely as White students to be suspended and half as likely to enroll in Advanced Placement classes. They perform two to three grade levels below their White peers in reading and math. On the NAEP, the nation's education report card, their fourth- and eighth-grade reading and math scores have consistently been the lowest in the nation. Their dropout rate is twice the national average, and only 72 percent graduate, the lowest percentage of any demographic group.[25]

Native American students and their families have experienced generations of overt discrimination, by both the federal government and school districts. There are few Native teachers, and the curriculum pays scant attention to their history and culture. According to Native Hope, an advocacy organization, these students are confronted with a world that does not understand them or their customs. Consequently, many of them are alienated, enveloped in an environment of isolation and self-doubt. The consequences of this maltreatment are dire. Not only are Native American students less well prepared academically, they are also 50 percent more likely to commit suicide than their White classmates.

Until 1978, the federal government relocated most Native children away from their families and tribal way of life to long-term boarding schools run by the Interior Department's Bureau of Indian Education (BIE) and Christian organizations. It is estimated that in 1973, sixty thousand children were enrolled in a boarding school. A graduate of one such school called them "institutions created to destroy and vilify Native culture, language, family, and spirituality." Survivors describe "a culture of pervasive physical and sexual abuse at the schools. Food and medical attention were often scarce; many students died."[26]

It was not until 1978 that, under the Indian Child Welfare Act, Native parents could legally refuse to have their children sent to one of those schools, and their enrollment declined rapidly in the 1980s. The BIE and Christian organizations still operate about two dozen boarding schools.

Today, more than 90 percent of Native students attend schools near or on reservations, often in rural areas, that are operated by school districts or the BIE. While the 1972 Indian Education Act was intended to give tribes more responsibility for educating their own children, districts have generally maintained control over curriculum, funding, and staffing.

Discrimination is so commonplace, one parent noted, that it is almost taken for granted. A three-year investigation of a rural Northern California school district, conducted by the US Department of Education, concluded in 2015, found that the school's principal called Native students a "pack of wolves." The district did not provide them with special education, and they were disciplined more harshly than their White classmates.[27]

Schools run by the BIE have also miseducated their students. A Government Accountability Office report found that the BIE had managed the schools it operates so badly that it had given them permission to use assessments that failed to meet federal requirements. Recently, a federal report found more than half of BIE-funded schools lacked the internet bandwidth and computer hardware to meet the requirements of new assessments aligned to college- and career-ready standards.[28]

Discrimination is also an issue in these schools. In one lawsuit, plaintiffs contended that an elementary school in rural Arizona with a predominantly Native enrollment, run by the BIE, was "persistently understaffed, lacked a functioning library and adequate textbooks, and provided inadequate special education services. Because of 'excessive exclusionary discipline,' some students barely attend classes." In a 2020 settlement, the federal government guaranteed that discrimination against students with disabilities at BIE-operated schools will be prohibited, as the law requires, and independent monitors will review the government's actions. Litigation continues regarding the other allegations.[29]

There are some encouraging examples of government agencies collaborating with Native American tribal leaders to provide a high-quality, culturally appropriate education. In Washington state, for instance, tribes have set up their own education programs, which receive state funding.[30]

The National Caucus of Native American Legislators has developed a multipronged strategy to overcome these problems:

- Ensure access for Native students to a curriculum that prepares them for the rigors of a new economy and college.
- Address the multidimensional, contextual problems associated with decreased achievement before students begin school.
- Offer an outstanding teaching force.
- Make schools more culturally relevant places for Native children.
- Ensure adequate distribution of resources.

That report was issued in 2008, but little progress has been made toward achieving these goals.

What are individual students' legal rights?

Until the 1960s, individual students had few legal rights. They could be suspended or expelled on the say-so of the principal, without any reason being given; they could only form clubs that received the principal's approval; their articles in the student newspaper could be censored because they were deemed offensive; and they could not express political viewpoints with which the administration disagreed.

In the landmark case *Tinker v. Des Moines School District* (1968), the Supreme Court declared that students do not "shed their constitutional rights to freedom of speech or expression at the schoolhouse gate."[31] High school students in Des Moines, Iowa, planned to come to school wearing armbands, as a silent protest against the Vietnam War. The principal, fearing that their armbands would "disrupt" classes, warned the students that they would be suspended. The justices ruled that mere suspicion wasn't a good enough reason to punish them. Before suspending a student, a school administrator had to show that the conduct would "materially and substantially interfere with the requirements of appropriate discipline in the operation of the school."[32]

The *Tinker* case was decided in an era when other historically disadvantaged groups—low-income students, English Language Learners, and students with disabilities—were pressing their claims in the courts. But until recently, *Tinker* was the high-water mark for student rights. While the "materially and substantially" disruption standard remained on the books, the Supreme Court repeatedly limited the scope of what students were constitutionally entitled to say or do. For instance, in *Bethel School District v. Fraser* (1986), the justices ruled that a high school student's sexual innuendo-laden speech during a school assembly was not constitutionally protected—*Tinker* protected political speech, not vulgarity.[33] Two years later, in *Hazelwood v. Kuhlmeier*, the justices upheld a principal's right to prevent a student newspaper from publishing articles about divorce and teenage pregnancy on the basis of "legitimate pedagogical concerns."[34]

From armbands protesting the Vietnam War to Confederate garb, lower federal courts relied on the "substantial disruption test" in ruling that schools could prohibit students from wearing clothing with Confederate symbols and, in another case, that a school could ban an American flag T-shirt on Cinco de Mayo because of a disruption that had taken place the previous year. However, a school that allowed its students to wear an "X" T-shirt, associated with Malcolm X and the Black Muslim movement, also had to allow students to wear shirts with Confederate symbols.

Courts are now being called on to determine whether students may be disciplined for what they say outside school on social media. In *Mahanoy Area School District v. B. L.* (2021), the Supreme Court sided with the student, holding that a Pennsylvania school district violated the First Amendment by punishing a student for a vulgar social media message sent while she was not on school grounds.[35] In that case, a student who was disappointed because she had failed to make the varsity team sent a Snapchat to about 250 friends, with an image of the student and a friend raising their middle fingers and a message that cursed out "school," "softball," "cheer," and "everything." To avoid "chaos," the principal banned the student from cheerleading for a year.

The Supreme Court reversed the principal's decision. While the justices did not establish a categorical ban on regulating student speech outside of school, citing the need of school systems to be able to deal with issues like bullying and threats, the decision stressed that courts should be skeptical of efforts to constrain off-campus speech.

"America's public schools are the nurseries of democracy," wrote Justice Stephen Breyer. "Our representative democracy only works if we protect the 'marketplace of ideas.' Schools have a strong interest in ensuring that future generations understand the workings in practice of the well-known aphorism, 'I disapprove of what you say, but I will defend to the death your right to say it.' " Where and how the student spoke was an important factor in the Supreme Court's ruling. "Her posts appeared outside of school hours from a location outside the school. She did not identify the school in her posts or target any member of the school community with vulgar or abusive language."

Students also challenged the schools' disciplinary regime, arguing that arbitrary suspension denied them their rights. In *Goss v. Lopez* (1975), the Supreme Court ruled that students were constitutionally entitled to a hearing under the due process clause.[36] However, the hearing to which students are entitled is a bare-bones proceeding. While they can tell their side of the story, students are not entitled to have a lawyer present or cross-examine witnesses. Two years later, the justices upheld paddling as a form of student discipline.[37]

Students have also challenged searches of their school lockers by school administrators or police, contending that the practice violates their constitutional right to privacy and protection against unwarranted searches and seizures. Here as well, students have not prevailed. In *New Jersey v. TLO* (1985), the Supreme Court ruled that the unique nature of the school setting justified abandoning the usual constitutional standard of probable cause, substituting the looser standard of "reasonable suspicion" and leaving enormous discretion in the hands of school officials and police.[38]

What is LGBTQ students' experience?

Until recently, most LGBTQ students remained in the closet because they were fearful about how they would be treated by fellow students, teachers, and staff. Now more of these youth are coming out, as social norms change and legislatures and courts establish their legal rights.

In the federal government's 2016 biennial Youth Risk Behavior Survey, which included 15,600 high school students ages fourteen to seventeen, 1.3 million students described themselves as gay, lesbian, or bisexual.[39] These students have long been the target of gay-bashing and other forms of discrimination. More than a third of the LGBTQ students in the 2016 survey reported that they had been bullied at school.

They were three times more likely than straight students to have been raped and twice as likely to have been attacked with a weapon. They skipped school far more often than their straight classmates because they felt unsafe. Classmates and teachers who witnessed these assaults rarely intervened.

The Youth Risk Behavior Survey also revealed the horrific impact of gay-bashing on LGBTQ students' mental health. LGBTQ students are estimated to be three to four times more likely to commit suicide than their straight classmates. During the year preceding the study, more than 40 percent of them had seriously considered suicide, and 29 percent had attempted suicide.[40]

Transgender youth are especially likely to be targeted. A 2009 study found that more than two-thirds felt unsafe in school because of their sexual orientation and the way they expressed their gender. In another survey, three-quarters of transgender students reported that they were frequently harassed; more than a third were attacked physically, and one in eight had been raped.[41]

A 2021 study concluded that "LGBTQ secondary students were at higher risk for bullying, chronic sadness, and thoughts of suicide, as well as poorer learning engagement and academic performance, compared to their straight and non-transgender peers." These students also reported receiving substantially less support from teachers. The study concluded that "if LGBTQ students experienced the same levels of support and safety at school as non-transgender and straight students, disparities [in rates such as suicidal ideation, chronic sadness, and harassment] would disappear or greatly diminish."[42]

Increasingly, states are taking steps to protect LGBTQ youth by including sexual orientation, gender identity, and gender expression in laws that protect students against discrimination and harassment. States differ widely in the scope and enforcement of this legislation. Forty-nine states have enacted antibullying laws, but most do not specifically mention sexual orientation or gender identity/expression.

Title IX of the 1972 Education Amendments bars schools that receive federal funds from discrimination based on sex. A school's obligation to protect students against sexual violence and support their continued access to education is the same regardless of students' sexual orientation, gender identity, and gender presentation. Schools must investigate and remedy instances of sexual violence against LGBTQ students, using the same approaches they rely on in responding to all complaints of sexual violence. In several court cases, LGBTQ students who have been the targets of sex discrimination and harassment have successfully relied on Title IX.

Transgender students can also claim legal protection. In 2021 the US Education Department asserted that transgender students are protected under Title IX. This position sets the stage for explosive political and legal battles, as a number of states have recently enacted legislation that requires transgender athletes to play on sports teams that align with their sex assigned at birth.

Every court that has addressed the restroom issue has ruled in favor of transgender students. In 2020, for example, a federal court of appeals found that prohibiting a transgender male student from using the boys' restroom violates the equal protection clause as well as Title IX.[43]

Courts have also sided with plaintiffs who challenge LGBT discrimination on constitutional grounds. In a landmark 1996 ruling, Jamie Nabozny successfully challenged the failure of high school administrators to intervene in the "relentless antigay verbal and physical abuse by fellow students" to which he had been subjected. This was the first case in which a court recognized that the equal protection clause of the Fourteenth Amendment applies to the mistreatment of gay and lesbian students.

The constitutional guarantees of freedom of speech and freedom of association in schools apply to LGBT student activities. LGBT campus organizations can hang posters, make announcements, and hold meetings on the same basis as other student organizations. If a school's dress code allows students to wear T-shirts with slogans, for example, they have the right to wear T-shirts that endorse gay pride.[44] Students may bring a same-sex date to the prom or homecoming. Schools can't create a dress code based on the stereotype that only girls can wear some types of clothing and only boys can wear other types. If a school permits clubs that aren't directly related to school classes, like a chess club, the federal Equal Access Act empowers students to form a Gay-Straight Alliance (GSA) or other LGBTQ-themed club, which provides a safe haven for LGBT youth and supportive classmates. A 2016 survey identified more than four thousand GSAs in middle schools and high schools.[45]

Seven states require (as of 2020) local school boards to enact antiharassment policies that specifically include sexual orientation and gender identity. Legislation in eight other states bars discrimination against students based on their sexual orientation and gender identity.

Four states require public schools to incorporate LGBT material in social sciences classes and prohibit discriminatory language in the curriculum. This issue, like the rights of transgender athletes, has generated fierce debate. Proponents argue that teaching LGBT-affirming topics will reduce homophobia. They point out that homophobic slurs and absenteeism have decreased in schools that have implemented an inclusive curriculum.[46] Opponents contend that including LGBT-positive material in the curriculum promotes a "homosexual agenda."[47] Beginning in 2021, a growing number of states adopted legislation aimed at restricting the discussion of LGBT topics in the classroom and banning books that address these issues.

6

THE IMPACT OF
THE PANDEMIC

How have schools responded to Covid-19?

Whether or not the threat posed by the pandemic has faded from the scene by the time you are reading this book, whether we are still in the midst of the pandemic or reckoning with the fallout, the impact of Covid-19 will be long-lasting.

The emergence of Covid in early 2020 reconfigured every aspect of schooling, even as it touched every aspect of our lives. In an attempt to halt the spread of the virus, principals, superintendents, and (later) governors closed the schools. The wave of closures began in February 2020, and by early May all but two states had ordered that schools be shut for the rest of the school year. The speed and magnitude of these changes was unprecedented; more than fifty million students and three million teachers found their lives turned upside down.

The pandemic proved to be a stress test for the schools. Every district had to respond to a cataclysmic set of events that demanded change-artist flexibility and speed. Not only did school systems have to rethink the way they educated their students, but they were also called upon to deliver essential services, like hot breakfasts and lunches, to children and families who otherwise would have gone hungry.

During the 2020–21 and 2021–22 school years, the nation's thirteen thousand school districts mostly had to decide for themselves the right course of action. The responses differed from district to district, and in different regions of the country. In some states, especially in the South, Midwest, and Great Plains, almost all students began the 2020–21 school year attending school in person, and they continued to do so, except for temporary closures during outbreaks. In many eastern and western states, most students were not in classrooms that entire year.[1]

The impact of Covid reaches far beyond the direct risk of infection. Racial and social class inequities that had long been glossed over surfaced as massive and highly visible problems. An education system that had relied on face-to-face interactions in classrooms had to operate almost entirely virtually.

During the period that schools were closed, many students lost ground academically; on average, they fell five months behind in mathematics and four months behind in reading.[2]

Those from low-income families suffered the most. Inadequate teaching, largely attributable to teachers' lack of preparation for distance learning; the lack or unreliability of laptops, iPads, and internet access; the jerry-built curriculum; the absence of conditions, such as a quiet place to study, that are conducive to learning—all these factors have taken their toll.[3] From the start of the pandemic through the 2020–21 school year, students in majority-Black schools lost six months in math, and those in low-income schools lost seven. High schoolers from low-income families were more likely to drop out of high school and less likely to enroll in college. Researchers feared that the result, not just in the United States but worldwide, would be a "lost COVID generation."[4]

Even before the pandemic, reading and math scores on the NAEP—the nation's "report card"—had declined for thirteen-year-olds, the first drop in a half century of measuring student proficiency in these subjects. Of even greater concern, the data from the 2019–20 tests showed that the pervasive achievement gap had widened. Test scores declined among the lowest-performing students, but not those at the top, setting off alarm bells among educators.

These grim realities presented districts with a dilemma: When should schools open again? How should the risk of spreading Covid to students and staff, through opening prematurely, be balanced against the learning loss that resulted from relying on online education?

Many districts that had reopened their schools in fall 2020 had to close them a month or two later, after an outbreak of Covid among students and teachers. Before the pandemic, pre-K–12 public school enrollment had been on a slight upward trajectory, but enrollment dropped by more than 1.3 million students between 2018–19 and 2020–21, a decline of 2.7 percent from 2018–19 enrollment. Enrollment in kindergarten dropped by more than 9 percent, likely because of the difficulties of virtual learning for younger students. More students attended charter schools, which were likelier to remain open, and more parents started to homeschool their children.[5]

Beyond its impact on academics, Covid has generated a host of less tangible, though more profound and long-lasting, effects.

When surveyed in 2020–21, more than a third of parents said they were very or extremely concerned about their children's mental health. School districts that reopened in fall 2021 reported more disruptive behavior. The pandemic was a traumatic time for many children because it upended their education, schedules, and social lives. Out of school for as long as two years, some of them had forgotten what it was like to be in a social setting.

A 2021 study, conducted by the US Department of Education, highlighted the adverse impact of school closures on particular groups of students.[6] For multilingual learners, who already faced the dual task of mastering grade-level content while learning English, "the abrupt shift to learning from home amid the challenges of the pandemic made that struggle even harder." LGBT students "lost regular access to affirming student organizations and supportive peers, teachers, and school staff." These students are also at an "increased risk of abuse from unsupportive or actively hostile family members." More students faced "sexual harassment, abuse, and violence from household members and intimate partners," as well as online harassment. Another report found that the disruption was especially devastating for students with disabilities, who often depend on structures and patterns for a secure sense of self.[7]

Covid has been particularly traumatic for students who have lost family members and friends and have had to come to terms with loss and grief.[8]

At the end of the tumultuous 2020–21 school year, it seemed that the worst of the pandemic was over. Almost all schools were slated to reopen in the fall of 2021. It was anticipated that by then staff, as well as students who were eligible to be vaccinated (a cohort that would in the near future include all school-aged children), would have been vaccinated, thus making the schools safe places. While students and teachers in some school districts would be required to wear masks, schools would operate more or less as they had before the pandemic.

The 2021–22 school year was supposed to restore normality for students. But in August 2021 one account noted that "as COVID cases rise, students across the country are seeing the start of their year disrupted by quarantines after they were exposed to COVID. Some schools are offering quarantining students live virtual instruction. But others are being sent home with only paper packets or are receiving no instruction at all— a worrying indication that many students could face another year of stop-and-start learning."[9] This unanticipated increase in infections brought with it a tidal wave of controversies over vaccination and masking requirements, school opening, and virtual learning. As had been the case since the early stage of the epidemic, the schools had to respond both to public health concerns and political cross-pressures.

Mask wearing was an especially explosive topic. Public health officials urged that in addition to maintaining social distancing and improving ventilation, masks should be mandated for students and staff. While a majority of teachers and parents supported that position, as did the teachers' unions, right-wing politicians and social activists contended that such a requirement was an infringement on liberty; parents, not school officials, should make the decision. Governors in several states, including Texas and Florida, demanded that no such requirements be imposed, on pain of school districts' losing state funding; for their part, some school districts decided to defy their governor, and the disputes moved into the courts.

In some communities, the attacks turned vicious, as school board meetings were overrun by protesters voicing mask-themed conspiracy theories and accusations of fascism. School board members were harassed and threatened; some of them quit, citing the toxic environment that made their job impossible to do. So menacing were these attacks that school officials sought help from the US Department of Justice in combating them.

As vaccines became widely available and judged to be safe for young children, another front opened in the political wars: Should school districts be allowed to require that, aside from those who had already been infected, staff and students be vaccinated or regularly tested for Covid?

While the public schools are no strangers to culture wars, these battles were particularly pernicious. The fights took their toll, as a larger than usual number of teachers and administrators opted to leave the profession. In Los Angeles, a quarter of administrators retired at the end of the 2020–21 school year. The educational challenges brought about by Covid were daunting; political fights were far more than educators bargained for when they entered the field.

What will Covid's long-term impact on schools be?

Covid has forced school districts to revisit, from top to bottom, their educational strategies. A 2021 survey of 375 public and charter school administrators concluded that most of these school leaders believed that public education would never be the same.[10]

In a 2021 survey of one thousand teachers, two-thirds reported that they will blend familiar teaching styles with strategies that they developed during Covid:

- 58 percent said they're more confident trying out new ideas to engage students.
- 56 percent are more confident about collaborating with their colleagues.
- 52 percent are more confident in communicating with families.
- 50 percent are more confident using technology to engage students.[11]

Making predictions is usually a perilous business, and that's certainly true in this instance. While the pull of the normal is strong, a cataclysmic event like Covid is likely to bring about some noteworthy reforms:

- *Technology will become increasingly important.* Covid obliged schools to expand their use of technology, and progress on this front will continue. The digital chasm, which school districts labored to overcome, will continue to shrink, as many more students have access to the internet and a laptop or iPad in school and at home than before the pandemic.
- *Virtual learning will increase.* Full-time online instruction was a stopgap solution to an immediate problem, and most students expressed a strong desire to return to school. But educators have learned that a one-size-fits-all

model is outmoded. Teachers acquired new pedagogical tools, and many of them are eager to continue using them. Districts will make greater use of distance learning, in combination with classroom instruction. More students will take some courses in the classroom and other courses online.

- *More schools will broaden their focus beyond academics.* During the high-stakes testing era of the NCLB Act, academic success was the sole metric against which schools were judged, and while the ESSA has added new metrics such as school climate, testing still holds pride of place. In the aftermath of the pandemic, schools will focus more on the noncognitive factors that shape students' lives.

During the pandemic, students' mental health became a source of serious concern, but most districts lacked the expertise to respond effectively. Lesson learned: more attention will be paid to students' mental well-being, and SEL will be integrated into academics. Trauma-informed education will increasingly become part of the schools' approach to learning, and mindfulness practice will also become more common. In schools where these practices are well implemented, the school climate—the quality and character of school life, based on assessments of students', parents', teachers', and administrators' experiences—will improve.

- *Prekindergarten programs will expand.* The learning loss for elementary schoolchildren caused by Covid confirmed what educators have long understood: pre-K provides a critical head start, both in academic skills and SEL.
- *There will be more community schools.* Many school districts gained a new appreciation for the fact that they are community hubs, a literal lifeline for families that depended on them to provide meals and other kinds of support. That realization will spark greater interest in the community school strategy, which is estimated to be used in five

thousand schools. The strategy incorporates an array of programs, ranging from health clinics to arts, academics, and sports, before and after school, on weekends and during the summer.

- *Schools will do a better job of helping students who have fallen behind.* To address the learning-loss problem, some districts will rely on tutoring, which has been shown to generate large achievement gains cost effectively.[12] Other schools will expand the time devoted to instruction.

- *Schools will forge closer ties with parents.* Covid prompted schools to do a better job of communicating with families, and parents will expect schools to continue being proactive in their outreach.

- *Students will have an increasing say about their education.* Students secured a level of independence during Covid— a capacity for time management and decision-making autonomy that isn't in the repertoire of the traditional school—and they will seek more such opportunities.[13]

- *The quality of implementation is the make-or-break factor.* This is one prediction that can confidently be made. Whether the topic is early childhood education or school climate, bilingual education or community schools, the research leads to the same conclusion: the success or failure of any program depends upon how well it is implemented.

NOTES

Preface

1 Linda Darling-Hammond, *The Flat World and Education: How America's Commitment to Equity Will Determine Our Future*, Multicultural Education Series (New York: Teachers College Press, 2010).

2 Leila Morsy and Richard Rothstein, *Five Social Disadvantages That Depress Student Performance: Why Schools Alone Can't Close Achievement Gaps*, Economic Policy Institute, June 10, 2015, https://www.epi.org/publication/five-social-disadvantages-that-depress-student-performance-why-schools-alone-cant-close-achievement-gaps; Richard Rothstein, *Class and Schools: Using Social, Economic, and Educational Reform to Close the Black-White Achievement Gap* (New York: Teachers College Press, 2004).

Introduction

1 Erin Duffin, "School Enrollment in the United States from 1965 to 2018 for All Levels of Public and Private Schools, with Projections up to 2029," Statista, June 2, 2021, https://www.statista.com/statistics/183826/us-school-enrollment-for-all-levels-of-public-and-private-schools/.

2 "State Education Practices (SEP): Table 1.3, Types of State and District Requirements for Kindergarten Entrance and Attendance, by State, 2020," Institute of Education Sciences, National Center for Education Statistics, 2020, https://nces.ed.gov/programs/statereform/tab1_3-2020.asp; and Bryan Kelley, Matt Weyer, Meghan McCann, Shanique Broom, and

Tom Keily, "50-State Comparison: State K–3 Policies," Education Commission of the States, September 28, 2020, https://www.ecs.org/kindergarten-policies/.

3 "The Federal Role in Education," US Department of Education, June 15, 2021, https://www2.ed.gov/about/overview/fed/role.html.

4 Stephen Sawchuk, "What Is Critical Race Theory, and Why Is It Under Attack?," *Education Week*, May 18, 2021, https://www.edweek.org/leadership/what-is-critical-race-theory-and-why-is-it-under-attack/2021/05.

5 Clark McKown and Rhona S. Weinstein, "The Development and Consequences of Stereotype Consciousness in Middle Childhood," *Child Development* 74, no. 2 (March 2003): 498–515, https://doi.org/10.1111/1467-8624.7402012.

6 Maureen Costello and Coshandra Dillard, *Hate in School Report*, Learning for Justice, 2018, https://www.learningforjustice.org/magazine/publications/hate-at-school-report.

7 Laura Meckler, "Utah School District Allowed 'Serious and Widespread Racial Harassment,' Justice Dept. Finds," *Washington Post*, October 21, 2021, https://www.washingtonpost.com/education/2021/10/21/utah-school-racial-discrimination/.

8 Ibram X. Kendi, *How to Be an Antiracist* (New York: One World, 2019).

9 Alex Spurrier, Sara Hodges, and Jennifer O'Neal Schiess, *Priced Out of Public Schools: District Lines, Housing Access, and Inequitable Educational Options*, Bellwether Education Partners, October 7, 2021, https://bellwethereducation.org/publication/priced-out.

10 David L. Kirp, *The Sandbox Investment: The Preschool Movement and Kids-First Politics* (Cambridge, MA: Harvard University Press, 2009); and Katherine A. Magnuson and Jane Waldfogel, "Early Childhood Care and Education: Effects on Ethnic and Racial Gaps in School Readiness," *Future of Children* 15, no. 1 (2005): 169–96, https://doi.org/10.1353/foc.2005.0005. We use "Latino," rather than "Hispanic," throughout the text. According to the US Census Bureau, Hispanic includes people with ancestry from Spain and Latin American Spanish-speaking countries, while Latino also includes people from Latin American countries that were formerly colonized by both Spain and Portugal.

11 National Center for Education Statistics, "Public High School Graduation Rates," US Department of Education, Institute of

Education Sciences, 2021, https://nces.ed.gov/programs/coe/indicator/coi.

12 "Higher Education for Foster Youth: The National Foster Youth Institute," National Foster Youth Institute, 2011, https://nfyi.org/issues/higher-education/; *Federal Data Summary: School Years 2014–15 to 2016–2017* (Browns Summit, NC: National Center for Homeless Education, 2019).

13 Bureau of Labor Statistics, US Department of Labor, "Median Weekly Earnings $606 for High School Dropouts, $1,559 for Advanced Degree Holders," *Economics Daily*, October 21, 2019, https://www.bls.gov/opub/ted/2019/median-weekly-earnings-606-for-high-school-dropouts-1559-for-advanced-degree-holders.htm.

14 David Kirp, *The College Dropout Scandal* (New York: Oxford University Press, 2019).

15 Jason A. Grissom and Christopher Redding, "Discretion and Disproportionality: Explaining the Underrepresentation of High-Achieving Students of Color in Gifted Programs," *AERA Open* 2, no. 1 (2016), https://doi.org/10.1177/2332858415622175.

16 US Government Accountability Office, *GAO K-12 Education: Discipline Disparities for Black Students, Boys, and Students with Disabilities* (report to congressional requesters §258, n.d.); and Libby Nelson and Dara Lind, "The School-to-Prison Pipeline, Explained," *Vox*, February 24, 2015, https://www.vox.com/2015/2/24/8101289/school-discipline-race.

17 Thomas B. Edsall, "Is Education No Longer the 'Great Equalizer'?," *New York Times*, June 23, 2021, https://www.nytimes.com/2021/06/23/opinion/education-poverty-intervention.html.

18 Nathan Glazer, "Towards an Imperial Judiciary?," *Public Interest* 41 (1975), https://www.nationalaffairs.com/storage/app/uploads/public/58e/1a4/bfc/58e1a4bfc7d30891958163.pdf.

19 "History," Mather Elementary School, accessed February 2, 2022, http://www.matherelementary.org/history.html.

20 Robert Bernstein, "U.S. Census Bureau Projections Show a Slower Growing, Older, More Diverse Nation a Half Century from Now," US Census Bureau, Public Information Office, December 12, 2012, https://www.census.gov/newsroom/releases/archives/population/cb12-243.html.

21 Steven A. Camatora, Bryan Griffith, and Karen Zeigler, *Mapping the Impact of Immigration on Public Schools*, Center for Immigration Studies, January 9, 2017, https://cis.org/Report/Mapping-Impact-Immigration-Public-Schools.

22 *The Next Era of Human Machine Partnerships: Emerging Technologies' Impact on Society & Work in 2030* (Palo Alto, CA: Institute for the Future, 2017).

23 Saheli Roy Choudhury, "A.I. and Robotics Will Create Almost 60 Million More Jobs Than They Destroy by 2022, Report Says," *CNBC*, September 17, 2018, https://www.cnbc.com/2018/09/17/wef-machines-are-going-to-perform-more-tasks-than-humans-by-2025.html.

Chapter 1

1 Mark G. Yudof, Betsy Levin, Rachel F. Moran, James E. Ryan, and Kristi L. Bowman, *Education Policy and the Law*, 5th ed. (Belmont, CA: Wadsworth/Cengage Learning, 2002).

2 Jay Caspian Kang, "Have We Failed Suburban Schools?," *New York Times*, September 23, 2021, https://www.nytimes.com/2021/09/23/opinion/suburban-schools-inner-city.html.

3 James S. Coleman, Ernest Q. Campbell, James McPartland, Alexander M. Mood, Frederic D. Weinfeld, and Robert L. York, *Equality of Educational Opportunity* (Washington, DC: National Center for Educational Statistics, 1966), https://files.eric.ed.gov/fulltext/ED012275.pdf.

4 Nancy H. St. John, "Desegregation and Minority Group Performance," *Review of Educational Research* 40, no. 1 (February 1, 1970): 111–33, https://doi.org/10.3102/00346543040001111.

5 "The Benefits of Socioeconomically and Racially Integrated Schools and Classrooms," The Century Foundation, April 29, 2019, https://tcf.org/content/facts/the-benefits-of-socioeconomically-and-racially-integrated-schools-and-classrooms/?agreed=1; M. Basile, "The Cost-Effectiveness of Socioeconomic School Integration," in *The Future of School Integration: Socioeconomic Diversity as an Education Reform Strategy*, ed. R. D. Kahlenberg, 121–51 (New York: The Century Foundation, 2012); and Sean F. Reardon, Ericka S. Weathers, Erin M. Fahle, Heewon Jang, and Demetra Kalogrides, *Is Separate Still Unequal? New Evidence on School Segregation and Racial Academic Achievement Gaps* (Palo Alto, CA: Stanford Center for Education

Policy Analysis, 2019), https://vtechworks.lib.vt.edu/bitstream/handle/10919/97804/SeparateStillEqual.pdf?se.

6 Rucker C. Johnson, "Long-Run Impacts of School Desegregation & School Quality on Adult Attainments" (working paper, National Bureau of Economic Research, Cambridge, MA, 2015).

7 Raj Chetty, Nathaniel Hendren, and Lawrence Katz, "The Effects of Exposure to Better Neighborhoods on Children: New Evidence from the Moving to Opportunity Experiment," *American Economic Review* 106, no. 4 (2016): 1–46, https://doi.org/10.3386/w21156.

8 Lyle Denniston, "Court Strikes Down School Integration Plans, Ends Term," *SCOTUSblog*, June 28, 2007, https://www.scotusblog.com/2007/06/court-strikes-down-school-integration-plans-ends-term/.

9 Richard D. Kahlenberg, Peter W. Cookson, Susan Shaffer, and Charo Basterra, *Socioeconomic Integration from an Equity Perspective*, ed. Phoebe Schlanger (Bethesda, MD: MAEC, 2017), https://files.eric.ed.gov/fulltext/ED585403.pdf.

10 Marco Basile, "The Cost-Effectiveness of Socioeconomic School Integration," in *The Future of School Integration: Socioeconomic Diversity as an Education Reform Strategy*, ed. Richard D. Kahlenberg, 127–51 (New York: Century Foundation Press, 2012).

11 These percentages represent the national average; specific state formulas for how schools are financed differ substantially.

12 "California's New School Finance Law: Local Control Funding Formula (LCFF)," Public Advocates, March 26, 2020, https://www.publicadvocates.org/our-work/education/public-school-funding/lcff/.

13 Emma Brown, "In 23 States, Richer School Districts Get More Local Funding Than Poorer Districts," *Washington Post*, March 12, 2015, https://www.washingtonpost.com/news/local/wp/2015/03/12/in-23-states-richer-school-districts-get-more-local-funding-than-poorer-districts/.

14 Bruce D. Baker, Danielle Farrie, and David Sciarra, *Is School Funding Fair? A National Report Card*, 7th ed. (Newark, NJ: Education Law Center, 2018), https://edlawcenter.org/assets/files/pdfs/publications/Is_School_Funding_Fair_7th_Editi.pdf.

15 Melanie Hanson, "U.S. Public Education Spending Statistics," Education Data Initiative, August 2, 2021, https://educationd

ata.org/public-education-spending-statistics#public-education-spending-statistics.

16   Krista Watson, "Why Richer Areas Get More School Funding Than Poorer Ones: What's behind the Great Divide of American Schools," Global Citizen, August 3, 2016, https://www.globalciti zen.org/en/content/cost-of-education-in-us/.

17   "Federal Role in Education," US Department of Education (ED), June 15, 2021, https://www2.ed.gov/about/overview/fed/role.html.

18   Larry J. Obhof, "School Finance Litigation and the Separation of Powers," *Mitchell Hamline Law Review*, 45, no. 2 (2019): 539.

19   Paul Minorini, Stephen D. Sugarman, Rosemary Chalk, and Janet S. Hansen, "Educational Adequacy and the Courts: The Promise and Problems of Moving to a New Paradigm," in *Equity and Adequacy in Education: Issues and Perspectives*, ed. Helen F. Ladd, 175–208 (Washington, DC: National Academy Press, 1999).

20   Ibid.

21   Ibid.

22   Valerie Strauss, "Michigan Settles Historic Lawsuit after Court Rules Students Have a Constitutional Right to a 'Basic' Education, Including Literacy," *Washington Post*, May 14, 2020, https://www.washingtonpost.com/education/2020/05/14/michigan-settles-historic-lawsuit-after-court-rules-students-have-constitutional-right-basic-education-including-literacy/.

23   Coleman et al., *Equality of Educational Opportunity*.

24   Eric A. Hanushek, "Introduction: Good Intentions Captured—School Funding Adequacy and the Courts," in *Courting Failure: How School Finance Lawsuits Exploit Judges' Good Intentions and Harm Our Children*, ed. Eric A. Hanushek, xiii–xxxii (Stanford, CA: Education Next Books, 2006).

25   Rob Greenwald, Larry V. Hedges, and Richard D. Laine, "The Effect of School Resources on Student Achievement," *Review of Educational Research* 66, no. 3 (1996): 361–96, https://doi.org/10.3102/00346543066003361.

26   Bruce D. Baker, *How Money Matters for Schools*, School Finance Series (Palo Alto, CA: Learning Policy Institute, 2018).

27   Kirabo C. Jackson, Rucke C. Johnson, and Claudia Persico, "Effects of School Spending on Educational and Economic Outcomes: Evidence from School Finance Reforms," National

Bureau of Economic Research. NBER, October 1, 2015, https://
www.nber.org/papers/w20847.

28 Baker, *How Money Matters for Schools*.

29 Rucker Johnson and Sean Tanner, *Money and Freedom: The Impact
of California's School Finance Reform* (Palo Alto, CA: Learning
Policy Institute, 2018).

30 "What Is School Choice?," EdChoice, June 28, 2021, https://
www.edchoice.org/school-choice/what-is-school-choice/.

31 "Just the FAQs—School Choice," Center for Education Reform,
accessed March 17, 2022, https://edreform.com/2011/
11/just-the-faqs-school-choice/#:~:text=The%20term%20
%E2%80%9Cschool%20choice%E2%80%9D%20means,the%20
schools%20their%20children%20attend.&text=People%20of%20
greater%20economic%20means,their%20children%20in%20priv
ate%20schools.

32 John E. Chubb and Terry M. Moe, *Politics, Markets, and America's
Schools* (Washington, DC: Brookings Institution, 1990).

Chapter 2

1 "What Are Magnet Schools," Magnet Schools of America, 2021,
http://magnet.edu/about/what-are-magnet-schools.

2 Donald Waldrip, "A Brief History of Magnet Schools," Magnet
Schools of America, accessed March 17, 2022, https://magnet.
edu/brief-history-of-magnets.

3 Adriana Prothero, "What Are Charter Schools?," *Education Week*,
August 9, 2019, https://www.edweek.org/policy-politics/what-
are-charter-schools/2018/08.

4 Richard D. Kahlenberg, *Tough Liberal: Albert Shanker
and the Battles over Schools, Unions, Race, and Democracy*
(New York: Columbia University Press, 2009).

5 Iris C. Rotberg and Joshua L. Glazer, eds. *Choosing Charters: Better
Schools or More Segregation?* (New York: Teachers College
Press, 2018).

6 Alyss Rafa, Bryan Kelley, and Micah Anne Wixom, "50-State
Comparison: Charter School Policies," Education Commission
of the States, January 28, 2020, https://www.ecs.org/charter-sch
ool-policies/.

7 National Alliance, *Estimated Charter Public School Enrollment,
2016–17* (Washington, DC: National Alliance for Public Charter
Schools, 2017), https://www.publiccharters.org/sites/default/

files/migrated/wp-content/uploads/2017/01/EER_Report_
V5.pdf.

8 Rebecca David, *National Charter School Management
   Overview: 2016–2017 School Year*, National Alliance for Public
   Charter Schools, August 27, 2018, https://www.publiccharters.
   org/sites/default/files/documents/2019-06/napcs_managem
   ent_report_web_06172019.pdf.

9 Laura Mckenna, "Why Don't Suburbanites Want Charter
   Schools? Politics and Personal Preferences Are at Play," *Atlantic*,
   October 1, 2015, https://www.theatlantic.com/education/arch
   ive/2015/10/why-dont-suburbanites-want-charter-schools/
   408307/; Kevin Helsa, Jamison White, and Adam Gerstenfeld,
   *A Growing Movement: America's Largest Charter Public School
   Communities*, 13th ed. (Washington, DC: National Alliance for
   Public Charter School, 2019), https://www.publiccharters.org/
   sites/default/files/documents/2019-03/rd1_napcs_enrollment_
   share_report%2003112019.pdf; and National Alliance, *Estimated
   Charter Public School Enrollment, 2016–17*.

10 Gene Glass, Kevin G. Weiner, and Justin Bathon, *Online K–12
   Schooling in the U.S.: Uncertain Private Ventures in Need of Public
   Regulation* (Boulder, CO: National Education Policy Center, 2011),
   https://nepc.colorado.edu/sites/default/files/NEPC-VirtSch
   ool-1-PB-Glass-Welner.pdf.

11 Mathematica, "Online Charter Schools Struggle to Engage Their
   Students New National Study Details the Operations and Effects
   of Online Charter Schools," *Mathematica: Progress Together* (blog),
   October 27, 2015, https://www.mathematica.org/news/online-
   charter-schools-struggle-to-engage-their-students.

12 Michael B. Henderson, David Houston, Paul E. Peterson, and
   Martin R. West, "Public Support Grows for Higher Teacher Pay
   and Expanded School Choice," *Education Next* 20, no. 1 (2020),
   https://www.educationnext.org/school-choice-trump-era-resu
   lts-2019-education-next-poll/.

13 "Urban Charter School Study Report on 41 Regions," Center
   for Research on Education Outcomes, accessed March 18, 2022,
   http://urbancharters.stanford.edu/download/Urban%20Char
   ter%20School%20Study%20Report%20on%2041%20Regions.
   pdf?_hsenc=p2ANqtz-9ihIRZN2YYgB1Bb04f2XPX2vJYKdoLbj_
   ViOpg9x001ZwtJlYLUxNX2ug8X18noySTc2ps-Pm43Ua65250v5_

uu0hMpNMGqvOsfHW8ufOkBK2tzks&_hsmi=34665222; Patrick Denice, *Are Charter Schools Working? A Review of the Evidence*, CRPE: Reinventing Public Education, August 2014, https://crpe. org/are-charter-schools-working-a-review-of-the-evidence/; Philip Gleason, Melissa Clark, and Christina Tuttle, "Charter Schools: Are They Effective?," Mathematica, 2019, https://math ematica.org/projects/charter-schools-are-they-effective#:~:text= We%20found%20that%3A,achievement%20in%20math%20 and%20reading.&text=Among%20subgroups%20of%20stude nts%2C%20impacts,when%20they%20entered%20charter%20 schools.

14 Ibid. A comparison between Los Angeles public schools and charter schools found that there was no significant difference in the performance of elementary school and high school students. However, charter middle schools had a modest positive impact on student achievement.

15 "Urban Charter School Study Report on 41 Regions."

16 Because coauthor Kevin Macpherson previously worked as a KIPP administrator, David Kirp wrote the section on KIPP. "The Kipp Approach: Learn More about What Makes Kipp Different," KIPP Public Charter Schools, July 27, 2021, https://www.kipp. org/approach/.

17 Thomas Coen, Ira Nichols-Barrer, and Philip Gleason, *Long-Term Impacts of KIPP Middle Schools on College Enrollment and Early College Persistence*, Mathematica, September 26, 2019, https:// mathematica.org/publications/long-term-impacts-of-kipp-mid dle-schools-on-college-enrollment-and-early-college-persiste nce; and Christina Clark Tuttle, Kevin Booker, Philip Gleason, Gregory Chojnacki, Virginia Kncechtel, Thomas Coen, Ira Nichols-Barrer, and Lisbeth Goble, *Understanding the Effect of KIPP as It Scales*, vol. I, *Impacts on Achievement and Other Outcomes*, Mathematica Policy Research Report, September 17, 2015, https://www.mathematica.org/news/kipp-i3-scale-up.

18 Noliwe Rooks, *Cutting School: The Segrenomics of American Education* (New York: The New Press, 2020).

19 Brian P. Gill, P. Mike Timpane, Karen E. Ross, Dominic J. Brewer, and Kevin Booker, *Rhetoric versus Reality: What We Know and What We Need to Know about Vouchers and Charter Schools* (Santa Monica, CA: Rand Education, 2007).

20   Zachary Jason, "The Battle over Charter Schools," *Harvard Ed Magazine*, Summer 2017, https://www.gse.harvard.edu/news/ed/17/05/battle-over-charter-schools.

21   Valerie Strauss, "John Oliver Hysterically Savages Charter Schools—and Charter Supporters Aren't Happy," *Washington Post*, August 22, 2016, https://www.washingtonpost.com/news/answer-sheet/wp/2016/08/22/john-oliver-hysterically-savages-charter-schools-and-charter-supporters-arent-happy/.

22   Chester E. Finn, Bruno V. Manno, and Brandon L. Wright, *Charter Schools at the Crossroads: Predicaments, Paradoxes, Possibilities* (Cambridge, MA: Harvard Education Press, 2016).

23   Carol Burris and Ryan Pfleger, *Broken Promises: An Analysis of Charter School Closures from 1999–2017*, Network for Public Education, accessed March 18, 2022, https://networkforpubliceducation.org/wp-content/uploads/2020/08/Broken-Promises-PDF.pdf.

24   Robin Lake, Ashley Jochim, Paul Hill, and Sivan Tuchman, *Charter Schools and District Enrollment Loss: California Charter Schools; Costs, Benefits, and Impact on School Districts* (Seattle, WA: Center on Reinventing Public Education, 2019), https://eric.ed.gov/?id=ED595191. The way facilities are allocated among schools also generates controversy, as charters are seen as claiming the space that rightfully belongs to public schools.

25   Chester E. Finn, Bruno V. Manno, and Brandon L. Wright, "Philanthropy and the Growth of Charter Schools: What Is the Right Role for Private Funders in the US Education System?," *Stanford Social Innovation Review* October 14, 2016, https://ssir.org/articles/entry/philanthropy_and_the_growth_of_charter_schools#; and Sally Ho, "Billionaires Fuel US Charter Schools Movement," *AP News*, July 16, 2018, https://apnews.com/article/melinda-gates-north-america-education-wa-state-wire-tx-state-wire-92dc914dd97c487a9b9aa4b006909a8c.

26   Christina A. Samuels, "Special Education Enrollment on Upward Trend in Charter Schools," *Education Week*, February 28, 2018, https://www.edweek.org/policy-politics/special-education-enrollment-on-upward-trend-in-charter-schools/2018/02.

27   Ashley Jochim and Lesley Lavery, *An Unlikely Bargain: Why Charter School Teachers Unionize and What Happens When They Do* (Bothell, WA: Center for Reinventing Public Education, 2019).

28 David Stuit and Thomas M. Smith, *Teacher Turnover in Charter Schools*, National Center on School Choice, Vanderbilt Peabody College, June 2010, https://files.eric.ed.gov/fulltext/ED543582.pdf.

29 Valerie Strauss, "Some 'No-Excuses' Charter Schools Say They Are Changing: Are They? Can They?," *Washington Post*, August 29, 2019, https://www.washingtonpost.com/education/2019/08/29/some-no-excuses-charter-schools-say-they-are-changing-are-they-can-they/; and Eliza Shapiro, "Why Some of the Country's Best Urban Schools Are Facing a Reckoning," *New York Times*, July 5, 2019, https://www.nytimes.com/2019/07/05/nyregion/charter-schools-nyc-criticism.html.

30 A 2021 report, *Chartered for Profit: The Hidden World of Charter Schools Operated for Financial Gain*, describes how National Heritage Academies (NHA), one of the country's largest education management organizations, "locks schools in with a 'sweeps contract' where virtually all revenue is passed to the for-profit management corporation, NHA, that runs the school"; Carol Burris and Darcie Cimarusti, *Chartered for Profit: The Hidden World of Charter Schools Operated for Financial Gain*, Network for Public Education, 2021, https://networkforpubliceducation.org/chartered-for-profit/; Peter Greene, "Four Truths about For-Profit Charter Schools," *Progressive Magazine*, August 2, 2019, https://progressive.org/public-schools-advocate/four-truths-about-for-profit-charter-schools-Greene-190802/.

31 Network for Public Education, *Do Charter Schools Profit from Educating Students?*, Network for Public Education, 2021, https://networkforpubliceducation.org/wp-content/uploads/2019/01/Do-charter-schools-profit-from-educating-students%C6%92.pdf.

32 Runyon v. McCrary, 427 U.S. 160 (1976).

33 Espinoza et al. v. Montana Department of Revenue et al., 591 U.S. __ (2020).

34 Joshua M. Cowen, David J. Fleming, John F. Witte, Patrick J. Wolf, and Brian Kisida, "School Vouchers and Student Attainment: Evidence from a State-Mandated Study of Milwaukee's Parental Choice Program," *Policy Studies Journal* 41, no. 1 (February 21, 2013): 147–68, https://doi.org/10.1111/psj.12006; John F. Witte, Patrick J. Wolf, Joshua M. Cowen, Deven E. Carlson, and David J. Fleming, "High-Stakes

Choice: Achievement and Accountability in the Nation's Oldest Urban Voucher Program," *Educational Evaluation and Policy Analysis* 36, no. 4 (2014): 437–56, https://doi.org/10.3102/01623 73714534521.

35 R. Joseph Waddington, and Mark Berends, "Impact of the Indiana Choice Scholarship Program: Achievement Effects for Students in Upper Elementary and Middle School," *Journal of Policy Analysis and Management* 37, no. 4 (August 8, 2018): 783–808, https://doi.org/10.1002/pam.22086; Jonathan Mills, and Patrick Wolf, *The Effects of the Louisiana Scholarship Program on Student Achievement after Four Years*, SSRN, accessed March 18, 2022, https://papers.ssrn.com/sol3/papers.cfm?abstract_id= 3376230; and David Figlio, and Krzysztof Karbownik, *Evaluation of Ohio's EdChoice Scholarship Program: Selection, Competition, and Performance Effects* (Columbus, OH: Thomas B. Fordham Institute, 2016), https://edex.s3-us-west-2.amazonaws.com/publication/ pdfs/FORDHAM%20Ed%20Choice%20Evaluation%20Report_ online%20edition.pdf.

36 Caroline Hoxby, "Rising Tide: New Evidence on Competition and the Public Schools," *Education Next*, July 19, 2006, https:// www.educationnext.org/rising-tide/; and Jay P. Greene and Marcus A. Winters, *When Schools Compete: The Effects of Vouchers on Florida Public School Achievement*, August 2003, https://citese erx.ist.psu.edu/viewdoc/download?doi=10.1.1.693.3956&rep= rep1&type=pdf.

37 Bayliss Fiddiman and Jessica Yin, "The Danger Private School Voucher Programs Pose to Civil Rights," *Center for American Progress*, May 13, 2019, https://www.americanprogress.org/arti cle/danger-private-school-voucher-programs-pose-civil-rights/ #:~:text=May%2013%2C%202019-,The%20Danger%20Private%20 School%20Voucher%20Programs%20Pose%20to%20Civil%20Rig hts,most%20vulnerable%20students%20from%20discrimination.

38 Michael J. Petrilli, "Are Private Schools Allowed to Discriminate?," *Education Next*, June 2017, https://www.educat ionnext.org/private-schools-allowed-discriminate/.

39 Nurse-Family Partnership, *Nurse-Family Partnership: Research Trials and Outcomes; The Gold Standard of Evidence* (Denver, CO: Nurse-Family Partnership, 2021), https://www.nursefa milypartnership.org/wp-content/uploads/2021/02/NFP-Research-Trials-and-Outcomes.pdf; and David L. Olds, Charles

R. Henderson, Robert Tatelbaum, and Robert Chamberlin, "Improving the Delivery of Prenatal Care and Outcomes of Pregnancy: A Randomized Trial of Nurse Home Visitation," *Pediatrics* 77, no. 1 (1986): 16–28, https://doi.org/10.1542/peds.77.1.16.

40 NAEYC National Governing Goard, *Developmentally Appropriate Practice: National Association for the Education of Young Children*, NAEYCDAP, n.d., https://www.naeyc.org/sites/default/files/globally-shared/downloads/PDFs/resources/position-stateme nts/dap-statement_0.pdf.

41 "Three Early Childhood Development Principles to Improve Child Outcomes" (working paper, Center on the Developing Child at Harvard University, April 23, 2021), https://developi ngchild.harvard.edu/resources/three-early-childhood-developm ent-principles-improve-child-family-outcomes/.

42 Allison Friedman-Krauss, W. Steven Barnett, and Milagros Nores, *How Much Can High-Quality Universal Pre-K Reduce Achievement Gaps?*, April 2016, https://cdn.americanprogress. org/wp-content/uploads/2016/04/01115656/NIEER-Achievem entGaps-report.pdf.

43 James J. Heckman, "The Hard Facts behind Soft Skills," Heckman: The Economics of Human Potential, February 6, 2017, https://heckmanequation.org/resource/the-hard-facts-behind-soft-skills/.

44 Marjorie Wechsler, Hanna Melnick, Anna Maier, and Joseph Bishop, "The Building Blocks of High-Quality Early Childhood Education Programs," Learning Policy Institute, April 20, 2016, https://learningpolicyinstitute.org/product/building-blo cks-high-quality-early-childhood-education-programs; and "Benchmarks for High-Quality Pre-k Checklist," NIEER, 2020, https://nieer.org/wp-content/uploads/2019/12/BENCHMA RKS-CHECK-LIST-PDF.pdf.

45 National Institute for Early Education Research (NIEER), Rutgers Graduate School of Education, November 20, 2020, https://nieer. org/state-preschool-yearbooks.

46 "Significant" is used in the statistical sense; that an effect is statistically significant means it is highly unlikely that it was a chance result.

47 Lawrence J. Schweinhart, Helen V. Barnes, and David P. Weikart, *Significant Benefits: The High/Scope Perry Preschool Study through*

Age 27, Monographs of the High/Scope Educational Research Foundation, No. Ten (Ypsilanti, MI: High/Scope Foundation, 1993); L. Schweinhart, J. Montie, Z. Xiang, W. Barnett, C. Belfield, and M. Nores, *Lifetime Effects: The High/Scope Perry Preschool Study through Age 40* (Ypsilanti, MI: High/Scope Educational Research Foundation, 2005), https://www.semanticscholar.org/paper/ Lifetime-Effects%3A-The-High%2FScope-Perry-Preschool-40- Schweinhart-Montie/37b2a6beba431f7d0e027adfd9f8c59e2d38b d93; and *Social Programs That Work Review: Evidence Summary for the Perry Preschool Project*, October 2021, https://evidenceba sedprograms.org/document/perry-preschool-project-evidence- summary/.

48   Michael L. Anderson, "Multiple Inference and Gender Differences in the Effects of Early Intervention: A Reevaluation of the Abecedarian, Perry Preschool, and Early Training Projects," *Journal of the American Statistical Association* 103, no. 484 (2008): 1481–95, https://doi.org/10.1198/016214508000000841.

49   Drew Bailey, Greg J. Duncan, Candice L. Odgers, and Winnie Yu, "Persistence and Fadeout in the Impacts of Child and Adolescent Interventions," *Journal of Research on Educational Effectiveness* 10, no. 1 (November 6, 2016): 7–39, https://doi.org/10.1080/19345 747.2016.1232459.

50   Diane Whitmore Schanzenbach, and Lauren Bauer, *The Long- Term Impact of the Head Start Program*, Brookings, August 19, 2016, https://www.brookings.edu/research/the-long-term-impact-of- the-head-start-program/.

51   Mark W. Lipsey, Dale C. Farran, and Kerry G. Hofer, *A Randomized Control Trial of a Statewide Voluntary Prekindergarten Program on Children's Skills and Behaviors through Third Grade*, Peabody Research Institute, September 29, 2015, https://files. eric.ed.gov/fulltext/ED566664.pdf; and Dale C. Farran, and Mark W. Lipsey, *Expectations of Sustained Effects from Scaled up Pre- K: Challenges from the Tennessee Study*, Brookings, October 8, 2015, https://www.brookings.edu/research/expectations-of-sustai ned-effects-from-scaled-up-pre-k-challenges-from-the-tennessee- study/.

52   Christina Weiland and Hirokazu Yoshikawa, "Impacts of a Prekindergarten Program on Children's Mathematics, Language, Literacy, Executive Function, and Emotional Skills," *Child*

Development 84, no. 6 (March 27, 2013): 2112–30, https://doi.org/10.1111/cdev.12099.

53 Guthrie Gray-Lobe, Parag A. Pathak, and Christopher R. Walters, *The Long-Term Effects of Universal Preschool in Boston* (Cambridge, MA: National Bureau of Economic Research, 2021), https://www.nber.org/papers/w28756.

54 "Inbrief: The Science of Early Childhood Development," Center on the Developing Child, 2007, https://developingchild.harvard.edu/resources/inbrief-science-of-ecd/; Jacqueline Bruce, Megan R. Gunnar, Katherine C. Pears, and Philip A. Fisher, "Early Adverse Care, Stress Neurobiology, and Prevention Science: Lessons Learned," *Prevention Science* 14, no. 3 (2013): 247–56, https://doi.org/10.1007/s11121-012-0354-6.

55 Charles A. Nelson, Nathan A. Fox, and Charles H. Zeanah, *Romania's Abandoned Children: Deprivation, Brain Development, and the Struggle for Recovery* (Cambridge, MA: Harvard University Press, 2014).

56 Arthur R. Jensen, "How Much Can We Boost IQ and Scholastic Achievement," US Department of Health, Education & Welfare, Office of Education, January 1, 1969, https://www.semanticscholar.org/paper/How-Much-Can-We-Boost-IQ-and-Scholastic-Achievement-Jensen/c0180db7ff784e3aa7ad4c089d3c7bced50303a4.

57 Jack P. Shonkoff and Pat Levitt, "Neuroscience and the Future of Early Childhood Policy: Moving from Why to What and How," *Neuron* 67, no. 5 (September 9, 2010): 689–91, https://doi.org/10.1016/j.neuron.2010.08.032; and David L. Kirp, *The Sandbox Investment: The Preschool Movement and Kids-First Politics* (Cambridge, MA: Harvard University Press, 2009).

58 This section draws on a variety of sources, including the chapter detailing community schools in David L. Kirp, *Kids First: Five Big Ideas for Transforming Children's Lives and America's Future* (New York: Public Affairs, 2012); and Anna Maier, Julia Daniel, Jeannie Oakes, and Livia Lam, "Community Schools as an Effective School Improvement Strategy: A Review of the Evidence" (working paper, Learning Policy Institute & National Education Policy Center, December 2017), https://learningpolicyinstitute.org/sites/default/files/product-files/Community_Schools_Effective_REPORT.pdf.

59 Abel McDaniels, *Building Community Schools Systems,* Center for American Progress, August 22, 2018, https://www.americanp rogress.org/article/building-community-schools-systems/ and https://www.americanprogress.org/issues/education-k-12/ reports/2018/08/22/454977/building-community-schools-systems/.

60 Robert Pondiscio, "No Apologies for 'No Excuses' Charter Schools," The Thomas B. Fordham Institute, July 7, 2019, https:// fordhaminstitute.org/national/commentary/no-apologies-no-excuses-charter-schools.

61 "Community Schools: Partnerships supporting students, families and communities," California School Boards Association, October 2010, https://www.csba.org/-/media/CSBA/Files/ GovernanceResources/PolicyNews_Briefs/CommunitySchools/ 2010_10_PolicyBrief_CommunitySchools.ashx?la=en&rev=ec0c6 be9ac6d4204ab9f9e5b1395833a.

62 David L. Kirp, "The Community School Comes of Age: The Model Is Expanding Rapidly; Is It a Fad, or the Future?," *New York Times,* January 10, 2019, https://www.nytimes.com/ 2019/01/10/opinion/community-school-new-york.html.

63 Maier et al., "Community Schools as an Effective School Improvement Strategy"; and Anne T. Henderson and Karen L. Mapp, *A New Wave of Evidence: The Impact of School, Family, and Community Connections on Student Achievement,* 2002, https:// sedl.org/connections/resources/evidence.pdf.

64 The senior author participated in the design of the research; Maier et al., "Community Schools as an Effective School Improvement Strategy."

65 Mary E. Walsh and Claire Foley, *City Connections: Intervention & Impact Progress Report 2020,* City Connects: Center for Optimized Student Support, 2020, https://www.bc.edu/content/dam/bc1/ schools/lsoe/sites/coss/City%20Connects%20progress%20rep ort%202020.pdf.

66 Leigh M. Parise, William Corrin, Kelly Granito, Zeest Haider, Marie-Andrée Somers, and Oscar Cerna, *Two Years of Case Management: Final Findings from the Communities in Schools Random Assignment Evaluation,* April 2017, https://www.mdrc. org/sites/default/files/CIS%20RCT%20Final%20Report-Web-REV.pdf.

67 Paul T. Hill, "How Home Schooling Will Change Public
    Education," Brookings, June 1, 2000, https://www.brookings.edu/
    articles/how-home-schooling-will-change-public-education/.

68 Moriah Balingit and Kate Rabinowitz, "Home Schooling
    Exploded among Black, Asian and Latino Students: But It Wasn't
    Just the Pandemic," *Washington Post*, July 27, 2021, https://www.
    washingtonpost.com/education/2021/07/27/pandemic-hom
    eschool-black-asian-hispanic-families/.

69 Rob Reich, "The Civic Perils of Homeschooling," *ASCD
    Educational Leadership*, April 1, 2002, https://www.ascd.org/el/
    articles/the-civic-perils-of-homeschooling.

70 Heath A. Brown, *Homeschooling the Right: How Conservative
    Education Activism Erodes the State* (New York: Columbia
    University Press, 2021); and Rachel Wise, "What Does the
    Research Say about the Impact of Homeschooling on Academics
    and Social Skills?," *Education and Behavior*, October 14, 2020,
    https://educationandbehavior.com/what-does-research-say-
    about-homeschooling/.

71 Brian D. Ray, "A Systematic Review of the Empirical Research on
    Selected Aspects of Homeschooling as a School Choice," *Journal
    of School Choice* 11, no. 4 (November 27, 2017): 604–21, https://
    doi.org/10.1080/15582159.2017.1395638.

72 Sandra Martin-Chang, Odette N. Gould, and Reanne E. Meuse,
    "The Impact of Schooling on Academic Achievement: Evidence
    from Homeschooled and Traditionally Schooled Students,"
    *Canadian Journal of Behavioural Science/Revue canadienne des
    sciences du comportement* 43, no. 3 (2011): 195–202, https://doi.
    org/10.1037/a0022697.

73 George W. Bush, "President Bush Addresses NAACP Annual
    Convention," Washington, DC, Convention Center, July 20, 2006.
    https://georgewbush-whitehouse.archives.gov/news/releases/
    2006/07/20060720.html.

74 Jane L. David, and Patrick M. Shields, *When Theory Hits
    Reality: Standards-Based Reform in Urban Districts; Final Narrative
    Report* (Arlington, VA: SRI International, 2001), https://files.eric.
    ed.gov/fulltext/ED480210.pdf.

75 Kenneth A. Sirotnik, "Promoting Responsible Accountability
    in Schools and Education," *Phi Delta Kappan* 83, no. 9 (May 1,
    2002): 662–73, https://doi.org/10.1177/003172170208300908.

76   Robert M. Hauser and Jay P. Heubert, *High Stakes: Testing for Tracking, Promotion, and Graduation* (Washington, DC: National Academy Press, 1999), https://nap.nationalacademies.org/read/6336/chapter/1#ii.

77   Stephen P. Klein, Laura S. Hamilton, Daniel F. McCaffrey, and Brian M Stecher, "What Do Test Scores in Texas Tell Us?" (working paper, RAND, 2000), https://doi.org/10.7249/IP202.

78   WestEd, *The High Stakes of High-Stakes Testing* (Palo Alto, CA: Author, 2000).

79   L. McNeil and A. Valenzuela, "The Harmful Impact of the TAAS System of Testing in Texas," in *Raising Standards or Raising Barriers? Inequality and High-Stakes Testing in Public Education*, ed. G. Orfield and M. L. Kornhaber (New York: Century, 2001).

80   Kathryn M. Doherty, "Poll: Teachers Support Standards-With Hesitation," *Education Weekly*, January 11, 2001, https://www.edweek.org/education/poll-teachers-support-standards-with-hesitation/2001/01.

81   Alan Blinder, "Atlanta Educators Convicted in School Cheating Scandal," *New York Times*, April 1, 2015, https://www.nytimes.com/2015/04/02/us/verdict-reached-in-atlanta-school-testing-trial.html.

82   Valerie Strauss, "Is Poverty Destiny? Ideology vs. Evidence in School Reform," *Washington Post*, September 19, 2015, https://www.washingtonpost.com/blogs/answer-sheet/post/is-poverty-destiny-ideology-vs-evidence-in-school-reform/2012/09/18/cf121d2e-0201-11e2-b257-e1c2b3548a4a_blog.html.

83   Daniel Denvir, "Atlanta's School Scandal Isn't Local How Education Reform's 'No Excuses' Motto Causes Cheating," *New Republic*, April 5, 2013, https://newrepublic.com/article/112844/atlanta-school-test-cheating-scandal-when-no-excuses-crime.

84   Dana Goldstein, "Michelle Rhee's Cheating Scandal: School Test Score Irregularities," *Daily Beast*, March 28, 2011, https://www.thedailybeast.com/michelle-rhees-cheating-scandal-school-test-score-irregularities.

85   Joan F. Goodman, "Charter Management Organizations and the Regulated Environment," *Educational Researcher* 42, no. 2 (March 2013): 89–96, https://doi.org/10.3102/0013189x12470856.

86   Joanne Golann and Mira Debs, "The Harsh Discipline of No-Excuses Charter Schools: Is It Worth the Promise?," *Education Week*, June 9, 2019.

87   "Development Process," Common Core State Standards
     Initiative, 2022, http://www.corestandards.org/about-the-
     standards/development-process/.
88   Frederick M. Hess, "How the Common Core Went Wrong,"
     National Affairs, Fall 2014, https://www.nationalaffairs.com/
     publications/detail/how-the-common-core-went-wrong.
89   "Standards in Your State," Common Core State Standards
     Initiative, 2013, http://www.corestandards.org/standards-in-
     your-state/.
90   Diane Ravitch, "The Common Core Costs Billions and Hurts
     Students," *New York Times*, July 23, 2016, https://www.nytimes.
     com/2016/07/24/opinion/sunday/the-common-core-costs-billi
     ons-and-hurts-students.html.
91   Mengli Song, Rui Yang, and Michael Garet, "Song: Did Common
     Core Standards Work? New Study Finds Small but Disturbing
     Negative Impacts on Students' Academic Achievement," *74
     Million*, June 4, 2019, https://www.the74million.org/article/
     song-did-common-core-standards-work-new-study-finds-small-
     but-disturbing-negative-impacts-on-students-academic-achi
     evement/.
92   Tom Loveless, *Between the State and the Schoolhouse: Understanding
     the Failure of Common Core* (Cambridge, MA: Harvard Education
     Press, 2021).
93   Alison DeNisco, "Common Core No More? New York and
     21 Other States Revise or Rename K12 Standards," District
     Administration, October 9, 2017, https://districtadministration.
     com/common-core-no-more-new-york-and-21-other-states-rev
     ise-or-rename-k12-standards/.
94   Neal McCluskey, "Has No Child Left Behind Worked?," CATO
     Institute, February 9, 2015, https://www.cato.org/testimony/
     has-no-child-left-behind-worked.
95   Linda Darling-Hammond, "Evaluating 'No Child Left Behind,'"
     Stanford Center for Opportunity Policy in Education, September
     12, 2017, https://edpolicy.stanford.edu/library/blog/873.
96   Chad Aldeman, Max Marchitello, and Kaitlin Pennington, *An
     Independent Review of ESSA State Plans*, accessed April 3, 2022,
     https://bellwethereducation.org/sites/default/files/Bellwethe
     r_ESSAReview_ExecSumm_Final.pdf; and Diane Whitmore
     Schanzenbach, Lauren Bauer, and Megan Mumford, "Lessons
     for Broadening School Accountability under the Every Student

Succeeds Act" (working paper, The Hamilton Project, October 2016), https://www.hamiltonproject.org/assets/files/lessons_ broadening_school_accountability_essa.pdf.

97 Matt Barnum, "No Child Left Behind Is Dead: But Have States Learned from It?," *Chalkbeat: Essential Education Reporting across America*, August 4, 2017, https://www.chalkbeat.org/2017/8/ 4/21102738/no-child-left-behind-is-dead-but-have-states-lear ned-from-it.

98 Susan Fuhrman, *Designing Coherent Education Policy: Improving the System* (San Francisco, CA: Jossey-Bass, 2010).

99 Marshall Smith and Jennifer O'Day, *Quality and Equality in American Education: Systemic Problems, Systemic Solutions*, Carnegie Foundation, February 2016, https://www.carnegiefou ndation.org/resources/publications/quality-and-equality-in- american-education-systemic-problems-systemic-solutions/.

100 Margaret Goertz Robert E. Floden, and Jennifer O'Day, *Studies of Education Reform: Systemic Reform*, vol. 1, *Findings and Conclusions*, July 1995, https://www2.ed.gov/PDFDocs/volume1.pdf.

101 M. D. Cohen, J. G. March, and J. P. Olsen, "A Garbage Can Model of Organizational Choice," *Administrative Science Quarterly* 17, no. 1 (1972): 1–25.

102 W. Edwards Deming, *Out of the Crisis* (Cambridge, MA: MIT Press, 2018).

103 "The Six Core Principles of Improvement," Carnegie Foundation for the Advancement of Teaching, 2022, https://www.carnegi efoundation.org/our-ideas/six-core-principles-improvement/.

104 Anthony S. Bryk, Louis M. Gomez, Alicia Grunow, and Paul G. LeMahieu, *Learning to Improve: How America's Schools Can Get Better at Getting Better* (Cambridge, MA: Harvard Education Press, 2017).

105 David L. Kirp, "Who Needs Charters When You Have Public Schools Like These?," *New York Times*, April 1, 2017, https:// www.nytimes.com/2017/04/01/opinion/sunday/who-needs- charters-when-you-have-public-schools-like-these.html.

Chapter 3

1 Dan Goldhaber, "In Schools, Teacher Quality Matters Most," *Education Next* 16, no. 22 (2016), https://www.educationnext. org/in-schools-teacher-quality-matters-most-coleman/; Eric A. Hanushek, John F. Kain, and Steven G. Rivkin, "Teachers,

Schools, and Academic Achievement" (working paper, National Bureau of Economic Research, August 1998), https://www.nber.org/papers/w6691.

2   Andy Jacob, Elizabeth Vidyarthi, and Kathleen Carroll, *The Irreplaceables: Understanding the Real Retention Crisis in America's Urban Schools*, 2012, https://tntp.org/assets/documents/TNTP_Irreplaceables_2012.pdf.

3   Raj Chetty, John N. Friedman, and Jonah E. Rockoff, "Measuring the Impacts of Teachers II: Teacher Value-Added and Student Outcomes in Adulthood," *American Economic Review* 104, no. 9 (September 2014): 2633–79, https://doi.org/10.3386/w19424; and Raj Chetty, John N. Friedman, Nathaniel Hilger, Ammanuel Saez, Diane Whitmore Schanzenbach, and Danny Yagan, "How Does Your Kindergarten Classroom Affect Your Earnings? Evidence from Project STAR" (working paper, National Bureau of Economic Research, September 2010), https://www.nber.org/papers/w16381.

4   C. Rubie-Davis, *Becoming a High Expectation Teacher: Raising the Bar* (London: Routledge, 2015).

5   Jeffrey Cornelius-White, "Learner-Centered Teacher-Student Relationships Are Effective: A Meta-Analysis," *Review of Educational Research* 77, no. 1 (2007): 113–43; and John Hattie, *Visible Learning: A Synthesis of over 800 Meta-Analysis Relating to Achievement*, 1st ed. (New York: Routledge, 2017), https://doi.org/10.3102/003465430298563.

6   Cynthia D. Prince, Julia Koppich, Tamara Morse Azar, Monica Bhatt, and Peter J Witham, "Research Synthesis," Center for Educator Compensation Reform, October 2006, https://www.leg.state.nv.us/App/NELIS/REL/76th2011/ExhibitDocument/OpenExhibitDocument?exhibitId=24129&fileDownloadName=h0416_hasjo4.pdf.

7   Raj Chetty, John N. Friedman, and Jonah E. Rockoff, "Measuring the Impacts of Teachers II: Teacher Value-Added and Student Outcomes in Adulthood," *American Economic Review* 104, no. 9 (September 2014): 2633–79, https://doi.org/10.3386/w19424.

8   Linda Darling-Hammond, "Evaluating Teacher Evaluation," Stanford Center for Opportunity Policy in Education, September 12, 2017, https://edpolicy.stanford.edu/library/blog/573; and Jesse Rothstein, "Student Sorting and Bias in Value Added Estimation: Selection on Observables and Unobservables,"

Education Finance and Policy 4, no. 4 (2009): 537–71, https://doi. org/10.3386/w14666.

9　Tara Kini and Anne Podolsky, "Does Teaching Experience Increase Teacher Effectiveness? A Review of the Research," Educator Quality, Learning Policy Institute, June 3, 2016, https:// learningpolicyinstitute.org/product/brief-does-teaching-experie nce-increase-teacher-effectiveness-review-research.

10　OECD, *PISA 2018 Results: Snapshot of Students' Performance in Reading, Mathematics and Science*, accessed April 8, 2022, https:// www.oecd.org/pisa/PISA-results_ENGLISH.png; Singapore and Finland are ranked second and seventh in 2018 reading scores, respectively. Amanda Ripley, *The Smartest Kids in the World: And How They Got That Way* (New York: Simon & Schuster, 2013).

11　Matthew Ronfeldt, Susanna Loeb, and James Wyckoff, "How Teacher Turnover Harms Student Achievement," *American Educational Research Journal* 50, no. 1 (February 2011): 4–36, https://doi.org/10.3386/w17176.

12　Anne Podolsky, Tara Kini, and Linda Darling-Hammond, "Solving the Teacher Shortage: How to Attract and Retain Excellent Educators," Educator Quality: Recruitment & Retention, Learning Policy Institute, September 15, 2016, https:// learningpolicyinstitute.org/product/solving-teacher-shortage.

13　Anne Konoske-Graf, Lisette Partelow, and Meg Benner, "To Attract Great Teachers, School Districts Must Improve Their Human Capital Systems," Center for American Progress, December 22, 2016, https://www.americanprogress.org/article/ to-attract-great-teachers-school-districts-must-improve-their-human-capital-systems/.

14　Illinois Network of Charter Schools, National Alliance for Public Charter Schools, and Ed Fuel, "National Best Practices: Teacher Recruitment and Pipelines," November 21, 2016, https://www. publiccharters.org/publications/national-practices-teacher-recr uitment-pipelines.

15　Dominic J. Brewer, "Career Paths and Quit Decisions: Evidence from Teaching," *Journal of Labor Economics* 14, no. 2 (1996): 313–39, https://doi.org/10.1086/209813.

16　Podolsky, Kini, and Darling-Hammond, "Solving the Teacher Shortage:"; and Michael L. Hansen, Diana S. Lien, Linda C. Cavalluzzo, and Jennie W. Wenger, "Relative Pay and Teacher Retention: An Empirical Analysis in a Large Urban District" (working paper, CNA Corporation, March 2004), https://files. eric.ed.gov/fulltext/ED485516.pdf.

17 Podolsky, Kini, and Darling-Hammond, "Solving the Teacher Shortage"; Ann Schimke, "Why School Districts Are Operating as Landlords," *Atlantic*, January 6, 2017, https://www.theatlan tic.com/education/archive/2017/01/why-school-districts-are-operating-as-landlords/512318/; and Lisa Fernandez, "1st of Its Kind: Oakland Expands Housing Program for Teachers of Color," KTVU FOX 2, September 29, 2021, https://www.ktvu. com/news/1st-of-its-kind-oakland-expands-housing-program-for-teachers-of-color.

18 "Key Elements for a Strong and Diverse Teaching Profession," Learning Policy Institute, n.d., https://learningpolicyinstitute. org/sites/default/files/product-files/Key-Elements-Strong-Dive rse-Teaching-Profession_INFOGRAPHIC.pdf.

19 Liana Loewus, "The Nation's Teaching Force Is Still Mostly White and Female," *Education Week*, August 15, 2017, https:// www.edweek.org/teaching-learning/the-nations-teaching-force-is-still-mostly-white-and-female/2017/08.

20 "Digest of Education Statistics, 2015," National Center for Education Statistics (NCES), US Department of Education, March 2016, https://nces.ed.gov/programs/digest/d15/tables/ dt15_105.40.asp.

21 Note that earlier research found few if any such benefits. Thomas Dee, "Teachers, Race and Student Achievement in a Randomized Experiment," *Review of Economics and Statistics*, February 1, 2004, https://cepa.stanford.edu/content/teachers-race-and-student-achievement-randomized-experiment; Travis J. Bristol and Javier Martin-Fernandez, "The Added Value of Latinx and Black Teachers for Latinx and Black Students: Implications for Policy," *Policy Insights from the Behavioral and Brain Sciences* 6, no. 2 (October 2, 2019): 147–53, https://doi.org/10.1177/23727 32219862573; and TNTP, *A Broken Pipeline: Teacher Preparation's Diversity Problem*, December 2, 2020, https://tntp.org/publicati ons/view/a-broken-pipeline.

22 Seth Gershenson, Cassandra M. D. Hart, Joshua Hyman, Constance Lindsay, and Nicholas W. Papageorge, "The Long-Run Impacts of Same-Race Teachers" (working paper, National Bureau of Economic Research, November 2018), https://www. nber.org/papers/w25254.

23 Linda Darling-Hammond and Joan C. Baratz-Snowden, *A Good Teacher in Every Classroom: Preparing the Highly Qualified Teachers Our Children Deserve*, vol. 1 (San Francisco, CA: Jossey-Bass, 2005).

24 Dan Goldhaber, John Krieg, Natsumi Naito, and Roddy Theobald, "Making the Most of Student Teaching: The Importance of Mentors and Scope for Change," *Education Finance and Policy* 15, no. 3 (2020): 581–91, https://doi.org/10.1162/edfp_a_00305.

25 Lauren Camera, "Sharp Nationwide Enrollment Drop in Teacher Prep Programs Cause for Alarm," *U.S. News and World Report*, December 3, 2019, https://www.usnews.com/news/education-news/articles/2019-12-03/sharp-nationwide-enrollment-drop-in-teacher-prep-programs-cause-for-alarm.

26 "California Teacher Workforce Trends Signal Worsening Shortages," Learning Policy Institute, February 8, 2017, https://learningpolicyinstitute.org/product/california-teacher-workforce-trends-signal-worsening-shortages-brief.

27 "Training Methods," Mississippi Teacher Corps, 2022, https://www.mtc.olemiss.edu/our-methods-1.

28 "Our Approach," Teach for America, accessed April 9, 2022, https://www.teachforamerica.org/what-we-do/approach; and Jack Schneider, "Rhetoric and Practice in Pre-Service Teacher Education: The Case of Teach for America," *Journal of Education Policy* 29, no. 4 (2014): 425–42, https://doi.org/10.1080/02680939.2013.825329.

29 Committee on the Study of Teacher Preparation Programs in the United States, *Preparing Teachers: Building Evidence for Sound Policy* (Washington, DC: National Academies Press, 2010). Summaries of studies using a range of designs suggest little to no difference between the two (Suzanne M. Wilson, Robert E. Floden, and Joan Ferrini-Mundy, *Teacher Preparation Research: Current Knowledge, Gaps, and Recommendations* [Seattle, WA: Center for the Study of Teaching and Policy, 2001]; Michael Allen, *Eight Questions on Teacher Preparation: What Does the Research Say? A Summary of the Findings* [Denver, CO: Education Commission of the States, 2003], https://files.eric.ed.gov/fulltext/ED479051.pdf), but several studies, including one that used a randomized control design (Paul T. Decker, Daniel P. Mayer, and Steven Glazerman, *The Effects of Teach for America*

on Students: Findings from a National Evaluation [Working paper, Institute for Research on Poverty, July 2004], https://citeseerx. ist.psu.edu/viewdoc/download?doi=10.1.1.217.2516&rep= rep1&type=pdf), have identified small differences (Donald J. Boyd, Pamela L. Grossman, Hamilton Lankford, Susanna Loeb, and James Wyckoff, "Teacher Preparation and Student Achievement," *Educational Evaluation and Policy Analysis* 31, no. 4 [2009]: 416–40, https://doi.org/10.3102/0162373709353129; Zeyu Xu, Jane Hannaway, and Colin Taylor, *Making a Difference? The Effects of Teach for America in High School* [Durham, NC: The Urban Institute and CALDER, 2007]).

30 Roneeta Guha, Maria E. Hyler, and Linda Darling-Hammond, *The Teacher Residency: An Innovative Model for Preparing Teachers*, Learning Policy Institute, September 15, 2016, https://learning policyinstitute.org/product/teacher-residency.

31 Diana Hasiotis, Erin Grogan, Karen Lawrence, Adam Maier, Alex Wilpon, Andy Jacob, and Kate McGovern, *The Mirage: Confronting the Hard Truth about Our Quest for Teacher Development*, TNTP: Reimagine Teaching, August 4, 2015, https://tntp.org/ publications/view/the-mirage-confronting-the-truth-about-our-quest-for-teacher-development.

32 Ibid.; and Jack Rhoton and Katherin E. Stiles, "Exploring the Professional Development Design Process: Bringing an Abstract Framework into Practice," *Science Educator* 1, no. 1 (2002): 1–8, https://eric.ed.gov/?id=EJ646157.

33 Linda Darling-Hammond, Maria E. Hyler, Madelyn Gardner, and Danny Espinoza, *Effective Teacher Professional Development*, Learning Policy Institute, June 2017, https://learningpolicyinstit ute.org/sites/default/files/product-files/Effective_Teacher_Prof essional_Development_REPORT.pdf.

34 Margarete Kedzior, "Teacher Professional Development," 2004, https://citeseerx.ist.psu.edu/viewdoc/download?doi= 10.1.1.622.3559&rep=rep1&type=pdf.

35 Miranda Bowman, "Teacher Mentoring as a Means to Improve Schools," *BU Journal of Graduate Studies in Education* 6, no. 1 (2014): 47–51, https://eric.ed.gov/?id=EJ1230726.

36 Randi Nevins Stanulis and Robert E. Floden, "Intensive Mentoring as a Way to Help Beginning Teachers Develop Balanced Instruction," *Journal of Teacher Education* 60, no. 2 (2009): 112–22, https://doi.org/10.1177/0022487108330553.

37 Matthew A. Kraft, David Blazar, and Dylan Hogan, "The Effect
of Teacher Coaching on Instruction and Achievement: A Meta-
Analysis of the Causal Evidence," *Review of Educational Research*
88, no. 4 (2018): 547–88, https://doi.org/10.3102/003465431
8759268.

38 Ibid.; and Elena Aguilar, *Art of Coaching: Effective Strategies for
School Transformation* (San Francisco, CA: Jossey-Bass, 2013).

39 Stephen Sawchuk, "Teacher Evaluation: An Issue Overview,"
Education Week, September 3, 2015, https://www.edweek.org/
teaching-learning/teacher-evaluation-an-issue-overview/2015/
09#:~:text=In%20general%2C%20teacher%20evaluation%20ref
ers,and%20guide%20their%20professional%20development.

40 Eric Hanushek, "The Trade-off between Child Quantity and
Quality," *Journal of Political Economy* 100, no. 1 (1992): 84–117,
https://doi.org/http://hanushek.stanford.edu/sites/default/
files/publications/Hanushek%201992%20JPE%20100(1).pdf.

41 Daniel Weisberg, Susan Sexton, Jennifer Mulhern, and David
Keeling, *The Widget Effect: Our National Failure to Acknowledge
and Act on Differences in Teacher Effectiveness*, TNTP, June 8, 2009,
https://tntp.org/publications/view/evaluation-and-deve
lopment/the-widget-effect-failure-to-act-on-differences-in-teac
her-effectiveness?/overview/; and *Waiting for "Superman"*
(Paramount Vantage, 2010).

42 Kate Taylor and Motoko Rich, "Teachers' Unions Fight
Standardized Testing, and Find Diverse Allies," *New York Times*,
April 20, 2015, https://www.nytimes.com/2015/04/21/educat
ion/teachers-unions-reasserting-themselves-with-push-against-
standardized-testing.html.

43 Thomas Toch, "A New Era for the Battle over Teacher
Evaluations," *Atlantic*, March 8, 2016, https://www.theatlantic.
com/education/archive/2016/03/a-new-era-for-the-battle-over-
teacher-evaluations/472602/.

44 Brian M. Stecher, Deboarh J. Holtzman, Michael S. Garet, Laura
S. Hamilton, John Engberg, Elizabeth D. Steiner, Abby Robyn,
et al. *Improving Teaching Effectiveness: Final Report, the Intensive
Partnerships for Effective Teaching through 2015–2016*, RAND
Corporation, 2018, https://www.rand.org/content/dam/rand/
pubs/research_reports/RR2200/RR2242/RAND_RR2242.pdf.

45 Valerie Strauss, "Bill Gates Spent Hundreds of Millions of
Dollars to Improve Teaching: New Report Says It Was a Bust,"

Washington Post, June 29, 2018, https://www.washingtonpost.com/news/answer-sheet/wp/2018/06/29/bill-gates-spent-hundreds-of-millions-of-dollars-to-improve-teaching-new-report-says-it-was-a-bust/.

46 Thomas S. Dee and Benjamin J. Keys, "Does Merit Pay Reward Good Teachers? Evidence from a Randomized Experiment," *Journal of Policy Analysis and Management* 23, no. 3 (2004): 471–88, https://doi.org/10.1002/pam.20022; Matthew G. Springer, Dale Ballou, Laura S. Hamilton, Vi-Nhuan Le, J. R. Lockwood, Daniel F. McCaffrey, Matthew Pepper, and Brian M. Stecher, *Teacher Pay for Performance Experimental Evidence from the Project on Incentives in Teaching*, The Rand Corporation, 2010, https://www.rand.org/pubs/reprints/RP1416.html; and Brian M. Stecher and John F. Pane, "Evaluating the Effectiveness of Teacher Pay-for-Performance," Rand Solution, accessed April 9, 2022, https://www.rand.org/capabilities/solutions/evaluating-the-effectiveness-of-teacher-pay-for-performance.html.

47 Kency Nittler and Nicole Gerber, "Tenure Decisions and Teacher Effectiveness," National Council of Teacher Quality, March 12, 2020, https://www.nctq.org/blog/Tenure-decisions-and-teacher-effectiveness.

48 Matt Barnum, "Fact-Check: Just How Many Tenured Teachers Are Fired Each Year Anyway? (Hint: Not Many)," *74 Million*, September 8, 2015, https://www.the74million.org/article/fact-check-just-how-many-tenured-teachers-are-fired-each-year-anyway-hint-not-many/; and Katherin O. Strunk, Nathan Barrett, and Jane Arnold Lincove, *When Tenure Ends: The Short-Run Effects of the Elimination of Louisiana's Teacher Employment Protections on Teacher Exit and Retirement*, Education Research Alliance for New Orleans, April 11, 2017, https://educationresearchalliancenola.org/files/publications/041217-Strunk-Barrett-Lincove-When-Tenure-Ends.pdf.

49 Hannah Putman, Kate Walsh, and Elizabeth Ross, *Making a Difference: Six Places Where Teacher Evaluation Systems Are Getting Results*, National Council of Teacher Quality, October 2018, https://www.nctq.org/publications/Making-a-Difference; and Linda Darling-Hammond, *Getting Teacher Evaluation Right: What Really Matters for Effectiveness and Improvement* (New York: Teachers College, 2013).

50 Jackie Mader, "The Rise of Teacher Unions: A Look at Union Impact over the Years," HechingerEd, September 19, 2012, http://hechingered.org/content/the-rise-of-teacher-unions-a-look-at-union-impact-over-the-years_5601/.

51 Steven Brill, "The Rubber Room: The Battle over New York City's Worst Teachers," *New Yorker*, August 24, 2009, https://www.newyorker.com/magazine/2009/08/31/the-rubber-room. Rubber rooms have since been discontinued after political backlash and criticism. Jennifer Medina, "Teachers Set Deal with City on Discipline Process," *New York Times*, April 10, 2010, https://www.nytimes.com/2010/04/16/nyregion/16rubber.html.

52 Jill Anderson and Martin West, "Harvard Edcast: The Complexities of Teacher Strikes," Harvard Graduate School of Education, March 13, 2019, https://www.gse.harvard.edu/news/19/03/harvard-edcast-complexities-teacher-strikes.

53 Eunice S. Han, "The Impact of Teachers Unions on Teachers' Well-Being under Various Legal Institutions: Evidence from District–Teacher Matched Data," *AERA Open* 5, no. 3 (2019), https://doi.org/10.1177/2332858419867291; and Agustina S. Paglayan, "Public-Sector Unions and the Size of Government," *American Journal of Political Science* 63, no. 1 (2018): 21–36, https://doi.org/10.1111/ajps.12388.

54 Johnathan Lott and Lawrence W. Kenny, "State Teacher Union Strength and Student Achievement," *Economics of Education Review* 35 (September 9, 2012): 93–103, https://doi.org/10.1016/j.econedurev.2013.03.006; and Robert M. Carini, Brian Powell, and Lara Carr Steelman, "Do Teacher Unions Hinder Educational Performance? Lessons Learned from State Sat and ACT Scores," *Harvard Educational Review*, November 30, 1999, https://eric.ed.gov/?id=EJ617440.

55 Liana Loewus, "Participation in Teachers' Unions Is Down, and Likely to Tumble Further," *Education Week*, October 12, 2017, https://www.edweek.org/leadership/participation-in-teachers-unions-is-down-and-likely-to-tumble-further/2017/10; and US Department of Education, National Center for Education Statistics, "National Teacher and Principal Survey: Total Number of Public School Teachers and Percentage of Public School Teachers in a Union or Employees' Association, by Selected

School Characteristics: 2015–16," 2016, https://nces.ed.gov/surv
eys/ntps/tables/Table_TeachersUnion.asp.

56 The Republic Staff, "A Year after the Teacher Walkout, a Timeline
of Arizona's #RedforEd Movement," *AZ Central*, April 11, 2019,
https://www.azcentral.com/story/news/local/arizona-educat
ion/2019/04/11/arizona-teacher-walkout-timeline-red-for-ed/
3337757002/; and Rachel M. Cohen, "Teacher Unrest Spreads
to Oklahoma, Where Educators Are 'Desperate for a Solution,'"
Intercept, March 6, 2018, https://theintercept.com/2018/03/06/
oklahoma-teacher-strike-west-virginia/.

57 Alex Ebert and Genevieve Douglas, "Teachers Leverage
#RedForEd Walkouts to Win Bigger Pay Boosts," *Bloomberg Law*,
January 21, 2020, https://news.bloomberglaw.com/daily-labor-
report/teachers-leverage-redfored-walkouts-to-win-bigger-pay-
boosts.

58 Valerie Strauss, "New Polls Find Most Americans Say Teachers
Are Underpaid—and Many Would Pay Higher Taxes to Fix
It," *New York Times*, June 1, 2018, https://www.washingtonp
ost.com/news/answer-sheet/wp/2018/06/01/new-polls-
find-most-americans-agree-teachers-are-underpaid-and-many-
would-pay-higher-taxes-to-fix-it/; and Tim Walker, "Poll: Public
Support for Teacher Strikes, Higher Pay Runs Wide and Deep,"
National Education Association, August 27, 2018, https://www.
nea.org/advocating-for-change/new-from-nea/poll-public-supp
ort-teacher-strikes-higher-pay-runs-wide-and.

59 Michèle Belot and Dinand Webbink, "Do Teacher Strikes
Harm Educational Attainment of Students?," *Labour*
24, no. 4 (2010): 391–406, https://doi.org/10.1111/
j.1467-9914.2010.00494.x.

60 For a general discussion of the role of the principal, see Jason
Grissom, Anna J. Egalite, and Constance A. Lindsay, *How
Principals Affect Students and Schools: A Systematic Synthesis of Two
Decades of Research* (New York: The Wallace Foundation, 2021).

61 Gerald C. Ubben, Larry W. Hughes, and Cynthia J. Norris, *The
Principal: Creative Leadership for Effective Schools* (Boston: Allyn
and Bacon, 2001).

62 The Wallace Foundation, ed., "Five Key Responsibilities—the
School Principal as Leader: Guiding Schools to Better Teaching
and Learning." Then Principal-Teacher Connection: A scholar's
view. January 1, 2013. https://www.wallacefoundation.org/

knowledge-center/pages/key-responsibilities-the-school-princi
pal-as-leader.aspx.

63 Eric A. Hanushek and Steven G. Rivkin, "Generalizations
about Using Value-Added Measures of Teacher Quality,"
American Economic Review 100, no. 2 (2010): 267–71, https://
doi.org/10.1257/aer.100.2.267; Jason A. Grissom, Demetra
Kalogrides, and Susanna Loeb, "Using Student Test Scores
to Measure Principal Performance," *Educational Evaluation
and Policy Analysis* 37, no. 1 (March 1, 2015): 3–28, https://
doi.org/10.3102/0162373714523831; and Ronald Williamson,
The Importance of the School Principal, Education Partnerships,
Inc., January 9, 2011, https://files.eric.ed.gov/fulltext/ED538
828.pdf.

64 Grissom, Egalite, and Lindsay, *How Principals Affect Students and
Schools.*

65 Andrew C. Porter, Joseph Murphy, Ellen Goldring, Stephen N.
Elliott, Morgan S. Polikoff, and Henry May, *Vanderbilt Assessment
of Leadership in Education: Technical Manual, Version 1.0* (Nashville,
TN: Vanderbilt University 2008).

66 Carmen Fariña and Laura Kotch, *A School Leader's Guide to
Excellence: Collaborating Our Way to Better Schools* (Portsmouth,
NH: Heinemann, 2014).

67 Karen Seashore Louis, Kenneth Leithwood, Kyla L.
Wahlstrom, and Stephen E. Anderson, Rep. *Learning from
Leadership: Investigating the Links to Improved Student Learning,*
Wallace, July 2010, https://www.wallacefoundation.org/knowle
dge-center/pages/investigating-the-links-to-improved-student-
learning.aspx.

68 Stephen Levin and Kathryn Bradley, *Understanding and
Addressing Principal Turnover: A Review of the Research,* NASSP,
Learning Policy Institute, March 19, 2019, https://learningpoli
cyinstitute.org/product/nassp-understanding-addressing-princi
pal-turnover-review-research-report.

69 Michael Wright and Rosemary Papa, "Sustaining and Sustainable
Superintendent Leadership," in *Oxford Research Encyclopedia of
Education*, August 27, 2020, https://doi.org/10.1093/acrefore/
9780190264093.013.788; and Louise Henry and Bonnie Reidy,
*Characteristics of Effective Superintendents: A Study to Identify
Qualities Essential to the Success of School Superintendents as Cited
by Leading Superintendents,* National School Public Relations

Association, June 2006, https://www.nspra.org/files/docs/CharacteristicsOfEffectiveSuperintendents.pdf.

70 "Superintendent of Schools—Job Description," Superintendent of Schools, 2020, https://www.superintendentofschools.com/resources/school-district-job-descriptions-bank/superintendent-of-schools-job-description/#:~:text=He%20is%20responsible%20for%20the,with%20respect%20to%20such%20activities.

71 Laura Ascione, "5 Key Priorities for Today's Superintendents," *ESchool News: Innovations in Educational Transformation*, September 17, 2018, https://www.eschoolnews.com/2018/09/17/5-key-priorities-for-todays-superintendents/2/.

72 GreatSchools Staff, "What Makes a Great Superintendent?," Great Schools.org, September 14, 2010, https://www.greatschools.org/gk/articles/what-makes-a-great-superintendent/.

73 Matthew M. Chingos, Grover J. (Russ) Whitehurst, and Katharine M. Lindquist, *School Superintendents: Vital or Irrelevant?*, Brookings, September 2014, https://www.brookings.edu/wp-content/uploads/2016/06/SuperintendentsBrown-Center9314.pdf.

74 Ibid.

75 The number of school districts has steadily declined, from 117,000 in 1940 to 13,500 today, as rural districts have been consolidated and the one-room schoolhouse has become a vanishing breed.

76 Katheryn W. Gemberling, Carl W. Smith, and Joseph S. Villani, *The Key Work of School Boards Guidebook. National School Boards Association* (Alexandria, CA: National School Boards Association, 2000), http://www.schoolinfosystem.org/archives/NSBA-KeyworkGuidebook.pdf.

77 Bob Luebke, "Why Conservatives Should Care about Local School Board Elections," Civitas Institute, October 20, 2020, https://www.nccivitas.org/2020/conservatives-care-local-school-board-elections/.

78 Ibid.

79 Michael Kirst and Katrina Bulkley, "'New, Improved' Mayors Take over City Schools," *Phi Delta Kappan* 81, no. 7 (March 2000): 542–46, https://www.jstor.org/stable/20439713.

80 Kenneth K. Wong and Francis X. Shen, *Mayoral Governance and Student Achievement: How Mayor-Led Districts Are Improving School and Student Performance*, Center for American Progress,

The Broad Foundation Education, March 2013, https://cdn.
americanprogress.org/wp-content/uploads/2013/03/Mayoral
Control-6.pdf?_ga=2.225950105.263700890.1597321580-954222
989.1597321580. For an example of a mayor who performs this
role exceptionally well, see David L. Kirp, *Improbable Scholars: The
Rebirth of a Great American School System and a Strategy for
America's Schools* (New York: Oxford University Press, 2013).

81 Stephen Sawchuk, "What Is Critical Race Theory, and Why Is It
Under Attack?," *Education Week*, May 18, 2021, https://www.
edweek.org/leadership/what-is-critical-race-theory-and-why-is-
it-under-attack/2021/05.

82 Hannah Natanson, "How and Why Loudoun County Became
the Face of the Nation's Culture Wars," *Washington Post*, July 5,
2021, https://www.washingtonpost.com/local/education/loud
oun-critical-race-theory-transgender-rights/2021/07/05/3dab0
1b8-d4eb-11eb-ae54-515e2f63d37d_story.html.

83 "Justice Department Addresses Violent Threats Against School
Officials and Teachers." The United States Department of Justice,
October 4, 2021, https://www.justice.gov/opa/pr/justice-dep
artment-addresses-violent-threats-against-school-officials-and-
teachers.

84 Jeffrey R. Henig, Rebecca Jacobsen, and Sarah Reckhow, *Outside
Money in School Board Elections: The Nationalization of Education
Politics* (Cambridge, MA: Harvard Education Press, 2019).

85 Howard Blume, "Charter Schools vs Teachers Union: A High
Stakes L.A. School Board Election Takes Shape," *Los Angeles
Times*, December 26, 2019, https://www.latimes.com/califor
nia/story/2019-12-26/high-stakes-lausd-elections-for-charters-
unions.

86 National PTA, *The PTA Story: A Century of Commitment to Children*
(Chicago: National PTA, 1997).

87 Rob Reich, "Not Very Giving," *New York Times*, September 4,
2013, https://www.nytimes.com/2013/09/05/opinion/not-
very-giving.html. *Nice White Parents*, a 2020 podcast, shows how
White parents with the best of intentions impeded the integration
of the schools their children attended by substituting their
priorities for the district's goals.

88 Catherine Brown, Scott Sargrad, and Meg Benner, *Hidden
Money: The Outsized Role of Parent Contributions in School Finance*,
Center for American Progress, April 8, 2017, https://www.ameri

canprogress.org/issues/education-k-12/reports/2017/04/08/428484/hidden-money/.

89 G. Packer, "Change the World: Silicon Valley Transfers Its Slogans—and Its Money—to the Realm of Politics," *New Yorker*, May 27, 2013.

90 R. Reich, "Not Very Giving," *New York Times*, September 4, 2013.

91 Lyndsey Layton, "How Bill Gates Pulled off the Swift Common Core Revolution," *Washington Post*, June 7, 2014, https://www.washingtonpost.com/politics/how-bill-gates-pulled-off-the-swift-common-core-revolution/2014/06/07/a830e32e-ec34-11e3-9f5c-9075d5508f0a_story.html.

92 Linda Shear, Barbara Means, Karen Mitchell, Ann House, Torie Gorges, Aasha Joshi, Becky Smerdon, and Jamie Shkolnik, "Contrasting Paths to Small-School Reform: Results of a 5-Year Evaluation of the Bill & Melinda Gates Foundation's National High Schools Initiative," *Teachers College Record: The Voice of Scholarship in Education* 110, no. 9 (February 1, 2022): 1986–2039, https://doi.org/10.1177/016146810811000903.

93 Frederick M. Hess, "The State of Education Philanthropy," American Enterprise Institute, March 18, 2019, https://www.aei.org/articles/the-state-of-education-philanthropy/.

94 Melissa Hruza, "How Much Do Teachers Spend on Supplies?," AdoptAClassroom.org, July 29, 2021, https://www.adoptaclassroom.org/2021/07/29/how-much-do-teachers-spend-on-supplies/.

95 Matt Barnum, "Big Education Funders Gates, Walton, and Chan Zuckerberg Are Coming Together to Seek 'Breakthroughs': Will It Work?," *Chalkbeat*, July 21, 2021, https://www.chalkbeat.org/2021/7/21/22587262/education-funders-gates-czi-walton-breakthroughs-aerdf-research-and-development.

Chapter 4

1 Sarah D. Sparks, "Training Bias out of Teachers: Research Shows Little Promise So Far," *Education Week*, November 7, 2020, https://www.edweek.org/leadership/training-bias-out-of-teachers-research-shows-little-promise-so-far/2020/11; and Lori Patton David and Samuel D. Museus, "Identifying and Disrupting Deficit Thinking," *Medium* (blog), July 19, 2019, https://medium.com/national-center-for-institutional-diversity/identifying-and-disrupting-deficit-thinking-cbc6da326995.

2 Jason A. Okonofua, David Paunesku, and Gregory M. Walton, "Brief Intervention to Encourage Empathic Discipline Cuts Suspension Rates in Half among Adolescents," *Proceedings of the National Academy of Sciences* 113, no. 19 (May 25, 2016): 5221–26, https://doi.org/10.1073/pnas.1523698113.

3 Research also demonstrates that unconscious racial and ethnic bias can be minimized through exposure to individuals who defy racial stereotypes.

4 Jason A. Okonofua, Gregory M. Walton, and Jennifer L. Eberhardt, "A Vicious Cycle: A Social–Psychological Account of Extreme Racial Disparities in School Discipline," *Perspectives on Psychological Science* 11, no. 3 (May 22, 2016): 381–98, https://doi.org/10.1177/1745691616635592; and David S. Yeager, Valerie Purdie-Vaughns, Sophia Yang Hooper, and Geoffrey L. Cohen, "Loss of Institutional Trust among Racial and Ethnic Minority Adolescents: A Consequence of Procedural Injustice and a Cause of Life-Span Outcomes," *Child Development* 88, no. 2 (2017): 658–76, https://doi.org/10.1111/cdev.12697.

5 Culturally responsive pedagogy or culturally sustaining pedagogy is a teaching style that focuses on how teachers interact with students and design their courses.

6 Zaretta Hammond, *Culturally Responsive Teaching and the Brain: Promoting Authentic Engagement and Rigor among Culturally and Linguistically Diverse Students* (Thousand Oaks, CA: Corwin, 2015).

7 Thomas Dee and Emily Penner, "The Causal Effects of Cultural Relevance: Evidence from an Ethnic Studies Curriculum," *American Educational Research Journal* 54, no. 1 (February 1, 2017): 127–66, https://doi.org/10.3386/w21865.

8 Kate Barrington, "The Pros and Cons of Tracking in Schools," *Public School Review* (blog),December 9, 2020, https://www.publicschoolreview.com/blog/the-pros-and-cons-of-tracking-in-schools.

9 Ibid.; and L. M. Terman, "A New Approach to the Study of Genius," *Psychological Review* 29, no. 4 (1922): 310–18, https://doi.org/10.1037/h0071072; and Ellwood Patterson Cubberley, *Changing Conceptions of Education* (Cambridge, MA: Houghton Mifflin, 1909).

10 Barrington, "Pros and Cons of Tracking in Schools."

11 Jeannie Oakes, *Keeping Track: How Schools Structure Inequality* (New Haven, CT: Yale University, 2005); Ray Rist, "Student Social Class and Teacher Expectations: The Self-Fulfilling Prophecy in Ghetto Education," *Harvard Educational Review* 40, no. 3 (1970): 411–51, https://doi.org/10.17763/haer.40.3.h0m02 6p670k618q3; James E. Rosenbaum, *Making Inequality the Hidden Curriculum of High School Tracking* (New York: Wiley, 1976); and David L. Kirp, "Schools as Sorters: The Constitutional and Policy Implications of Student Classification," *University of Pennsylvania Law Review* 121, no. 4 (1973): 705, https://doi.org/10.2307/ 3311135.

12 Christine M. Rubie-Davies, *Becoming a High Expectation Teacher: Raising the Bar* (London: Routledge, 2015).

13 Claude M. Steele and Joshua Aronson, "Stereotype Threat and the Intellectual Test Performance of African Americans," *Journal of Personality and Social Psychology* 69, no. 5 (1995): 797–811, https://doi.org/10.1037/0022-3514.69.5.797; and Claude Steele, *Whistling Vivaldi: How Stereotypes Affect Us and What We Can Do* (New York: W. W. Norton, 2010).

14 Matthew McBee, "Examining the Probability of Identification for Gifted Programs for Students in Georgia Elementary Schools: A Multilevel Path Analysis Study," *Gifted Child Quarterly* 54, no. 4 (2010): 283–97, https://doi.org/10.1177/0016986210377927; and Matthew T. McBee, "A Descriptive Analysis of Referral Sources for Gifted Identification Screening by Race and Socioeconomic Status," *Journal of Secondary Gifted Education* 17, no. 2 (2006): 103–11, https://doi.org/10.4219/jsge-2006-686.

15 Eric A. Hanushek, "Assessing the Effects of School Resources on Student Performance: An Update," *Educational Evaluation and Policy Analysis* 19, no. 2 (1997): 141–64, https://doi.org/10.3102/ 01623737019002141; Eric A. Hanushek, "Evidence, Politics, and the Class Size Debate" (working paper, ResearchGate, January 2000), https://www.researchgate.net/profile/Eric-Hanushek/ publication/246118091_Evidence_Politics_and_the_Class_Size _Debate/links/551427810cf2eda0df304791/Evidence-Politics- and-the-Class-Size-Debate.pdf; and Caroline Hoxby, "The Effects of Class Size and Composition on Student Achievement: New Evidence from Natural Population Variation," *Quarterly Journal of Economics* 115, no. 4 (November 2000): 1239–85, https://doi.org/ 10.3386/w6869.

16 Frederick Mosteller, "The Tennessee Study of Class Size in the
    Early School Grades," *Future of Children* 5, no. 2 (1995): 113–28,
    https://doi.org/10.2307/1602360.

17 Elizabeth Graue, Kelly Hatch, Kalpana Rao, and Denise Oen,
    "The Wisdom of Class-Size Reduction," *American Educational
    Research Journal* 44, no. 3 (September 2007): 670–700, https://doi.
    org/10.3102/0002831207306755.

18 Emily Richmond, "Is It Better to Have a Great Teacher or a Small
    Class?," *Atlantic*, November 2013, https://www.theatlantic.
    com/education/archive/2013/11/is-it-better-to-have-a-great-
    teacher-or-a-small-class/281628/; and Michael Hansen, *Right-
    Sizing the Classroom: Making the Most of Great Teachers*, Fordham
    Institute, November 18, 2013, https://fordhaminstitute.org/
    national/research/right-sizing-classroom-making-most-great-
    teachers#:~:text=That's%20the%20intriguing%20question%20t
    hat,fewer%E2%80%94then%20see%20what%20happens.

19 Christopher Jepsen and Steven Rivkin, *Class Size Reduction,
    Teacher Quality, and Academic Achievement in California Public
    Elementary Schools*, Public Policy Institute of California, 2002,
    https://www.ppic.org/publication/class-size-reduction-teacher-
    quality-and-academic-achievement-in-california-public-element
    ary-schools/.

20 "What Is School Climate?," National School Climate Center at
    Ramapo for Children, August 19, 2021, https://schoolclimate.
    org/about/our-approach/what-is-school-climate/; and Ming-
    Te Wang and Jessica L. Degol, "School Climate: A Review of the
    Construct, Measurement, and Impact on Student Outcomes,"
    Educational Psychology Review 28, no. 2 (2016): 315–52, https://
    doi.org/10.1007/s10648-015-9319-1.

21 Alexandra Loukas, "What Is School Climate," *Leadership Compass*
    5, no. 1 (2007), https://pdf4pro.com/view/what-is-school-clim
    ate-naesp-61a7a3.html.

22 Dakari Aarons, Brigid Ahern, Jenn Alexander, Elisha Arillaga,
    Carmen Ayala, Jim Balfanz, Jillian Balow, Brad Bernatek,
    and Megan Blanco, *Creating Conditions for Student Success: A
    Policymakers' School Climate Playbook*, Aspen Institute, January
    26, 2021, https://www.aspeninstitute.org/publications/creat
    ing-conditions-for-student-success-a-policymakers-school-clim
    ate-playbook/.

23 National School Climate Council, *The School Climate
    Challenge: Narrowing the Gap between School Climate Research
    and School Climate Policy, Practice Guidelines and Teacher
    Education Policy*, 2007, https://schoolclimate.org/wp-cont
    ent/uploads/2021/05/school-climate-challenge-web.pdf;
    Ruth Berkowitz, Hadass Moore, Ron Avi Astor, and Rami
    Benbenishty, "A Research Synthesis of the Associations between
    Socioeconomic Background, Inequality, School Climate, and
    Academic Achievement," *Review of Educational Research* 87, no. 2
    (2016): 425–69, https://doi.org/10.3102/0034654316669821; and
    Amrit Thapa, Jonathan Cohen, Ann Higgins-D'Alessandro, and
    Shawn Guffey, *School Climate Research Summary*, National School
    Climate Center, 2012, https://files.eric.ed.gov/fulltext/ED573
    683.pdf.

24 Matthew A. Kraft, William H. Marinell, and Darrick Shen-
    Wei Yee, "School Organizational Contexts, Teacher Turnover,
    and Student Achievement," *American Educational Research
    Journal* 53, no. 5 (2016): 1411–49, https://doi.org/10.3102/
    0002831216667478; and Rebecca J. Collie, Jennifer D. Shapka,
    and Nancy E. Perry, "School Climate and Social–Emotional
    Learning: Predicting Teacher Stress, Job Satisfaction, and
    Teaching Efficacy," *Journal of Educational Psychology* 104, no. 4
    (2012): 1189–204, https://doi.org/10.1037/a0029356.

25 Stephen Kostyo, Jessica Cardichon, and Linda Darling-
    Hammond, "Making ESSA's Equity Promise Real: State
    Strategies to Close the Opportunity Gap Building a Positive
    School Climate," Learning Policy Institute, 2018, https://lear
    ningpolicyinstitute.org/sites/default/files/product-files/ESSA_
    Equity_Promise_Climate_BRIEF.pdf.

26 "Summary Table of Office of Safe and Healthy Students
    Approved School Climate Surveys (as of October 22, 2018)," Safe
    Supportive Learning, accessed April 10, 2022, https://safesup
    portivelearning.ed.gov/sites/default/files/Summary%20Ta
    ble%20of%20OSHS%20Approved%20School%20Climate%20Su
    rveys_languages%20added%203.27.20.pdf.

27 Jonathan Cohen and Amrit Thapa, "School Climate
    Improvement: What Do U.S. Educators Believe, Need and
    Want?," *International Journal on School Climate and Violence
    Prevention* 2, no. 1 (2017): 90–116, https://www.researchgate.net/

publication/318542257_SCHOOL_CLIMATE_IMPROVEMENT_
WHAT_DO_US_EDUCATORS_BELIEVE_NEED_AND_WANT.

28 National School Climate Council, *School Climate Challenge*.

29 Linda Darling-Hammond and Channa Cook-Harvey, "Educating
the Whole Child: Improving School Climate to Support
Student Success," Learning Policy Institute, September 7,
2018, https://learningpolicyinstitute.org/product/educat
ing-whole-child-brief.

30 "Discipline," National Center on Safe Supportive Learning
Environments (NCSSLE), American Institute of Research, 2022,
https://safesupportivelearning.ed.gov/topic-research/environm
ent/discipline.

31 Jacob Middleton, "The Experience of Corporal Punishment
in Schools, 1890–1940," *History of Education* 37, no. 2 (April 3,
2008): 253–75, https://doi.org/10.1080/00467600701607882.

32 Elizabeth T. Gershoff and Sarah A. Font, "Corporal Punishment
in U.S. Public Schools: Prevalence, Disparities in Use, and
Status in State and Federal Policy," *Social Policy Report* 30, no. 1
(2016): 1–26, https://doi.org/10.1002/j.2379-3988.2016.tb00086.x.

33 Jacqueline M. Nowicki, *K–12 Education: Discipline Disparities for
Black Students, Boys, and Students with Disabilities*, US Government
Accountability Office, 2018; and US Department of Education,
Corporal Punishment, by School District, InformED, 2014, https://
www2.ed.gov/policy/gen/guid/school-discipline/images/
2013-14-crdc-corporal-punishment-map-1200.png.

34 Juvenile Justice: School-to-Prison Pipeline," American Civil
Liberties Union, April 4, 2022, https://www.aclu.org/issues/
juvenile-justice/juvenile-justice-school-prison-pipeline.

35 Russell J. Skiba, "Zero Tolerance, Zero Evidence: An Analysis of
School Disciplinary Practice" (working paper, Lilly Endowment,
Inc., August 2000), https://web.archive.org/web/20140824031
650/http://www.indiana.edu/~safeschl/ztze.pdf; and "K–12
Education: Discipline Disparities for Black Students, Boys, and
Students with Disabilities," US Government Accountability
Office, April 10, 2018, https://www.gao.gov/products/
gao-18-258.

36 US Department of Education Office for Civil Rights, "Civil
Rights Data Collection: Data Snapshot; School Discipline," 2014,
https://ocrdata.ed.gov/assets/downloads/CRDC-School-Dis
cipline-Snapshot.pdf.

37 Charles Bell, "School Suspensions Don't Just Unfairly Penalize
     Black Students—They Lead to Lower Grades and 'Black Flight,'"
     The Conversation (blog), accessed April 10, 2022, https://thec
     onversation.com/school-suspensions-dont-just-unfairly-penal
     ize-black-students-they-lead-to-lower-grades-and-black-flight-
     150240; and Linda Jacobson, "Study: In 28 Districts, Middle and
     High School Students Lose More Than a Year of Learning Due to
     Suspensions," *74 Million*, October 12, 2020, https://www.the74
     million.org/article/study-in-28-districts-middle-and-high-sch
     ool-students-lose-more-than-a-year-of-learning-due-to-susp
     ensions/.
38 Matt Barnum and Kalyn Belsha, "Behind the Scenes, Civil Rights
     Groups Urge Biden Administration to Place Limits on School
     Police," *Chalkbeat*, June 29, 2021, https://www.chalkbeat.org/
     2021/6/29/22554788/biden-cardona-schools-police-discipline-
     education-trust.
39 Matt Barnum, "Do Police Keep Schools Safe? Fuel the School-to-
     Prison Pipeline? Here's What Research Says," *Chalkbeat*, June 23,
     2020, https://www.chalkbeat.org/2020/6/23/21299743/police-
     schools-research.
40 US Department of Education, National Center for Education
     Statistics, "Table 233.70, Percentage of Public Schools with
     Security Staff Present at Least Once a Week, and Percentage with
     Security Staff Routinely Carrying a Firearm, by Selected School
     Characteristics: 2005–06 through 2017-18," August 2019, https://
     nces.ed.gov/programs/digest/d19/tables/dt19_233.70.asp.
41 Barnum and Belsha, "Behind the Scenes, Civil Rights Groups
     Urge Biden Administration to Place Limits on School Police";
     Mark Keierleber, "Police-Free Schools? This Suburban
     Minneapolis District Expelled Its Cops Years Ago," *74 Million*,
     July 8, 2020, https://www.the74million.org/article/police-free-
     schools-this-suburban-minneapolis-district-expelled-its-cops-
     years-ago/; and Lauren Camera, "The End of Police in Schools,"
     U.S. News and World Report, June 12, 2020, https://www.usnews.
     com/news/the-report/articles/2020-06-12/schools-districts-end-
     contracts-with-police-amid-ongoing-protests.
42 Louis Freedberg, "California to Extend Ban on Pushing Students
     out of School for Disruptive Behavior," *EdSource*, September 9,
     2019, https://edsource.org/2019/california-to-ban-pushing-
     students-out-of-school-for-disruptive-behavior/617326.

43   Gregory Austin, Thomas Hanson, Alexis Stern, Gary Zhang, and Rebeca Cerna, *How Are Suspensions Related to School Climate in California Middle Schools?*, WestEd, 2020, https://www.wested. org/resources/suspensions-and-school-climate/#.

44   University of Missouri-Columbia, "Rethinking School Suspensions: School Climate Offers a Clue," *ScienceDaily*, December 12, 2018, https://www.sciencedaily.com/releases/ 2018/12/181212121901.htm.

45   Ibid.; and Jason A. Okonofua, Gregory M. Walton, and Jennifer L. Eberhardt, "A Vicious Cycle: A Social–Psychological Account of Extreme Racial Disparities in School Discipline," *Perspectives on Psychological Science* 11, no. 3 (May 22, 2016): 381–98, https:// doi.org/10.1177/1745691616635592; and David L. Kirp, "Don't Suspend Students. Empathize," *New York Times*, September 2, 2017, https://www.nytimes.com/2017/09/02/opinion/sunday/ dont-suspend-students-empathize.html.

46   "Indicator 15: Retention, Suspension, and Expulsion," National Center for Education Statistics, February 2019, https://nces. ed.gov/programs/raceindicators/indicator_rda.asp.

47   Office for Civil Rights, *An Overview of Exclusionary Discipline Practices in Public Schools for the 2017–18 School Year* (Washington, DC: US Department of Education, 2021); and "CRDC Data Reports and Presentations," Civil Rights Data Collection, accessed April 10, 2022, https://ocrdata.ed.gov/resources/data reports.

48   OECD iLibrary, December 2019, https://doi.org/10.1787/acd78 851-en.

49   Dewey G. Cornell and Susan P. Limber, "Do U.S. Laws Go Far Enough to Prevent Bullying at School?," *CE Corner*, American Psychological Association, February 2016, https://www.apa. org/monitor/2016/02/ce-corner.

50   "Bullying at School and Electronic Bullying," Institute of Education Sciences, National Center for Education Statistics, May 2021, https://nces.ed.gov/programs/coe/indicator/a10; and "Youth Risk Behavior Surveillance System (YRBSS)," Centers for Disease Control and Prevention, October 27, 2020, https://www. cdc.gov/healthyyouth/data/yrbs/index.htm.

51   "Bullying Statistics," PACER Center—Champions for Children with Disabilities, November 2020, https://www.pacer.org/bully ing/info/stats.asp.

52 "Bullying," American Psychological Association, 2022, https://
    www.apa.org/topics/bullying.

53 Rachel C. Vreeman and Aaron E. Carroll, "A Systematic Review
    of School-Based Interventions to Prevent Bullying," *Archives of
    Pediatrics & Adolescent Medicine* 161, no. 1 (January 2007): 78–88,
    https://doi.org/10.1001/archpedi.161.1.78.

54 Diana Divecha, "What Are the Best Ways to Prevent Bullying in
    Schools?," *Greater Good Magazine*, October 29, 2019, https://grea
    tergood.berkeley.edu/article/item/what_are_the_best_ways_
    to_prevent_bullying_in_schools.

55 This section draws heavily on stopbullying.gov, a useful guide to
    all aspects of bullying.

56 Chris Glavin, "History of School Shootings in the United States,"
    K12 Academics, July 26, 2018, https://www.k12academics.com/
    school-shootings/history-school-shootings-united-states.

57 One shooting occurred at my high school when I was a student,
    when a suspended student fatally shot his teacher.

58 Bryan Vossekuil, Robert Fein, Marisa Reddy, Randy Borum,
    and William Modzeleski, *The Final Report and Findings of the Safe
    School Initiative: Implications for the Prevention of School Attacks
    in the United States* (Washington, DC: US Secret Service and US
    Department of Education, 2004).

59 "We Came to Learn: A Call to Action for Police-Free Schools,"
    Advancement Project, January 29, 2019, https://advancement
    project.org/wecametolearn/; and Anya Kamenetz, "Here's
    How to Prevent the Next School Shooting, Experts Say," *NPR*,
    March 7, 2018, https://www.npr.org/sections/ed/2018/03/
    07/590877717/experts-say-here-s-how-to-prevent-the-next-sch
    ool-shooting.

60 Philip J. Cook, *Gun Debate: What Everyone Needs to Know®*
    (London: Oxford University Press, 2020).

61 John E. Eck and Ronald V. Clarke, "Situational Crime
    Prevention: Theory, Practice and Evidence," *Handbooks of
    Sociology and Social Research* (2019): 355–76, https://doi.org/
    10.1007/978-3-030-20779-3_18.

62 "Number of Armed Guards at US Schools Is Rising, Study
    Finds," *Associated Press*, March 29, 2018, https://www.theguard
    ian.com/us-news/2018/mar/29/number-of-armed-guards-at-
    us-schools-is-rising-study-finds.

63 David Kirp, Marjorie Wechsler, Madelyn Gardner, and Titilayo Tinubu Ali, *Disrupting Disruption The Steady Work of Transforming Schools* (Oxford: Oxford University Press, 2022).

64 Caitlin Moe and Ali Rowhani-Rahbar, "What We Know about School Mass Shootings since Columbine and How to Prevent Them," K-12 School Shooting Database, September 15, 2020, https://www.chds.us/ssdb/what-we-know-about-school-mass-shootings-since-columbine-and-how-to-prevent-them/; and "A Comprehensive Plan for Preventing Mass Shootings and Ending All Gun Violence in American Schools," Everytown for Gun Safety, April 19, 2020, https://everytownresearch.org/report/preventing-gun-violence-in-american-schools/#a-comprehensive-plan.

65 Herbert Marsh and Sabina Kleitman, "Extracurricular School Activities: The Good, the Bad, and the Nonlinear," *Harvard Educational Review* 72, no. 4 (2002): 464–515, https://doi.org/10.17763/haer.72.4.051388703v7v7736.

66 Margo Gardner, Jodie Roth, and Jeanne Brooks-Gunn, "Adolescents' Participation in Organized Activities and Developmental Success 2 and 8 Years after High School: Do Sponsorship, Duration, and Intensity Matter?," *Developmental Psychology* 44, no. 3 (2008): 814–30, https://doi.org/10.1037/0012-1649.44.3.814.

67 "The Association Between School-Based Physical Activity, Including Physical Education, and Academic Performance 2010," US Department of Health and Human Services, Centers for Disease Control and Prevention, https://www.cdc.gov/healthyyouth/health_and_academics/pdf/pa-pe_paper.pdf. The quality of this research is open to question. Amika Singh, Léonie Uijtdewilligen, Jos W. R. Twisk, Willian vanMechelen, and Mai J. M. Chinapaw, "Physical Activity and Performance at School: A Systematic Review of the Literature Including a Methodological Quality Assessment," *Archives of Pediatrics & Adolescent Medicine* 166, no. 1 (January 2012): 49–55, https://doi.org/10.1001/archpediatrics.2011.716.

68 However, a close-grained reanalysis of this research concludes that "the positive association . . . can, in large part, be explained by individual [differences], as opposed to academic spillovers." Daniel I. Rees and Joseph J. Sabia, "Sports Participation and Academic Performance: Evidence from the National

Longitudinal Study of Adolescent Health," *Economics of Education Review* 29, no. 5 (2010): 751–59, https://doi.org/10.1016/j.eco nedurev.2010.04.008.

69 Suzie Boss, "Technology Integration: A Short History," Edutopia, George Lucas Educational Foundation, September 7, 2011, https://www.edutopia.org/technology-integration-history; Alia Wong, "Children's TV—Left Behind," *Atlantic*, July 16, 2015, https://www.theatlantic.com/education/archive/2015/07/the-1960s-experiment-childrens-tv/398681/; Alia Wong, "The Sesame Street Effect," *Atlantic*, June 17, 2015, https://www.thea tlantic.com/education/archive/2015/06/sesame-street-presch ool-education/396056/; and Center for Children and Technology, *Television Goes to School: The Impact of Video on Student Learning in Formal Education*, CPB, January 2004, https://cct.edc.org/sites/cct.edc.org/files/publications/PBS_tv-school.pdf.

70 Thomas D. Cook, *"Sesame Street" Revisited* (New York: Russell Sage Foundation, 1975); Mabel L. Rice, Aletha C. Huston, Rosemarie Truglio, and John Wright. "Words from 'Sesame Street': Learning Vocabulary While Viewing," American Psychological Association, 1990, https://psycnet.apa.org/rec ord/1990-19464-001; Boss, "Technology Integration" ; Wong, "Children's TV—Left Behind"; Stephen J. Ceci and Paul B. Papierno, "The Rhetoric and Reality of Gap Closing: When the 'Have-Nots' Gain but the 'Haves' Gain Even More," *American Psychologist* 60, no. 2 (2005): 149–60, https://doi.org/10.1037/0003-066x.60.2.149.

71 Harold Wenglinsky, *Does It Compute? The Relationship between Educational Technology and Student Achievement in Mathematics*, ETS Policy Information Center, 1998, https://www.ets.org/resea rch/policy_research_reports/publications/report/1998/cneu.

72 David L. Kirp, *Improbable Scholars: The Rebirth of a Great American School System and a Strategy for America's Schools* (New York: Oxford University Press, 2013).

73 "The Evolution of Technology in the Classroom," *Purdue Online Blog*, 2022, https://online.purdue.edu/blog/education/evolution-technology-classroom; "The Condition of Education 2021 (NCES 2021-144), Children's Internet Access at Home," US Department of Education, National Center for Education Statistics, 2021, https://nces.ed.gov/fastfacts/display.asp?id=

46&_ga=2.172788131.1486922700.1630685120-1771454718.162
9431374.

74   Jeremy M. Roschelle, Roy D. Pea, Christopher M. Hoadley,
Douglas N. Gordin, and Barbara M. Means, "Changing How
and What Children Learn in School with Computer-Based
Technologies," *Future of Children* 10, no. 2 (2000): 76–101, https://
doi.org/10.2307/1602690.

75   Cassandra M. D. Hart, Dan Berger, Brian Jacob, Susanna Loeb,
and Michael Hill, "Online Learning, Offline Outcomes: Online
Course Taking and High School Student Performance," *AERA
Open* 5, no. 1 (2019), https://doi.org/10.1177/2332858419832852.

76   "La Public Schools to Deploy 31K Apple Ipads This Year, Supply
All 640K Students in 2014," AppleInsider Forums, 2013, https://
forums.appleinsider.com/discussion/comment/2368514/.

77   Natasha Singer, "How Google Took over the Classroom,"
New York Times, May 13, 2017, https://www.nytimes.com/2017/
05/13/technology/google-education-chromebooks-schools.html.

78   John F. Payne, Elizabeth D. Steiner, Matthew D. Baird, Laura S.
Hamilton, and Joseph D. Pane, *How Does Personalized Learning
Affect Student Achievement?*, Rand Corporation, 2017, https://
www.rand.org/pubs/research_briefs/RB9994.html.

79   Education Elements, *The Core Four of Personalizing Learning*,
Education Elements, 2016, https://www.edelements.com/lp-the-
core-four-of-personalizing-learning-white-paper?hsCtaTracking=
a8e78e88-1bfa-4246-9799-a628f341812d%7C6913b33a-29bb-41b1-
ba1f-9e1ddd7c55a9.

80   Anthony G. Picciano and Jeff Seaman, "K–12 Online Learning: A
Survey of U.S. School District Administrators," Sloan Consortium
(NJ1), November 30, 2006, https://eric.ed.gov/?id=ED530103.

81   Barbara Means, Yukie Toyama, Robert Murphy, Marianna Bakia,
and Karla Jones, *Evaluation of Evidence-Based Practices in Online
Learning: A Meta-Analysis and Review of Online Learning Studies*,
US Department of Education, Office of Planning, Evaluation,
and Policy Development, Policy and Program Studies Service,
September 2010, https://www2.ed.gov/rschstat/eval/tech/
evidence-based-practices/finalreport.pdf.

82   "Deeper Learning Competencies: April 2013," Hewlett
Foundation, 2013, https://hewlett.org/wp-content/uploads/
2016/08/Deeper_Learning_Defined__April_2013.pdf.

83 "Deeper Learning," Learning Policy Institute, 2022, https://lear
    ningpolicyinstitute.org/topic/deeper-learning?page=14&gclid=
    Cj0KCQjwkZiFBhD9ARIsAGxFX8ClYjroxolDd36wu_AsCzE
    nhwyfJQ-uiAjHooZKtPSiNWX6EDMmAMwaAj0eEALw_wcB;
    "What Is PBL?," PBLWorks, Buck Institute for Education, 2022,
    https://www.pblworks.org/what-is-pbl; Jal Mehta and Sarah M.
    Fine, *In Search of Deeper Learning: The Quest to Remake the American
    High School* (Cambridge, MA: Harvard University Press, 2020);
    and Zachary Jason, "Bored Out of Their Minds," *Harvard Ed.
    Magazine*, Winter 2017, https://www.gse.harvard.edu/news/
    ed/17/01/bored-out-their-minds.

84 "Transforming Education from the Classroom to Congress,"
    all4ed.org, Future Ready Schools, 2022, https://all4ed.org/fut
    ure-ready-schools/; and Lucas Education Research, January 31,
    2022, https://www.lucasedresearch.org/.

85 Kristina Zeiser, "Study of Deeper Learning: Opportunities and
    Outcomes," American Institutes for Research, 2022, https://
    www.air.org/project/study-deeper-learning-opportunities-and-
    outcomes.

86 David L. Kirp, "Who Needs Charters When You Have Public
    Schools Like These?," *New York Times*, April 1, 2017, https://
    www.nytimes.com/2017/04/01/opinion/sunday/who-needs-
    charters-when-you-have-public-schools-like-these.html.

87 *Rising above the Gathering Storm: Energizing and Employing
    America for a Brighter Economic Future* (Washington, DC: National
    Academies Press, 2007), https://nap.nationalacademies.org/
    read/11463/chapter/1#iii.

88 "Current State of STEM Education in the US: What Needs to Be
    Done?," Mand Labs: Step by Step, May 6, 2022, https://www.
    mandlabs.com/current-state-of-stem-education-in-us-what-
    needs-to-be-done/.

89 Leslie Morrison Gutman and Ingrid Schoon, "A Synthesis
    of Causal Evidence Linking Non-Cognitive Skills to Later
    Outcomes for Children and Adolescents," *Non-cognitive Skills and
    Factors in Educational Attainment* (March 2013): 171–98, https://
    doi.org/10.1007/978-94-6300-591-3_9.

90 James J. Heckman, John Eric Humphries, and Tim Kautz, *The
    Myth of Achievement Tests: The GED and the Role of Character in
    American Life* (Chicago: University of Chicago Press, 2015).

91 Valerie Strauss, "The Surprising Thing Google Learned about Its Employees—and What It Means for Today's Students," *Washington Post*, December 20, 2017, https://www.washingtonp ost.com/news/answer-sheet/wp/2017/12/20/the-surprising-thing-google-learned-about-its-employees-and-what-it-means-for-todays-students/.

92 C. Kirabo Jackson, Shanette C. Porter, John Q. Easton, Alyssa Blanchard, and Sebastián Kiguel, "School Effects on Socio-Emotional Development, School-Based Arrests, and Educational Attainment" (working paper, National Bureau of Economic Research, February 2020), 10.3386/w26759, https://www.nber. org/papers/w26759.

93 Emma García, *Inequalities at the Starting Gate: Cognitive and Noncognitive Skills Gaps between 2010–2011 Kindergarten Classmates*, Economic Policy Institute, June 17, 2015, https:// www.epi.org/publication/inequalities-at-the-starting-gate-cognitive-and-noncognitive-gaps-in-the-2010-2011-kindergarten-class/.

94 Bettina L. Love, "'Grit Is in Our DNA': Why Teaching Grit Is Inherently Anti-Black," *Education Week*, February 12, 2019, https://www.edweek.org/leadership/opinion-grit-is-in-our-dna-why-teaching-grit-is-inherently-anti-black/2019/02.

95 Marcus Credé, Michael C. Tynan, and Peter D. Harms, "Much Ado about Grit: A Meta-Analytic Synthesis of the Grit Literature," *Journal of Personality and Social Psychology* 113, no. 3 (2017): 492–511, https://doi.org/10.1037/pspp0000102.

96 Gregory M. Walton, "The New Science of Wise Psychological Interventions," *Current Directions in Psychological Science* 23, no. 1 (February 3, 2014): 73–82, https://doi.org/10.1177/096372141 3512856.

97 "What Is Social and Emotional Learning?," CASEL Guide to Schoolwide SEL, 2022, https://schoolguide.casel.org/what-is-sel/what-is-sel/.

98 Joseph A. Durlak, Roger P. Weissberg, Allison B. Dymnicki, Rebecca D. Taylor, and Kriston B. Schellinger, "The Impact of Enhancing Students' Social and Emotional Learning: A Meta-Analysis of School-Based Universal Interventions," *Child Development* 82, no. 1 (2011): 405–32, https://doi.org/10.1111/ j.1467-8624.2010.01564.x.

99 Individuals who believe their talents can be developed through
    hard work have a growth mindset. They tend to achieve more
    than those with a more fixed mindset, who believe their talents
    are innate. Carol S. Dweck, *Mindset: The New Psychology of Success*
    (New York: Ballantine Books, 2006).

100 R. H. Thaler and C. R. Sunstein, *Nudge: Improving Decisions about
    Health, Wealth, and Happiness* (New Haven, CT: Yale University
    Press, 2008).

101 Lindsay C. Page, Benjamin L. Castleman, and Katharine Meyer,
    "Customized Nudging to Improve FAFSA Completion and
    Income Verification," *Educational Evaluation and Policy Analysis* 42,
    no. 1 (2019): 3–21, https://doi.org/10.3102/0162373719876916.

102 Brian A. Jacob and Kelly Lovett, "Chronic Absenteeism: An Old
    Problem in Search of New Answers," *Brookings* (blog), 2017,
    https://www.brookings.edu/research/chronic-absenteeism-an-
    old-problem-in-search-of-new-answers/.

103 Phyllis W. Jordan, *Nudging Students and Families to Better
    Attendance* (blog), Education Next, November 5, 2018, https://
    www.educationnext.org/nudging-students-families-better-att
    endance/.

104 Todd Rogers and Avi Feller, "Reducing Student Absences at Scale
    by Targeting Parents' Misbeliefs," *Nature Human Behaviour* 2, no.
    5 (2018): 335–42, https://doi.org/10.1038/s41562-018-0328-1.

105 Gregory M. Walton, "The New Science of Wise Psychological
    Interventions," *Current Directions in Psychological Science* 23, no.
    1 (February 3, 2014): 73–82, https://doi.org/10.1177/096372141
    3512856.

106 Lisa S. Blackwell, Kali H. Trzesniewski, and Carol Sorich
    Dweck, "Implicit Theories of Intelligence Predict Achievement
    across an Adolescent Transition: A Longitudinal Study and an
    Intervention," *Child Development* 78, no. 1 (2007): 246–63, https://
    doi.org/10.1111/j.1467-8624.2007.00995.x.

107 Carol S. Dweck, *Mindset: The New Psychology of Success*
    (New York: Ballantine Books, 2006).

108 David S. Yeager, David Paunesku, Gregory M. Walton, and Carol
    S. Dweck, "Research Library: How Can We Instill Productive
    Mindsets At Scale? A Review of the Evidence and an Initial R&D
    Agenda" (white paper prepared for the White House meeting
    on "Excellence in Education: The Importance of Academic
    Mindsets," 2013), https://studentexperiencenetwork.org/resea

rch_library/how-can-we-instill-productive-mindsets-at-scale-a-review-of-the-evidence-and-an-initial-rd-agenda-a-white-paper-prepared-for-the-white-house-meeting-on-excellence-in-educat ion-the-importa/#.

109 David S. Yeager, Paul Hanselman, Gregory M. Walton, Jared S. Murray, Robert Crosnoe, Chandra Muller, Elizabeth Tipton, et al., "A National Experiment Reveals Where a Growth Mindset Improves Achievement," *Nature* 573, no. 7774 (2019): 364–69, https://doi.org/10.1038/s41586-019-1466-y.

110 Susana Claro, David Paunesku, and Carol S. Dweck, "Growth Mindset Tempers the Effects of Poverty on Academic Achievement," *Proceedings of the National Academy of Sciences* 113, no. 31 (2016): 8664–68, https://doi.org/10.1073/pnas.1608207113.

111 Victoria F. Sisk, Alexander P. Burgoyne, Jingze Sun, Jennifer L. Butler, and Brooke N. Macnamara, "To What Extent and under Which Circumstances Are Growth Mind-Sets Important to Academic Achievement? Two Meta-Analyses," *Psychological Science* 29, no. 4 (2018): 549–71, https://doi.org/10.1177/09567 97617739704.

112 Brooke Macnamara, "Schools Are Buying 'Growth Mindset' Interventions Despite Scant Evidence That They Work Well," *The Conversation* (blog), June 26, 2018, https://theconversation.com/schools-are-buying-growth-mindset-interventions-despite-scant-evidence-that-they-work-well-96001.

113 David S. Yeager and Carol S. Dweck, "What Can Be Learned from Growth Mindset Controversies?," *American Psychologist* 75, no. 9 (December 2020): 1269–84, https://doi.org/10.1037/amp 0000794.supp.

114 Greg M. Walton, "The Many Questions of Belonging," in *Handbook of Competence and Motivation: Theory and Application*, ed. Shannon T. Brady (New York: Guilford Press, 2017), 272–93.

115 Elizabeth Linos, Vikash Reddy, and Jesse Rothstein, *Increasing the Take-up of Cal Grants*, November 2018, https://www.capolicylab. org/wp-content/uploads/2019/06/Increasing-the-Take-up-of-Cal-Grants.pdf.

116 David S. Yeager and Gregory M. Walton, "Social-Psychological Interventions in Education," *Review of Educational Research* 81, no. 2 (2011): 267–301, https://doi.org/10.3102/0034654311405999.

117 Greg M. Walton, "The Many Questions of Belonging," in *Handbook of Competence and Motivation: Theory and Application*,

ed. Shannon T. Brady (New York: Guilford Press, 2017), 272–93; and Gregory M. Walton and David S. Yeager, "Seed and Soil: Psychological Affordances in Contexts Help to Explain Where Wise Interventions Succeed or Fail," *Current Directions in Psychological Science* 29, no. 3 (2020): 219–26, https://doi.org/10.1177/0963721420904453.

118   "Public High School Graduation Rates," US Department of Education, National Center for Education Statistics, Institute of Education Sciences, 2021, https://nces.ed.gov/programs/coe/indicator/coi.

119   Douglas N. Harris, "Are America's Rising High School Graduation Rates Real—or Just an Accountability-Fueled Mirage?," Brown Center Chalkboard, Brookings, March 2, 2020, https://www.brookings.edu/blog/brown-center-chalkboard/2020/03/02/are-americas-rising-high-school-graduation-rates-real-or-just-an-accountability-fueled-mirage/.

120   James J. Heckman, John Eric Humphries, and Tim Kautz, *The Myth of Achievement Tests: The GED and the Role of Character in American Life* (Chicago: University of Chicago Press, 2015).

121   Jeanne Gubbels, Claudia E. van der Put, and Mark Assink, "Risk Factors for School Absenteeism and Dropout: A Meta-Analytic Review," *Journal of Youth and Adolescence* 48, no. 9 (2019): 1637–67, https://doi.org/10.1007/s10964-019-01072-5.

122   Melisa Roderick, Thomas Kelley-Kemple, David W. Johnson, and Nicole O. Beechum, *Preventable Failure: Improvements in Long-Term Outcomes When High Schools Focused on the Ninth Grade Year*, April 2014, https://files.eric.ed.gov/fulltext/ED553174.pdf; and Andrew Sum, Ishwar Khatiwada, Joseph McLaughlin, and Sheila Palma, *The Consequences of Dropping Out of High School*, October 2009, http://www.precaution.org/lib/consequences_of_dropping_out_of_high_school.090601.pdf.

123   Elaine Allensworth, "The Use of Ninth-Grade Early Warning Indicators to Improve Chicago Schools," *Journal of Education for Students Placed at Risk* 18, no. 1 (2013): 68–83, https://doi.org/10.1080/10824669.2013.745181; and Nikolas Pharris-Ciurej, Charles Hirschman, and Joseph Willhoft, "The 9th Grade Shock and the High School Dropout Crisis," *Social Science Research* 41, no. 3 (2012): 709–30, https://doi.org/10.1016/j.ssresearch.2011.11.014.

124 Roderick, Kelley-Kemple, Johnson, and Beechum, *Preventable Failure*; Sum et al., *Consequences of Dropping Out of High School*; and "Mayor Lightfoot and Chicago Public Schools Announce Record-High Graduation Rate," Chicago Public Schools, September 4, 2020, https://www.cps.edu/press-releases/mayor-lightfoot-and-chicago-public-schools-announce-record-high-graduation-rate/.

125 "The Condition of Education 2021 (2021-144), Immediate College Enrollment Rate," US Department of Education, National Center for Education Statistics, 2021, https://nces.ed.gov/fastfacts/display.asp?id=51.

126 Karen Levesque, Jennifer Laird, Elisabeth Hensley, Susan P. Choy, and Emily Forrest Cataldi, *Career and Technical Education in the United States: 1990 to 2005 Statistical Analysis Report*, US Department of Education, National Center for Education Statistics, July 2008, https://nces.ed.gov/pubs2008/2008035.pdf; and Emily Hanford, "The Troubled History of Vocational Education," *APM Reports: Illuminating Journalism from American Public Media* (blog), September 9, 2014, https://www.apmreports.org/episode/2014/09/09/the-troubled-history-of-vocational-education.

127 David Kirp, Marjorie Wechsler, Madelyn Gardner, and Titilayo Tinubu Ali, *Disrupting Disruption: The Steady Work of Transforming Schools* (Oxford: Oxford University Press, 2022).

128 James J. Kemple, *Career Academies: Long-Term Impacts on Labor Market Outcomes, Educational Attainment, and Transitions to Adulthood*, MDRC, June 2008, https://www.mdrc.org/publication/career-academies-long-term-impacts-work-education-and-transitions-adulthood.

129 Daniel Kreisman and Kevin Stange, "Depth over Breadth: The Value of Vocational Education in U.S. High Schools," *Education Next* 19, no. 4 (2019), https://www.educationnext.org/depth-over-breadth-value-vocational-education-u-s-high-schools/.

Chapter 5

1 Andrew M. I. Lee, "The 13 Disability Categories under IDEA," Understood: School Supports, 2019, https://www.understood.org/articles/en/conditions-covered-under-idea.

2 National Center for Education Statistics, "The NCES Fast Facts Tool Provides Quick Answers to Many Education Questions

(National Center for Education Statistics)." "Students with Disabilities," Condition of Education. US Department of Education, Institute of Education Sciences, January 10, 2021, https://nces.ed.gov/programs/coe/indicator/cgg.

3 The senior author was co-counsel in the *PARC* case.

4 Diane Ravitch and Tom Loveless, "Broken Promises: What the Federal Government Can Do to Improve American Education," *Brookings* (blog), March 1, 2000, https://www.brookings.edu/articles/broken-promises-what-the-federal-government-can-do-to-improve-american-education/; National Education Association, "Special Education," *Issue Explainer* (blog), December 2, 2021, https://www.nea.org/advocating-for-change/action-center/our-issues/special-education; Tom Zembar, *Special Education Grants to States: IDEA Funding Gap*, National Education Association, Education Policy & Practice Department, Center for Great Public Schools, April 4, 2018, https://www.nea.org/sites/default/files/2020-06/IDEA-Funding-Gap-FY2017-with-State-Table.pdf.

5 Diana Lambert, "Amid Shortages, Schools Settle for Underprepared Special Education Teachers," *EdSource: Highlighting Strategies for Student Success*, January 10, 2020, https://edsource.org/2020/amid-shortages-schools-settle-for-underprepared-special-education-teachers/621656.

6 Nora Gordon, *Race, Poverty, and Interpreting Overrepresentation in Special Education*, Brookings, September 20, 2017, https://www.brookings.edu/research/race-poverty-and-interpreting-overrepresentation-in-special-education/.

7 Paul L. Morgan, George Farkas, Marianne M. Hillemeier, Richard Mattison, Steve Maczuga, Hui Li, and Michael Cook, "Minorities Are Disproportionately Underrepresented in Special Education," *Educational Researcher* 44, no. 5 (2015): 278–92, https://doi.org/10.3102/0013189x15591157; Beth Harry and Janette K. Klingner, *Why Are so Many Minority Students in Special Education? Understanding Race & Disability in Schools* (New York: Teachers College Press, 2014).

8 Valerie Strauss, "No, Special Education Does Not Treat Disability Like a Disease and Is Not 'Obsessed' with Forcing Students to Conform," *Washington Post*, February 25, 2019, https://www.washingtonpost.com/education/2019/02/25/no-special-educat

ion-does-not-treat-disability-like-disease-is-not-obsessed-with-forcing-students-conform/.

9 Carola Suarez-Orozco and Marcelo Suárez-Orozco, *Children of Immigration* (Cambridge, MA: Harvard University Press, 2002).

10 Plyler v. Doe 457 U.S. 202 (1982).

11 "Immigrant Children," Child Trends, 2018, https://www.childtre nds.org/indicators/immigrant-children. This document is the source for most of the demographic information in this chapter.

12 Anne Morese, "A Look at Immigrant Youth: Prospects and Promising Practices" (working paper, NCSL's Children's Policy Initiative, David and Lucile Packard Foundation, March 2005), https://www.ncsl.org/research/immigration/a-look-at-immigr ant-youth-prospects-and-promisin.aspx.

13 David L. Kirp, *Improbable Scholars: The Rebirth of a Great American School System and a Strategy for America's Schools* (New York: Oxford University Press, 2013).

14 Suarez-Orozco and Suárez-Orozco, *Children of Immigration*.

15 Ibid.

16 Jannie Tankard Carnock, "How Young Children of Immigrants Face Discrimination at School," *New America* (blog), September 18, 2015, https://www.newamerica.org/education-policy/ edcentral/early-discrimination/; Annette Lin, "Teen Immigrants Bullied Because of Culture, Language, and More," *Teen Vogue*, October 30, 2019, https://www.teenvogue.com/story/ teen-immigrants-bullied-because-of-culture-language-and-more; and OECD, *The Resilience of Students with an Immigrant Background: Factors That Shape Well-Being*. OECD: Better Policies for Better Lives, March 19, 2018, https://www.oecd.org/educat ion/the-resilience-of-students-with-an-immigrant-background-9789264292093-en.htm.

17 Marta Miklikowska, Jochem Thijs, and Mikael Hjerm, "The Impact of Perceived Teacher Support on Anti-Immigrant Attitudes from Early to Late Adolescence," *Journal of Youth and Adolescence* 48, no. 6 (2019): 1175–89, https://doi.org/10.1007/ s10964-019-00990-8. International studies have shown that teachers' attitudes have a direct impact as well. A study of Swedish schools found that "classrooms where students shared an experience of teacher support were lower in prejudice than classrooms with weaker teacher support. . . . Teachers can counteract the development of prejudice and facilitate social

trust in adolescents by being supportive of them." What's more, teachers' biases may affect their academic performance. A study of Italian schoolteachers found that they give lower grades to immigrant students compared to native Italians who have the same performance on standardized, blindly graded tests." Encouragingly, the study found that "teachers informed of their stereotypes before term grading increase grades assigned to immigrants." Marco De Benedetto and Maria De Paola, *Immigration and Teacher Bias towards Foreign Students*, Seventy-Fifth Economic Policy Panel Meeting, April 2022, https://www.economic-policy.org/wp-content/uploads/2022/03/De_Benedetto_De_Paola__full_paper.pdf.

18 Georges Vernez, Allan Abrahamse, and Denise D. Quigley, *How Immigrants Fare in U.S. Education*, Rand Corporation, 1996, https://www.rand.org/pubs/monograph_reports/MR718.html.

19 Caroline Berner, "Diversity in Schools: Immigrants and the Performance of U.S. Born Students," *FutureEd* (blog), March 3, 2021, https://www.future-ed.org/diversity-in-schools-imm igrants-and-the-performance-of-u-s-born-students/; and David N. Figlio, Paola Giuliano, Riccardo Marchingiglio, Umut Özek, and Paola Sapienza, "Diversity in Schools: Immigrants and the Educational Performance of U.S. Born Students" (working paper, National Bureau of Economic Research, March 2021), 10.3386/w28596, https://www.edworkingpapers.com/sites/default/files/ai21-368.pdf.

20 David L. Kirp, "How a School Network Helps Immigrant Kids Learn," *New York Times*, May 30, 2015, https://www.nytimes.com/2015/05/31/opinion/sunday/how-a-school-network-helps-immigrant-kids-learn.html?searchResultPosition=1.

21 "Our Nation's English Learners," Department of Education, 2022, https://www2.ed.gov/datastory/el-characteristics/index.html#intro.

22 Erika Hoff, *Language Development*, 5th ed. (Belmont, CA: Wadsworth, 2014).

23 Diane August, Timothy Shanahan, and Kathy Escamilla, "English Language Learners: Developing Literacy in Second-Language Learners—Report of the National Literacy Panel on Language-Minority Children and Youth," *Journal of Literacy Research* 41, no. 4 (2009): 432–52, https://doi.org/10.1080/10862960903340 165; and Diane August, and Timothy Shanahan, *Developing*

Literacy in Second-Language Learners: Report of the National Literacy Panel on Language-Minority Children and Youth, 1st ed. (Mahwah, NJ: Lawrence Erlbaum, 2006).

24 Corey Mitchell, "'English-Only' Laws in Education on Verge of Extinction," *Education Week*, October 23, 2019, https://www.edw eek.org/teaching-learning/english-only-laws-in-education-on-verge-of-extinction/2019/10; Andrew Meyers, "Two-Language Instruction Best for English-Language Learners, Stanford Research Suggests," Research Stories, Stanford Graduate School of Education, March 25, 2014, https://ed.stanford.edu/news/students-learning-english-benefit-more-two-language-progr ams-english-immersion-stanford; Kathy Hoffman, "Arizona Is the Only State with an English-Only Education Law: It's Time to Repeal It," *AZ Central*, November 17, 2019, https://www. azcentral.com/story/opinion/op-ed/2019/11/17/arizona-only-state-english-only-law-we-repeal-it/2564675001/; and Jennifer L. Steele, Robert Slater, Gema Zamarro, Trey Miller, Jennifer J. Li, Susan Burkhauser, and Michael Bacon, *Dual-Language Immersion Programs Raise Student Achievement in English*, RAND Corporation, 2017, https://www.rand.org/pubs/research_bri efs/RB9903.html.

25 Much of this section is drawn from Erica L. Green and Annie Waldman, "'I Feel Invisible': Native Students Languish in Public Schools," *New York Times*, December 28, 2018, https://www. nytimes.com/2018/12/28/us/native-american-education.html; and Rebecca Clarren, "How America Is Failing Native American Students," *Nation*, July 24, 2017, https://www.thenation.com/article/archive/left-behind/.

26 Mary Anette Pember, "Death by Civilization," *Atlantic*, March 8, 2019, https://www.theatlantic.com/education/archive/2019/03/traumatic-legacy-indian-boarding-schools/584293/. The senior author participated in a lawsuit against the Intermountain Indian School. Among the issues raised in that lawsuit was the misuse of Ritalin to control the students. The school closed in 1984.

27 Laura Faer, Letter to John Sutter, Superintendent, re: case number 09-14-1111, United States Department of Education: Office for Civil Rights, November 22, 2017, https://www2.ed.gov/about/offices/list/ocr/docs/investigations/more/09141111-a.pdf.

28 The White House, *2014 Native Youth Report*, Executive Office of the President, 2014, https://obamawhitehouse.archives.gov/sites/default/files/docs/20141129nativeyouthreport_final.pdf.

29 Joanne Newman, "Native American Students with Disabilities and Denied Their Educational Rights, Reach a Landmark Settlement with the Federal Government, Clearing a Path toward Greater Equity," *SLS Blog: Mills Legal Clinic of Stanford Law School*, October 7, 2020, https://law.stanford.edu/2020/10/07/native-american-students-with-disabilities-and-denied-their-educatio nal-rights-reach-a-landmark-settlement-with-the-federal-gov ernment-clearing-a-path-toward-greater-equity/.

30 Leticia De La Vara, "Giving Native Communities a Seat at the Education Policy Table," *TNTP Blog*, January 31, 2017, https://tntp.org/blog/post/giving-native-communities-a-seat-at-the-education-policy-table.

31 In *West Virginia v. Barnett*, decided amid the patriotic fervor of World War II, the justices had earlier decided that students could not be compelled to salute the American flag. 319 U.S. 624 (1943).

32 Tinker v. Des Moines Independent Community School District, 393 U.S. 503 (1969), Justia Law, 1969, https://supreme.justia.com/cases/federal/us/393/503/.

33 Tinker v. Des Moines Independent Community School District 193 U.S. 503 (1969); and Bethel School District v. Fraser 478 U.S. 675 (1986).

34 Hazelwood School District v. Kuhlmeier 484 U.S. 260 (1988).

35 Mahanoy Area School District v. B.L., 594 U.S. ___ (2021).

36 Goss v. Lopez 419 U.S. 565 (1975).

37 Ingraham v. Wright, 430 U.S. 651 (1977).

38 New Jersey v. TLO, 469 U.S. 325 (1985).

39 "Adolescent and School Health: Health Considerations for LGBTQ Youth," Centers for Disease Control and Prevention, December 20, 2019, https://www.cdc.gov/healthyyouth/disp arities/health-considerations-lgbtq-youth.htm?CDC_AA_refVal= https%3A%2F%2Fwww.cdc.gov%2Fhealthyyouth%2Fdisparit ies%2Fsmy.htm.

40 Several other surveys have generated similar findings. In a 2011 national survey of some eighty-six hundred LGBT students, ages thirteen to twenty, from more than three thousand school districts, 85 percent reported frequently hearing "gay" used negatively, and more than half of them heard teachers or other

school staff make homophobic remarks. Afraid that they would be beaten up, more than a third of them avoided bathrooms and locker rooms. A 2019 national school climate survey found that 70 percent of LGBTQ students were verbally bullied and 29 percent beaten up because of their sexual orientation; 59 percent were verbally bullied and 29 percent physically bullied because of their gender expression. Nearly half of the LGBTQ students who considered dropping out said that such harassment was the reason.

41 Emily A. Greytak, Joseph G. Kosciw, and Elizabeth M. Diaz, *Harsh Realities: The Experience of Transgender Youth in Our Nation's Schools*, A Report from the Gay, Lesbian and Straight Education Network, 2009, https://files.eric.ed.gov/fulltext/ED505687.pdf; and Thomas Hanson, Gary Zhang, Rebeca Cerna, Alexis Stern, and Gregory Austin, *Understanding the Experiences of LGBTQ Students in California*, WestEd, 2021, https://www.wested.org/wp-content/uploads/2021/11/CHKS-2017-19-RaceEthnicity_LGBTQ_High-School_Final-FINAL.pdf.

42 Hanson et al., *Understanding the Experiences of LGBTQ Students in California*.

43 Suzanne Eckes and Maria Lewis, *The Complex and Dynamic Legal Landscape of LGBTQ Student Rights*, October 19, 2020, https://www.brookings.edu/blog/brown-center-chalkboard/2020/10/19/the-complex-and-dynamic-legal-landscape-of-lgbtq-student-rights/.

44 "How the Law Protects LGBTQ Youth," Lambda Legal, 2022, https://www.lambdalegal.org/know-your-rights/article/youth-how-the-law-protects.

45 Alexander Gabriel, Brandon Stratford, and Heather Steed, "Only 9 States and DC Report That More Than Half of Secondary Schools Have a Gender and Sexuality Alliance," *Child Trends* (blog), September 10, 2021, https://www.childtrends.org/blog/only-9-states-and-the-district-of-columbia-report-that-more-than-half-of-secondary-schools-have-a-gender-and-sexuality-alliance; and "Know Your Rights: Students & LGBTQ Rights at School," Southern Poverty Law Center, 2022, https://www.splcenter.org/know-your-rights-students-lgbtq-rights-school.

46 Martha Langmuir, "Improving School Climate for LGBT Youth: How You Can Make Change Now!," *QED: A Journal*

of GLBTQ Worldmaking, no. 1 (2013): 37–41, https://doi.org/
10.1353/qed.2013.0000.

47   "Wikipedia: Gay Agenda," Wikimedia Foundation, January 20,
2022, https://en.wikipedia.org/wiki/Gay_agenda.

Chapter 6

1   Kate Taylor, "13,000 School Districts, 13,000 Approaches to
Teaching during Covid," *New York Times*, January 21, 2021,
https://www.nytimes.com/2021/01/21/us/schools-coronavi
rus.html?referringSource=articleShare.

2   Emma Dorn, Bryan Hancock, Jimmy Sarakatsannis, and Ellen
Viruleg, "COVID-19 and Education: The Lingering Effects of
Unfinished Learning," *McKinsey & Company* (blog), July 27, 2021,
https://www.mckinsey.com/industries/education/our-insig
hts/covid-19-and-education-the-lingering-effects-of-unfinished-
learning.

3   Victoria Collis and Emma Vegas, *Unequally Disconnected: Access
to Online Learning in the US* (blog), June 22, 2020, https://www.
brookings.edu/blog/education-plus-development/2020/06/22/
unequally-disconnected-access-to-online-learning-in-the-us/.

4   Indermit Gill and Jamiee Saavedra, "We Are Losing a
Generation," *Brookings* (blog), January 28, 2022, https://www.
brookings.edu/blog/future-development/2022/01/28/we-are-
losing-a-generation.

5   Hailly T. N. Korman, Bonnie O'Keefe, and Matt Repka, *Missing in
the Margins 2020: Estimating the Scale of the COVID-19 Attendance
Crisis*, October 21, 2020, https://bellwethereducation.org/publ
ication/missing-margins-estimating-scale-covid-19-attendance-
crisis.

6   Susan B. Goldberg, *Education in a Pandemic: The Disparate Impacts
of COVID-19 on America's Students*, Department of Education,
Office for Civil Rights, June 9, 2021, https://www2.ed.gov/
about/offices/list/ocr/docs/20210608-impacts-of-covid19.pdf.

7   Hannah Natanson, Valerie Strauss, and Katherine Frey, "How
America Failed Students with Disabilities during the Pandemic,"
Washington Post, May 20, 2021.

8   NYU Langone Health, "Trauma in Children during the COVID-
19 Pandemic," *Patient Care/COVID-19 Mental Health Resources
for Families 2020* (blog), News Hub, 2020, https://nyulangone.
org/news/trauma-children-during-covid-19-pandemic#:~:text=

%E2%80%9CSome%20children%20may%20become%20overwhel
med,%2C%20or%20having%20sleep%20difficulties.%E2%80%9D.

9   Kalyn Belsha and Matt Barnum, "As Quarantines Send Students
Home, What's the Plan to Keep Them Learning?," *Chalkbeat*,
August 17, 2021, https://www.chalkbeat.org/2021/8/17/22628
684/quarantine-schools-covid-delta-cdc.

10 Peggy Barmore, "Schooling Has Changed Forever: Here's What
Will Stay When Things Go Back to Normal," *Hechinger Report*,
March 16, 2021, https://hechingerreport.org/schooling-has-
changed-forever-heres-what-will-stay-when-things-go-back-to-
normal/.

11 Joann Muller, "Teachers' Lessons from the Pandemic Will Last,
Survey Says," *Axios Navigate* (blog), October 5, 2021, https://
www.axios.com/teachers-pandemic-lessons-22d396c6-4fe8-4bfb-
8234-48ab97904999.html.

12 Jonathan Guryan, Jens Ludwig, Monica P. Bhatt, Philip J. Cook,
Jonathan M. V. Davis, Kenneth Dodge, George Farkas, et al. "Not
Too Late: Improving Academic Outcomes Among Adolescents"
(working paper, National Bureau of Economic Research, March
2021), https://www.nber.org/papers/w28531.

13 Barmore, "Schooling Has Changed Forever."

INDEX

For the benefit of digital users, indexed terms that span two pages (e.g., 52–53) may, on occasion, appear on only one of those pages.

ability grouping
 tracking vs., 89
 whole-class instruction vs., 90
absenteeism
 community schools, 46
 ESSA ratings, 57
 high school completion
  and, 117
 LGBTQ students, 138
 noncognitive skills, 111
 nudges, 113
Achievement First, 52
achievement gap, 87–89
 additional funding, 27–28
 Covid-19 pandemic, 140–41
 culturally responsive
  (sustaining) pedagogy, 88–
  89, 180n.5
 high-stakes
  accountability, 48–49
 mayoral-run urban districts, 79
 No Child Left Behind
  Act, 55, 56
 "no excuses" strategy, 51–52
 prioritizing equity, 87–88

showing students they
 belong, 88
staff training, 88
tracking, 90
Addams, Jane, 44
Advanced Education Research &
 Development Fund, 85
advanced placement classes
 Native American students, 130
 nudges, 113
 socioeconomic integration, 21
African American students. *See*
 Black students
Alaska Native students. *See*
 Native American students
American Federation of Teachers
 (AFT), 32, 71, 72
American Indian students. *See*
 Native American students
American Legislative Exchange
 Council (ALEC), 79
American Psychological
 Association, 99–100
Americans with Disabilities
 Act, 123

Anastasiou, Dimitris, 125
artificial intelligence, 12
Asian American students
  achievement gap, 87
  educational outcomes, 8–9
  homeschooling, 47
  immigrant students, 127
  Mather School, 11
  percentage of student
    population, 11–12
Asian American teachers, 64
Aspire Public Schools, 33
Astor, Ronald, 103
attendance zones and boundaries,
  6–7, 15, 18, 19, 21

belonging experiences, 88,
  115–16
Bethel School District v. Fraser, 133
BIE (Bureau of Indian
  Education), 130–32
bilingual and multilingual
  students, 8, 129–30, 141–42,
  146. *See also* English language
  learners
Black students
  achievement gap, 87
  charter schools, 33
  college enrollment, 9
  Covid-19 pandemic, 140
  effects of increased funding, 28
  gifted programs, 9
  graduation rates, 8–9
  Head Start, 42
  homeschooling, 47
  Jim Crow era, 15–16
  legal rights of students, 133–34
  Mather School, 11
  percentage of student
    population, 11–12
  police on campus, 96
  prejudice, discrimination, and
    violence, 7
  pre-K, 8

racial integration, 5, 18, 19–
  20, 23
secession from school districts, 18
socioeconomic integration, 22
socioeconomic status, 22
special education, 125
student discipline, 9, 95–96
Black teachers, 64–65
Bradley v. Milliken, 17
Breyer, Stephen, 134–35
Brookings Institution, 78, 83–84
Brown, Heath, 48
Brown University, ix
Brown v. Board of Education, xi,
  3–4, 6, 10, 16, 17–18, 23, 24–
  25, 121–22
Bryk, Anthony, 59–60
bullying, 98–102
  antibullying curricula and
    strategies, 100–1
  cyberbullying, 98–100, 108–9
  effect of school climate, 93
  effects of, 100
  increased concern over, 99
  LGBTQ students, 135–36
  physical, 98–99
  prevalence of, 99–100
  race and ethnicity, 101
  state legislation, 101
  verbal, 98–99
Bureau of Indian Education
  (BIE), 130–32
Bush, George H. W. and Bush
  administration, 52–53
Bush, George W. and Bush
  administration
  focus of secretary of
    education, 3
  high-stakes accountability, 49
busing, 16, 17

California Supreme Court, 25
Capitalism and Freedom
  (Friedman), 37

career education (vocational
    education), 117–19
  benefits of, 119
  criticism of, 118
  history of, 3, 24, 117–18
  premise of, 117
  research findings, 118
  tracking, 89, 90
Carnegie Foundation for
    the Advancement of
    Teaching, 59–60
CCNX (City Connects), 46
CCSS. *See* Common Core State
    Standards
Centers for Disease Control and
    Prevention (CDC), 105
Chan Zuckerberg Initiative, 85
charter schools, 2, 32–36
  academic achievement, 33–34
  accountability, 32, 34–35
  arguments in favor of, 33–34,
    155n.14
  Covid-19 pandemic, 141
  criticism of, 34–36, 156n.24
  defined, 32
  failed, 35
  independent charters vs.
    nonprofit and for-profit
    entities, 33
  market-based drivers, 35
  "no excuses" strategy, 36, 52
  number of, 33
  number of students, 33
  origin of concept, 32
  politically polarized
    opinions of, 33
  for-profit charters, 33, 36, 157n.30
  promoting diversity, 19
  school board elections, 81–82
  social-emotional learning, 36
  socioeconomic integration, 21
  unions and, 36, 72
  virtual, 33
  Walton Family Foundation, 84

CIS (Communities in
    Schools), 46–47
City Connects (CCNX), 46
civic participation, 12–13
Civil Rights Act, 3, 16
  Title VI, 39
  Title IX, 39
class size, 91–92
  assigning more students to
    highly effective teacher, 91–92
  effect on student
    achievement, 91–92
  reduction of, 91, 92
  research findings, 91, 92
Cold War, 3, 24
Coleman, James, x–xi
Coleman Report ("Equality of
    Educational Opportunity"),
    x–xi, 8–9, 19, 27
college preparation and enrollment
  belonging experiences, 115–16
  bullying, 100
  career education, 117–18
  charter schools, 34, 36
  community colleges, 9, 118
  community schools, 46
  Covid-19 pandemic, 140
  deeper learning, 110
  early childhood education,
    41, 42, 43
  Every Student Succeeds Act, 57
  extracurricular activities, 104–5
  graduate earnings, 9, 72–73
  high school completion, 116
  highly effective teachers, 61
  housing vouchers, 20
  immigrant students, 127, 128
  Native American students,
    131, 132
  noncognitive skills, 111
  percentage of students who do
    not attend college, 117
  race and ethnicity, 9, 19–20,
    87, 127

college preparation and
enrollment (*cont.*)
　school voucher, 37
　standards-based education, 53
　teacher preparation, 65
　tracking, 89
Columbine High School shooting,
　99, 102
Common Core State Standards
　(CCSS), 53
　arguments in favor of, 53
　criticism of, 53, 83–84
　research findings, 53
"common school" movement, x, 21
Communities in Schools
　(CIS), 46–47
community colleges, 9, 118
community schools, xi, 44–47
　components of, 45
　continuous improvement
　　strategy, 60
　number of, 44
　operating calendar, 45
　origin of concept, 44
　parents and, 45
　partners, 45
　post-pandemic increase, 145–46
　research findings, 46–47
　scope and role of, 44–45
　systemic reform strategy, 58
conflict resolution, 101–2
continuous improvement
　strategy, 59–60
　arguments in favor of, 60
　community schools, 60
　"garbage can" model vs., 59
　highly effective teachers, 62
　origin of concept, 59
　Plan-Do-Study-Act inquiry
　　cycle, 59–60
　premise of, 59
　systemic reform strategy, 58
"controlled choice"
　assignment, 19

corporal punishment, 95, 135
Council of Chief State School
　Officers, 53
Covid-19 pandemic, xii, 139–46
　charter schools and, 33
　culture wars, threats, and
　　violence, 143
　effects of disruption, 141–42
　English language
　　learners, 141–42
　homeschooling, 47
　LGBTQ students, 141–42
　long-term impact of, 144–46
　mask requirements, 4, 142–43
　mental health concerns, 145
　post-pandemic educational
　　strategies, 144
　post-pandemic
　　predictions, 144–46
　quarantining, 142
　school board elections and
　　recalls, 80–81
　school closures, 139, 141
　school response to, 139–43
　socioeconomic status, 140
　teachers, 64, 65
　technology and, 12
　vaccinations, 142–43
　varied responses, 139–40
"critical race theory," 2–3, 4, 80
culturally responsive (sustaining)
　pedagogy, 88–89, 180n.5
cyberbullying, 98–100, 108–9

Darling-Hammond, Linda, 75
*Davis v. Monroe County Board of
　Education*, 99
deeper learning, 109–10
　defined, 109
　effects of, 110
　example of, 109
　shallow learning vs., 109
　STEM education, 110
Deming, C. Edwards, 59

disabilities, students with, 95–96
  BIE-operated schools, 131–32
  bullying, 99, 101
  charter schools, 35–36
  Covid-19 pandemic, 141–42
  early childhood education, 41
  federal underwriting of
    educational initiatives, 3, 8
  legal rights of students, 133
  police on campus, 96
  prejudice and
    discrimination, 3
  school vouchers, 39
  special education, 121–25
  student discipline, 95–96
Drewery, Julie, 118
Duncan, Arne, 23–24, 51, 53

early childhood education
  (ECE), 39–44, 146. See also
  prekindergarten; preschool
  child care vs., 39–40
  criteria for, 40
  defined, 39
  developmental stage and mode
    of teaching, 39
  Early Head Start, 24
  "fadeout" contention, 42
  Head Start, 24, 42, 43–44
  high quality, 40–41
  neuroscience and
    genetics, 43–44
  parenting programs vs., 39–40
  research findings, 41–43
  teacher-child relationship,
    39–40
Early Head Start, 24
Edsall, Thomas, 9–10
Education Act, 130–31
Education Amendments Title
  IX, 137
education policies, 2, 4–6
  belief that expertise is irrelevant
    in setting, 4

data-free zone, 5
  defined, 4
  disputes over, 4
  ethics and constitutional
    principles as drivers of, 5
  evidence-based choices, 5–6, 27
  examples of choices in, 4
  federal government's role, 3–4
  hunches and ideologies as
    drivers of, 5
  influence of philanthropy
    on, 83–85
  role of judiciary, 10–11
  school board's role, 2
  school district's role, 1–2, 5
  school's role, 2
  state's role, 2–3
EEO. See equality of educational
  opportunity
Elementary and Secondary
  Education Act (ESEA), 3,
  24, 27, 54
Endrew F. v. Douglas County School
  District, 122
English language learners
  (ELLs), 129–30
  charter schools, 33–34
  Covid-19 pandemic, 141–42
  defined, 129
  federal underwriting of
    educational initiatives, 8
  graduation rates, 128
  immigrant students, 12, 126–
    27, 128
  Internationals Network
    schools, 128–29
  language immersion and
    bilingualism, 129–30
  legal rights of students, 133
  No Child Left Behind Act, 54
  political debate over, 129–30
  socioeconomic integration, 22
  teacher bias, 127
  teacher preparation, 65

English Plus, 129–30
Equal Access Act, 137–38
"Equality of Educational
    Opportunity" (Coleman
    Report), x–xi, 8–9, 19, 27
equality of educational
    opportunity (EEO), x–xi, 6–
    10, 15–29
  additional funding, 27–28
  aspiration vs. reality, 6
  racial integration, 6–8, 15–20
  school choice, 28–29
  school finance, 8, 22–27
  socioeconomic
    integration, 20–22
ESEA (Elementary and Secondary
    Education Act), 3, 24, 27, 54
Every Student Succeeds Act
    (ESSA), 24, 52, 56–58, 145
  federal vs. state role, 57
  No Child Left Behind Act
    vs., 57–58
  school climate, 93
  school "report cards," 57
  STEM education, 110–11
expulsion, 95–96
  antibullying strategies, 101
  defined, 95
  legal rights of students, 132–33
  race and ethnicity, 95–96
  reduction in, 96, 98
  zero-tolerance discipline, 95–96
extracurricular activities, 104–5
  deeper learning, 109
  effects of, 104–5
  homeschooling, 48
  level of participation, 104–5
  physical education, 105
  research findings, 104–5,
    188–89n.68

Farmington, Utah, school
    district, 7
FBI, 80

First Amendment, 73, 134
Floyd, George, 96
foster children
  federal underwriting of
    educational initiatives, 8
  graduation rates, 8–9
Fourteenth Amendment, 5, 137
Fox News, 80
Friedman, Milton, 37

"garbage can" model of
    organizational behavior, 59
Garland, Merrick B., 80
Gates Foundation, 51, 70, 83–
    84, 85
Gay-Straight Alliance
    (GSA), 137–38
General Educational
    Development (GED)
    test, 116
Google, 107, 111
Goss v. Lopez, 135
Government Accountability
    Office, 131
grade retention, 98
Gray-Lobe, Guthrie, 42–43
Green v. New Kent County, 16
group therapy, 102
growth mindset, 114–15
  effects of, 115
  fixed and mixed mindsets vs.,
    114–15, 193n.99
  research findings, 115
GSA (Gay-Straight
    Alliance), 137–38

Hall, Beverly, 50
Hartzler, Kirt, 104
Harvard Center for the
    Developing Child, 40
Hayakowa, S. I., 129–30
Hazelwood v. Kuhlmeier, 133
Head Start, 24, 42, 43–44
Heckman, James, 116

high school completion and
    graduation, 116–17
achievement gap, 87–88
additional funding, 28
college enrollment, 9
community schools, 46
criteria for, 2–3
dropouts, 116–17
early childhood education,
    41, 42, 43
early intervention, 117
ESSA ratings, 57
GED, 116
growth mindset, 115
immigrant students, 128
Native American students, 130
noncognitive skills, 111
race and ethnicity, 8–9, 87–88
rates of, 116
school vouchers, 37
socioeconomic
    integration, 21–22
warning signs, 117
high-stakes accountability, 48–
    51, 145
allegations of cheating, 50–51
arguments in favor of, 49, 50
criticism of, 49–50
defined, 48–49
"drill and kill" approach, 50
Every Student Succeeds
    Act, 57
homeless students
    federal underwriting of
        educational initiatives, 8
    graduation rates, 8–9
homeschooling, 47–48
    collaboration with public and
        private schools, 48
    criticism of, 48
    defined, 47
    funding, 47
    number of students, 1, 47
    outcomes, 48

race and ethnicity, 47
reasons for, 47
regulation, 2–3, 47
Homeschooling on the Right
    (Brown), 48
housing vouchers, 20
Hull House, 44

IDEA. See Individuals with
    Disabilities Education Act
IDEA Public Schools, 33
IEPs (Individualized Education
    Plans), 122–23
Imagine Schools, 33
immigration and
    immigrants, 125–29
    age on arrival, 128
    classroom composition, 12
    effect on nonimmigrant
        students, 127–28
    federal underwriting of
        educational initiatives, 8
    languages, 126–27, 128–29
    motivation to immigrate, 125
    number of immigrant
        students, 126
    obligation to educate, 125
    prejudice and
        discrimination, 127
    socioeconomic status, 126, 128
    teacher bias, 127, 198–99n.17
    undocumented immigrants,
        125, 126–27
Indian Child Welfare Act, 131
Individualized Education Plans
    (IEPs), 122–23
Individuals with Disabilities
    Education Act (IDEA), 122–24
    cost of, 123–24
    demand on teachers, 124
    due process, 123
    evaluations, 122
    free and appropriate
        education, 122

Individuals with Disabilities
  Education Act (IDEA) (*cont.*)
  implementation, 123–24
  Individualized Education
    Plans, 122–23
  least restrictive
    environment, 123
  parent participation, 123
  support and service
    access, 123
Ingraham v. Wright, 95
Internationals Network for Public
  Schools, 128–29

Janus v. American Federation of
  State, County, and Municipal
  Employees Council 31, 72–73
Jensen, Arthur, 43–44
Johnson, Lyndon B., 24
judiciary, 1–2. *See also* US Supreme
  Court; *names of specific cases*
  challenge of implementation, 11
  education policies, 10–11
  increased involvement, 10
  judicial activism, 10–11
  legal rights of students, 133–35,
    201n.31
  LGBTQ students, 137
  Native American students, 10
  racial integration, 6–7,
    15–18
  role of, 10–11
  school finance and
    funding, 24–27
  special education, 121–22
  special needs, 10
  symbolic and substantive
    impact, 10

Kauffman, Jim, 125
Kennedy, Anthony, 18
Kennedy, Ted, 55
Keyes v. Denver Unified School
  District, 16–17

kindergarten
  absenteeism, 113
  charter schools, 52
  class size reduction, 91
  Covid-19 pandemic, 141
  ESSA ratings, 57
  highly effective teachers, 61
  high-quality pre-K, 8
  race and ethnicity, 40
  skills upon entering, 40
  state requirements, 2
Knowledge Is Power Program
  (KIPP), 33, 34, 52
knowledge workers, 12

Latino students
  achievement gap, 87
  bilingualism, 129–30
  charter schools, 33
  college enrollment, 9
  ethnic studies, 89
  gifted programs, 9
  graduation rates, 8–9
  Hispanic vs. Latino, 148n.10
  homeschooling, 47
  immigrant students, 127
  Mather School, 11
  percentage of student
    population, 11–12
  police on campus, 96
  pre-K, 8
  racial integration, 18
  secession from school districts, 18
  socioeconomic integration, 22
  special education, 125
  student discipline, 95–96
  technology, 106
Latino teachers, 64
LAUSD (Los Angeles Unified
  School District), 107
Learning Policy Institute, 41, 46,
  75
legal rights of students, 132–35
  early lack of, 132–33

judicial decisions, 133–35, 201n.31
locker searches, 135
speech outside school on social
    media, 134–35
student discipline, 135
"substantial disruption
    test," 133–34
LGBTQ students, 135–38
antiharassment policies, 138
Covid-19 pandemic, 141–42
freedom of speech and of
    association, 137–38
judicial decisions, 137
legislative protections, 136–37
LGBT-affirming curricula, 138
number of, 135–36
prejudice, discrimination, and
    violence, 135–36, 201–2n.40
restroom issue, 137
school vouchers, 39
transgender students, 136, 137, 138
locker searches, 135
Los Angeles Unified School
    District (LAUSD), 107
Loveless, Tom, 83–84
low-income students. *See*
    socioeconomic status
lunch programs, 12, 82, 128, 139

magnet schools, 2, 18, 31–32
arguments in favor of, 31
criticism of, 31–32
defined, 31
origin of concept, 31
*Mahanoy Area School District v. B.
    L.*, 134–35
Mann, Horace, 6
Marjory Stoneman Douglas High
    School shooting, 102
Mather School, 11–12
*Mills v. Board of Education v.
    District of Columbia*, 121–22
Mississippi Teacher Corps, 66
Moving to Opportunity (MTO), 20

Nabozny, Jamie, 137
National Assessment of
    Educational Progress
    (NAEP), 54–55, 130, 140–41
National Association for the
    Advancement of Colored
    People (NAACP), 16
National Association for the
    Education of Young Children
    (NAEYC), 40
National Caucus of Native
    American Legislators, 132
National Center for Education
    Statistics, 121
National Coalition of Community
    Schools, 44
National Defense Education Act, 3
National Education Association
    (NEA), 72
National Governors Association, 53
National Heritage Academies
    (NHA), 157n.30
National Institute for Early
    Education Research (NIEER), 41
National Parent Teacher
    Association, 82
National Rifle Association, 103
National School Administrators
    Association, 96
Native American students, 130–32
academic disparities, 130
achievement gap, 87
boarding schools, 130–31
federal underwriting of
    educational initiatives, 8
graduation rates, 8–9
number of, 130
prejudice and discrimination,
    72, 130–32
role of judiciary, 10
socioeconomic integration, 22
strategies for overcoming
    problems, 132
student discipline, 130, 131–32

Native Hawaiian students. *See*
    Native American students
Native Hope, 130
NCLB Act. *See* No Child Left
    Behind Act
NEA (National Education
    Association), 72
New Jersey v. TLO, 135
New Teacher Project, The
    (TNTP), 69–70
New York Times, 9–10
New Yorker, 72
NHA (National Heritage
    Academies), 157n.30
NIEER (National Institute for
    Early Education
    Research), 41
No Child Left Behind (NCLB)
    Act, 24, 44–45, 54–56
    adequate yearly progress, 54
    arguments in favor of, 55
    criticism of, 55–56
    "drill and kill" approach, 50
    Every Student Succeeds Act
        vs., 57–58
    high-stakes accountability, 48–
        49, 145
    premise of, 54
    results of, 54–55
    school funding, 56
    standards-based
        education, 52–53
    state testing, 54
    teacher shortages, 56
    "no excuses" strategy, xi,
        36, 51–52
    adoption of, 52
    criticism of, 52
    Michelle Rhee, 51–52
    premise of, 51
noncognitive skills, 111–12
    cognitive skills vs., 111
    defined, 111
    effects of, 111

grit, 112
    policymaking and, 112
    research findings, 111
nudges, 113–14
    absenteeism, 113
    cost of, 113
    defined, 113
    increasing use of, 113
    social-psychological strategies
        vs., 113
Nurse-Parent Partnership, 39–40

Oakes, Jeannie, 90
Obama, Barack and Obama
    administration
    focus of secretary of
        education, 3
    Race to the Top, 51, 70
    school shootings, 102
    student discipline, 96
Office of Civil Rights, 3,
    95–96, 98
Organisation of Economic Co-
    operation and Development
    (OECD), 98–99
Ozarks Teaching Corps, 66

PACs (political action
    committees), 81
parent teacher student
    associations (PTSAs), 82
parent-teacher associations
    (PTAs), 1–2, 24, 81–82, 83
Park, Soyoung, 125
Pathak, Parag, 42–43
pay-for-performance
    evaluation, 70–71
Payzant, Tom, 77
PD. *See* professional development
PDSA (Plan-Do-Study-Act)
    inquiry cycle, 59–60
peer mediation, 101–2
*Pennsylvania Association for
    Retarded Citizens (PARC)*

*v. the Commonwealth of
Pennsylvania*, 121–22
Perry Preschool Project, 41–42, 44
philanthropy, 1–2, 83–85
    Advanced Education Research
        & Development Fund, 85
    allocation of, 84–85
    criticism of, 83, 84–85
    Gates Foundation, 83–84, 85
    PTAs and school-based
        foundations, 83
    Walton Family Foundation,
        83–84, 85
PISA (Programme for
    International Student
    Assessment) exams,
    63, 110–11
Plan-Do-Study-Act (PDSA)
    inquiry cycle, 59–60
Plessy v. Ferguson, 15–16
police and armed guards on
    campus, 96–97, 103
political action committees
    (PACs), 81
pregnancy, 61, 133
prekindergarten (pre-K)
    criticism of, 42
    effect of high quality, 8, 41–42
    post-pandemic expansion, 145
    research findings, 41–43
preschool
    benefits of, 42–43
    immigrant students, 128
    Perry Preschool Project, 41–
        42, 44
    race and ethnicity, 8, 9
    state education agencies, 2–3
    student discipline, 9
principals
    Covid-19 pandemic, 139
    leadership role, 75–76
    legal rights of students, 132–
        33, 134
    No Child Left Behind Act, 51

parental involvement, 76
prejudice and
    discrimination, 131
retention and turnover, 76
school climate, 94
student achievement, 75
support for teachers, 64,
    69, 75, 76
teacher evaluation, 69
vision of success, 75
private schools
    homeschooling collaboration
        with, 48
    number of students, 1
    regulation, 2–3
    school vouchers, 37, 38–39
    wealthy families, 33, 124
professional development
    (PD), 67–69
    coaching, 68–69
    coherent and integrated
        development, 68
    collaboration, 68
    content-oriented focus, 67
    embedding in daily
        work, 68
    inquiry-based development, 68
    mentoring, 68–69
    ongoing and extended
        development, 67
    teacher-driven development, 68
Programme for International
    Student Assessment (PISA)
    exams, 63, 110–11
Proposition 13, 23
PTAs (parent-teacher
    associations), 1–2, 24, 81–
        82, 83
PTSAs (parent teacher student
    associations), 82
public schools, xii. *See also* magnet
    schools; school districts
    charter schools vs., 32–36
    Covid-19 pandemic, 141

public schools (*cont.*)
   equality of educational
      opportunity, 6
   high-stakes accountability, 50
   homeschooling collaboration
      with, 48
   homeschooling vs., 48
   immigrant students, 125–26
   LGBTQ students, 138
   Native American students, 130
   number of public school
      students, 1
   number of students, 1
   operating calendar, 44
   parent-teacher
      associations, 82, 83
   philanthropy, 84
   racial diversity of teachers, 64
   racial integration, 15, 16
   regulation, 2–3
   residence requirements, 6–7
   school choice, 28–29
   school vouchers vs., 37–39
   socioeconomic integration, 21
   special education, 12, 121
   tracking, 89

race and ethnicity, 6–8. *See also*
      racial integration; *names*
      of specific races and ethnicities
   achievement gap, 87–89
   bullying, 101
   college enrollment, 9
   culturally responsive
      (sustaining) pedagogy, 88–
      89, 180n.5
   demographics, 11–12
   early childhood education, 40
   ethics and constitutional
      principles as drivers of policy, 5
   federal underwriting of
      educational initiatives, 8
   geographically based
      attendance zones, 6–7

gifted programs, 9
graduation rates, 8–9
Mather School, 11
neighborhood secession from
      school districts, 18
pre-K quality, 8
prioritizing equity, 87–88
racism and racial animus, 7
school district
      composition, 18–19
school funding, 23
school vouchers, 39
"separate but equal"
      doctrine, 15–16
showing students they
      belong, 88
special education, 125
of teachers, 64
training to reduce bias and
      create empathy, 88
within-school
      segregation, 18–19
zoning laws and covenants, 6–7
Race to the Top, 51, 70
racial integration, xi, 15–20
   attendance zones, 19
   benefits of, 5, 19–20
   desegregation vs.
      integration, 15
   ethics and constitutional
      principles as drivers of
      policy, 5
   impact of zoning laws and
      covenants, 6–7
   Jim Crow era, 15
   likelihood of attending racially
      and economically segregated
      school, 18
   outlawing segregation, 3–4, 6
   post-*Brown* resistance to
      desegregation, 16–17
   role of federal government, 16
   role of judiciary, 6–7,
      15–18

school board elections and
    recalls, 80–81
school vouchers, 37, 38–39
shift to socioeconomic
    integration, xi, 6–7, 18, 20
tools for promoting, 19
RAND Corporation, 84
Rehabilitation Act, 123
Reich, Rob, 83
religious schools
    homeschooling, 47
    school vouchers, 38–39
restorative justice programs,
    36, 94, 97
Rhee, Michelle, 51–52, 77
Roanoke, Virginia school
    system, 118
robotics, 12
Rodriguez v. San Antonio
    Independent School District, 25
"Rubber Room, The" (Brill), 72
rubber rooms, 174n.51

San Antonio Independent School
    District v. Rodriguez, 5
Sandy Hook Elementary School
    shooting, 102
school administration and
    administrators. *See also*
    principals; school boards;
    school districts
    bullying prevention, 100–1
    continuous improvement
        strategy, 59
    Covid-19 pandemic, 143, 144
    high-stakes
        accountability, 49, 50
    legal rights of students, 133, 135
    LGBTQ students, 137
    No Child Left Behind Act, 54
    PTAs and school-based
        foundations, 82
    Race to the Top, 70
    racial hate and bias, 7, 9

school climate, 94
    student discipline, 97
    unions, 72
school boards, 2
    culture wars, threats, and
        violence, 80
    elections, 79, 81–82
    influence of outside
        money, 81–82
    mayoral appointment, 79
    recalls, 80–81
    role, 79–81
school choice. *See* school
    strategies
school climate, 92–94
    achievement gap, 88
    adoption of measures, 93–94
    bullying prevention, 100–1
    coaching, 69
    community schools, 46
    defined, 92–93
    effect of, 93
    ESSA ratings, 57
    flexibility, 94
    homeschooling, 47
    improvement
        recommendations, 94
    positive, 93
    positive behavioral intervention
        support, 97
    post-Covid predictions, 145, 146
    principals, 76
    replacing police officers on
        campus, 96–97
    research findings, 94
    school shootings, 104
    social-emotional learning, 112
    suspension, 96
    teacher retention, 64
school district superintendents
    Covid-19 pandemic, 139
    effective, 77
    high-stakes accountability, 50
    hiring, 79

school district superintendents
  (*cont.*)
  nudges, 114
  passion for the job, 77
  retention and turnover, 78
  role of, 2, 76–78
  school shootings, 104
  student achievement, 78
school districts, 1–2, 131. *See also*
  education policies; school
  boards; school district
  superintendents; school
  finance and funding; *names of
  specific types of schools*
  achievement gap, 87–88
  bullying prevention, 101
  centralized offices, 2
  continuous improvement
  strategy, 59–60
  Covid-19 pandemic, 139–40,
  141, 142, 143, 144–46
  decline in number of, 177n.75
  effect of decisions by, 5
  equality of educational
  opportunity, 6–8
  Every Student Succeeds
  Act, 57
  hiring practices, 63
  immigrant students, 126
  Native American students, 130
  neighborhood secession
  from, 18
  No Child Left Behind Act, 56
  number of, 1
  prioritizing equity, 87–88
  racial and ethnic composition
  of, 18–19
  racial integration, 16–19
  school board and, 2
  school shootings, 103, 104
  scope of authority, 1–2
  socioeconomic integration, 20–21
  special education, 121–
  22, 123–24

student discipline, 96–97, 98
teacher evaluation, 69–70, 71
teacher professional
  development, 67
teacher recruitment and
  retention, 63–64
technology, 106–7, 108
tools for promoting
  integration, 19
unions and strikes, 72,
  73, 74
school finance and funding, xi,
  5, 22–27
  additional funding, 27–28
  adequacy standard, 26
  charter schools, 35
  equality and, 8
  federal funding, 22, 23–24
  federal policies, 24
  federal underwriting of
  educational initiatives, 8
  homeschooling, 47
  local funding, 22
  national education budget, 1
  No Child Left Behind Act, 56
  per-pupil spending among
  states, 23–24
  per-school spending within
  districts, 24
  philanthropy, 83–85
  PTAs and school-based
  foundations, 83
  racial disparities, 23
  role of judiciary, 24–27
  state funding, 22, 23–24
  taxes, 22–23
  threat of litigation, 10
school practitioners, xi, 61–85
  effective teachers, 61–63
  influence of outside money
  on school board
  elections, 81–82
  influence of philanthropy on
  education policy, 83–85

parent-teacher associations, 81–82
principal's leadership
  role, 75–76
school board's role, 79–81
school district superintendent's
  leadership role, 76–78
school-based
  foundations, 82–83
teacher evaluation, 69–71
teacher preparation, 65–67
teacher professional
  development, 67–69
teachers recruitment and
  retention, 63–65
teachers strikes, 73–74
teachers' unions, 71–73
school shootings, 102–4, 187n.57
armed security guards, 103
arming teachers, 103
common motives, 103
history of, 102
increase in, 103
protective measures, 103
school climate, 104
school strategies, xi, 31–60
charter schools, 32–36
community schools, 44–47
competition-based
  drivers, 28–29
continuous improvement
  strategy, 59–60
early childhood
  education, 39–44
Every Student Succeeds
  Act, 56–58
high-stakes
  accountability, 48–51
homeschooling, 47–48
magnet schools, 31–32
No Child Left Behind Act, 54–56
"no excuses" strategy, 51–52
school choice, 28–29
school vouchers, 37–39
standards-based education, 52–53

school transfer requests
No Child Left Behind Act, 54,
  55
racial integration, 19
socioeconomic integration, 21
school vouchers, 37–39
arguments in favor of, 38
criticism of, 38–39
defined, 37
market-based drivers, 38
number of students using, 37
racial and socioeconomic
  segregation, 37, 38–39
research findings, 37–38
school-based foundations, 82–83
secretaries of education, 3
SEL. See social-emotional learning
"separate but equal"
  doctrine, 15–16
Serrano v. Priest, 25, 26
SES. See socioeconomic status
Sesame Street, 106
Shanker, Albert, 32
Smith-Hughes Act, 3, 24, 117–18
social changes, 11–13
social-emotional learning
  (SEL), 112–13
bullying, 100
Covid-19 pandemic, 145
school climate, 94
social-psychological
  strategies, 114–16
belonging experiences, 115–16
growth mindset, 114–15
nudges vs., 114
socioeconomic integration, 20–22
attendance zones, 19
benefits of, 19–21, 22
generating racial integration
  through, 22
growth in, 21
school vouchers, 38–39
shift from racial integration, xi,
  6–7, 18, 20

socioeconomic status (SES)
  career education, 118
  classroom composition, 12
  community colleges, 9
  Covid-19 pandemic, 140
  digital divide, 106
  early childhood education,
    40, 42–43
  effects of increased funding, 28
  effects of moving to lower-
    poverty neighborhoods, 20
  ethics and constitutional
    principles as drivers of
    policy, 5
  federal underwriting of
    educational initiatives, 3, 8
  geographically based
    attendance zones, 6–7
  high-poverty schools that
    serve primarily minority
    students, 18
  immigrant students,
    126, 127–28
  income as major predictor of
    student success, 8–9
  lunch programs, 12
  No Child Left Behind Act, 55–56
  pre-K, 8
  school district concentration, 8
  special education, 124
  student discipline, 95–96
  zoning laws and covenants, 6–7
special needs and special
    education services, 121–25
  accuracy of diagnoses, 125
  charter schools, 35–36
  classroom composition, 12
  cost of, 123–24
  debate over, 125
  defined, 121
  demand on teachers, 124
  Individualized Education
    Plans, 122–23
  judicial decisions, 121–22

  mainstreaming, 12
  number of students
    receiving, 121
  role of judiciary, 10
  school vouchers, 39
  specialists, 121
  teacher training, 65
standards-based education, 52–53
  arguments in favor of, 53
  Common Core State
    Standards, 53
  criticism of, 53
  defined, 52
  research findings, 53
  teacher's role, 52
Stanford University, 83
STAR (Students-Teacher
    Achievement Ratio) study, 91
state education agencies, role
    of, 2–3
statistical significance, 159n.46
STEAM education, 110
STEM education, 110–11
  career education, 117
  defined, 110
  expansion of offerings, 12
  need for, 110–11
stereotype vulnerability, 88,
    90–91
Stevens, John Paul, 17
Stewart, Potter, 5, 25
strikes, 73–74
  history of, 73
  objectives of, 73, 74
  public support for, 74
  recent wave of, 73–74
  student achievement and, 74
student discipline, 94–98
  charter schools, 36
  corporal punishment, 95, 135
  effect of school climate, 93
  effects of, 96
  expulsion, 95–97, 98
  grade retention, 98

legal rights of students, 135
Native American students,
    130, 131–32
No Child Left Behind Act, 56
police on campus, 96
positive behavioral intervention
    support, 97
racial disparities, 9, 95–96
restorative justice
    programs, 36, 97
social psychology strategies, 98
suspension, 95–97
"zero-tolerance" approach, 5–6
zero-tolerance discipline, 95–
    96, 97
Students-Teacher Achievement
    Ratio (STAR) study, 91
Success Academy, 52
suspension, 95–97
    defined, 95
    effects of, 96
    number of, 95–96
    police and, 96–97
    race and ethnicity, 95–96
    reduction of, 97
    zero-tolerance discipline, 97
sustaining (culturally responsive)
    pedagogy, 88–89, 180n.5
Swann v. Charlotte-Mecklenburg
    County, 16
systemic reform strategy, 58–59
    arguments in favor of, 58
    continuous improvement
        strategy, 58
    premise of, 58
    research findings, 58–59

Tartans Rural Teacher
    Corps, 66
Teach for America (TFA), 66
teachers, xi
    alternative pathway
        programs, 66–67
    arming, 103

charter schools, 32, 34, 36
content knowledge, 62
continuous improvement
    strategy, 59, 60, 62
credentials, licensing, and
    certificates, 64–65, 66
demographics, 64
early childhood education,
    39–41, 42
effect of school climate, 93
evaluation, 69–71
evaluation of, 62–63
Every Student Succeeds
    Act, 58–59
gender of, 64
high expectations of their
    students, 61–62
highly effective, 61–63
high-stakes accountability,
    48–51, 69
housing subsidies, 64
immigrant students, 127,
    198–99n.17
magnet schools, 31–32
No Child Left Behind Act, 54–
    55, 56
number of, 1
post-Covid educational
    strategies, 144
preparation and training, 63,
    65–67, 170–71n.29
professional collaboration, 62
professional
    development, 67–69
race and ethnicity of, 64–65
racial integration, 15–16
recruitment of, 63–65
relationship building, 62
residency programs, 66–67
responsiveness to student
    needs, 62
retention and turnover, 63–65
salaries and compensation, 24,
    28, 63–64, 65–66, 71–74

teachers (*cont.*)
  school climate, 64
  signing bonuses, 64
  socioeconomic integration, 21
  special education, 124
  standards-based
    education, 52, 53
  strikes, 73–74
  strong teaching pedagogy, 62
  supervised teaching, 65
  support from principals, 64,
    69, 75, 76
  tenure, 71
  training to reduce bias and
    create empathy, 88, 98, 180n.3
  unions, 1–2, 36, 70, 71–73
teacher's aides, 71–72, 91, 122–23
technology, 105–9
  computers, 106
  criticism of, 107
  digital divide, 106
  ed-tech market, 107, 108
  effects of, 106
  history of, 105–6
  personalized curricula, 107–8
  post-Covid educational
    strategies, 144–45
  teaching responsible use
    of, 108–9
  virtual and online learning, 107,
    108, 144–45
testing and test scores
  achievement gap, 87
  class size reduction, 92
  community schools, 44, 46
  continuous improvement
    strategy, 59–60
  Covid-19 pandemic, 140–41
  credentials, licensing, and
    certificates, 65
  deeper learning, 110
  Every Student Succeeds Act, 57
  GED, 116–17
  growth mindset, 114–15

highly effective teachers, 62–63
high-stakes accountability, xi,
  3, 48–51
homeschooling, 47
immigrant students, 128
No Child Left Behind Act,
  54, 55–56
"no excuses" strategy, xi, 51–52
noncognitive skills, 111–12
philanthropy, 84
post-Covid predictions, 145
pre-K, 43
racial integration, 19–20
school vouchers, 37–38
social-emotional learning, 113
socioeconomic integration, 21
special education, 123
standards-based
  education, 52–53
teacher evaluation, 69, 70
technology, 106
TFA (Teach for America), 66
Till, Frank, 77
Time, 51
*Tinker v. Des Moines School
  District*, 133
TNTP (The New Teacher
  Project), 69–70
Tom Brown's Schooldays, 98–99
tracking, 89
  ability grouping vs., 89
  arguments in favor of, 90
  criticism of, 90
  defined, 89
  effects of, 90–91
  history of, 89
transgender students, 136, 137, 138
Trump, Donald and Trump
  administration
  charter schools, 33
  focus of secretary of
    education, 3
  school vouchers, 38
tutoring, 54, 55, 123, 146

UCLA, 90, 103
Uncommon Schools, 33, 52
Union, Oklahoma, school district,
    60, 104
unions, 1–2, 71–73
    American Federation of
    Teachers, 72
    charter schools, 36, 72
    civil rights, 72
    Covid-19 pandemic, 143
    decline in membership, 73
    National Education
        Association, 72
    objectives of, 36
    police on campus, 96
    school board elections, 81–82
    strikes, 73–74
    student achievement and, 73
    teacher evaluation, 70
University of Chicago, 116
US Attorneys' Offices, 80
US Department of Education, 3,
    56, 64, 95–96, 98, 101, 108,
    131, 137, 141–42
US Department of Justice, 7,
    101, 143
US Department of the
    Interior, 130–31
U.S. English, 129–30
US Supreme Court. *See also names
    of specific cases*
    increasing conservatism, 11, 17
    racial segregation and voucher
        plans, 37
    role in racial integration, 6–7,
        15–18, 20–21
    school funding, 25
    skepticism of constitutionality
        of integration, 17–18

value-added modeling
    methodology, 62–63
virtual and online learning, 33,
    107, 108, 144–45

vocational education. *See* career
    education

Waiting for Superman, 51, 70
Walters, Christopher, 42–43
Walton Family Foundation,
    83, 84, 85
War on Poverty, 24
Ward, Lester, ix
Wardlow, Ty, 104
Washington, D.C., school district, 51
Washington Post, 80
Weingarten, Randi, 71
West, Martin, 72–73
West Virginia v. Barnett, 201n.31
White students
    achievement gap, 87, 88
    benefits of integration, 19–20
    busing, 17
    college enrollment, 9
    community schools, 60
    "critical race theory," 80
    early childhood education, 40
    gifted programs, 9
    graduation rates, 8–9
    Jim Crow era, 15–16
    likelihood of attending racially
        and economically segregated
        school, 18
    Mather School, 11
    pre-K, 8
    public school composition, 11–12
    racial integration, 5, 16, 17,
        18–20, 23
    secession from school
        districts, 18
    student discipline, 9, 95–96,
        130, 131
White teachers, 64
Wiley, Andrew, 125

YES Prep, 52
Youth Risk Behavior Survey,
    135–36